Spinnin' the Web
Designing & Developing Web Projects

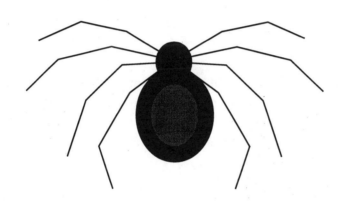

Written by
Annette Lamb

Dedicated to

Larry

First Printing: 1998

Copyright © 1998 by Annette Lamb.

All rights reserved. No part of this book may be reproduced or transmitted in any form or by any means now known or to be invented, electronic or mechanical, including photocopying, recording, or by any information storage or retrieval system without written permission from the authors or publisher, except for the brief inclusion of quotations in a review.

Permission is given for individual classroom teachers, computer coordinators, and library/media specialists to reproduce pages for classroom use. Contact the publisher for other types of copyright permissions.

The information and resources contained in this book are true, complete, and accurate to the best of our knowledge. All recommendations and suggestions are made without any guarantees on the part of the author or publishing company.

Printed in the United States of America.
ISBN 0-9641581-9-1

For additional information or to place an order:
Vision to Action
Order and Distribution Center
PO Box 2003
Emporia, Kansas 66801
Voice/FAX   (316) 343-7989
email   vision2a@cadvantage.com
website   http://cadvantage.com/~vision2a
For course information and web-based activities   http://magic.usi.edu

Table of Contents

Preface iii

Part I: **Exploring Schools on the Web** 1

    Chapter 1: School Web Pages 3

    Chapter 2: Classroom Web Pages 25

    Chapter 3: Online Newspapers 41

    Chapter 4: Project Pages 57

    Chapter 5: Student Pages 73

Part II: **Selecting Powerful Projects** 81

    Chapter 6: Large-Scale, Ongoing Projects 83

    Chapter 7: Small-Scale, Short-Term Projects 97

Part III: **Planning & Implementing Internet-based Project** 145

    Chapter 8: Planning Web-based Learning Environments 147

    Chapter 9: Designing Web Pages 181

    Chapter 10: Creating Web Pages 217

    Chapter 11: Designing & Developing School Web Sites 255

    Chapter 12: Implementing and Evaluating Project 269

Index 289

About the Author

Dr. Annette Lamb is a Professor of Teacher Education at the University of Southern Indiana in Evansville. She teaches and writes in the areas of Educational Technology Integration, Educational Computing, and Library/Media Management. Prior to higher education, she was an elementary media specialist and computer teacher. Annette Lamb received her Ph. D. in Instructional Technology from Iowa State University and has been active in both state and national educational technology associations. During the past several years, Dr. Lamb has made over 400 state, regional, national, and international presentations. She has published numerous articles in the educational computing and library/media areas. She has written nearly a dozen books on topics including Internet, multimedia, and technology integration. Her latest books are **Building Treehouses for Learning: Integrating Technology into Today's Classrooms, Magic Carpet Ride, MacPac for Teachers,** and new editions of **Cruisin' the Information Highway** and **Surfin' the Internet.**

Acknowledgements

I would like to thank web developers everywhere who have created a whole new world for educators over the past few years. Web names and URLs are provided with each example. We've included the lastest information on each site at the time of printing. We apologize for dated information, but that's life on the ever - changing information highway.

Preface

If you've been cruising the information highway and surfing the Internet, it's time to spin your own web. Web development is easier than you may think. Creating a web page is as easy as using a word processor.

Exploring the Book

Before jumping into the development of web projects, we'll explore schools on the web. The first five chapters focus on teacher and student produced web projects. You'll start by exploring school district and building level web sites. Within these sites you'll find classroom and department pages. Many schools are producing online newspapers, yearbooks, and electronic magazines called ezines. Finally, find out how students around the world are sharing their ideas through student web pages.

The second section of the book will help you select a powerful project for your classroom. We'll explore large-scale, ongoing projects as well as small-scale, short term projects.

Planning and implementing Internet-based projects is the focus of the third section. You'll learn to plan web-based learning environments and design web projects. Next, you'll identify web development tools and create your own web pages. You'll also learn to produce school web sites. The final chapter involves implementing and evaluating a web-based project.

Using the Book

You can't just read about the Internet, you need to do it. Get online and sit this book next to the computer. Visit the sites discussed and read the online articles suggested. Use the lists of web addresses throughout the book as additional resources.

The spider logo is used to highlight key ideas found throughout the book. Overviews, reviews, definitions, key words, and reminders can be found in these areas.

In each chapter you'll find **Idea Exploration** activities. The exercises are identified by a "light bulb" graphic and will help you develop the skills needed to design and develop your own site. You'll also find charts that can be used as worksheets to brainstorm ideas and make plans for your projects.

Although developing web projects can be lots of fun, they can also be frustrating. With this in mind, you'll find **Real World Considerations** areas at the end of many chapters. These sections focus on common problems and practical solutions.

Spinnin' the Web

Twenty years ago I began using a word processor. It was a great way to "type up" term papers. By the late 1980s, students started developing multimedia reports in HyperCard and HyperStudio. The next millennium promises a revolution in the way learners express their ideas and communicate with other students. No longer are children bound by the paper in their notebooks and the wall of their classrooms. They can reach outside their school and share their creativity with others around the global.

I hope you enjoy spinning the web as much as I do. From one web master to another, happy spinning!

Annette Lamb
Spring 1998

Part I: Exploring Schools on the Web

In this section, you'll explore how students are using the tools of technology to reach beyond the walls of the school. You'll also compare and contrast the approaches taken by different teachers and the varied roles of students.

The Internet has become a common tool for information and communication in schools. Many students and teachers are involved with developing web projects that are posted on a school web server.

Let's explore some ways that schools are developing their web presence. We'll examine each of the following areas.

Schools on the Web

School Web Pages
Classroom Web Pages
Newspapers
Project Pages
Student Pages

School District and Building Level Web Pages
Classroom Web Pages
Online School Newspapers and Magazines
Project Pages
Student Pages

School District and Building Level Web Pages. We'll start our exploration by examining school district and building level web pages. While you may not be involved in the development of the district page, you may be in charge of designing your building level page. What goes into a school building page?

Classroom Web Pages. Second graders, middle schoolers, and high school seniors can all be involved with the development of a classroom page. Whether the page will post homework or be used to share student poetry, classroom pages are a great way to break down the walls of your classroom.

Online School Newspapers and Magazines. Many schools have a newspaper, but does your school publish an online newspaper or ezine? Explore what schools are doing with electronic publishing.

Project Pages. Projects are a popular way to connection with classrooms around the world. They can also bring authentic, real-world materials, issues, and debates into your classroom. This chapter explores the range of projects across subject areas.

Student Pages. Children and teens love the Internet. Many students are developing pages on their own at home, while others are creating pages at school. Explore the elements of a student web page as well as issues related to posting student information on the Internet.

Chapter 1:
School District and
Building Level Web Pages

What should be put in a school web site?
Is updating important?
Do I need to get permission from parents to publish student photos?

In this chapter, you'll explore school district and building level web pages. Developing a school web page has become a popular practice in many schools. Most large school corporations and school districts have a central web page that leads to specific school pages. For example, **Evansville Vanderburgh School Corporation** (Figure 1-1a) contains general system information as well as an area called SchoolZone that links to individual school sites. Many schools are still in the process of developing their first web pages.

School Corporation and District Web Sites

Atlanta Area, Georgia Schools	http://www.atlanta.k12.ga.us/
Austin Independent School, Texas Schools	http://www.austin.isd.tenet.edu/
Cherry Creek, Colorado Schools	http://www.ccsd.k12.co.us/
Chico, California Schools	http://www.cusd.chico.k12.ca.us/
Evansville Area, Indiana Schools	http://www.evsc.k12.in.us/
Internet for Minnesota Schools	http://informns.k12.mn.us/

List 1-1. School Corporation and District Web Sites.

http://www.evsc.k12.in.us/   http://www.atlanta.k12.ga.us/

Figure 1-1a,b. Large School Systems.

Look beyond the flashy exterior of the school's first page.

School Corporation & District Web Sites

As you explore state agency, school corporation, and school district web pages, notice the kinds of information provided at this level. Rather than focusing on "student" oriented issues, these sites tend to provide general school information, resources for parents and the community, as well as links to specific schools. Although the focus of the Altanta Public Schools (see Figure 1-1b) web site is on information and resources for adults, the graphics show the system's learner-centered focus. Explore a few school corporation and district web sites. What's the purpose of the centralized web site? Who is the audience? Is it easy to access information about each school building?

Many of the larger school systems contain flashy front-ends. In other words, the school system invested in a professional designer and webmaster to make the first few pages look high quality. Unfortunately many of these sites lack depth. For example, there may be a nice index page, but the rest of the pages may be under construction or rarely updated. As you evaluate a site be certain to look at the depth and breadth of the site rather than just the flashy exterior. Also remember that your site doesn't need to have sound, animation, and other fancy features to look professional.

Your school site should reflect the philosophy of your administration, parents, teachers, and students. Is your school, teacher or student-focused? Is it an exciting place to work and learn? These questions should be answered with the first screen that is presented to the user.

School Web Sites

Many schools have developed building-level school web sites. What kinds of things do schools put on their web pages? Why? Who do you think looks at these pages? Explore some of the school web sites provided. Elementary, middle, and high school sites are listed in List 1-2. Figure 1-2 shows screens from sample schools.

Idea Exploration: School Web Page
Brainstorm a list of the elements you find in most school web pages. Create an evaluation form that contains a list of key features to look for in a school web page. What are the most important characteristics of an effective school web site?

Select a school from the ones in List 1-2. Create a web page that shows your evaluation form. It should also provide a review of one of the school pages.

Idea Exploration

Avocado Elementary School in Figure 1-2a shows its student-oriented focus by using a cartoon figure on the first page in addition to the photograph of the school. Also notice that the page is simple and easy to use.

Desert View High School (see Figure 1-2b) is interesting because it focuses on information of interest to students such as sports and clubs.

The Falcon's Nest in Figure 1-2c is an excellent example of a web page that has become an important element in the school. It is continuously updated and contains information related to the community as well as classroom projects. It's clear that students play an active role in the information found at this site.

Look for:
 Simplicity
 Ease of Use
 Student Focus
 Updating
 Timelines
 Clear Misson
 Good Links

School Web Pages

Alta Elementary School	http://cyberfair.gsn.org/altakcusd/
Arbor Heights School	http://www.halcyon.com/arborhts/arborhts.html
Armadillo: Texas	http://www.halcyon.com/arborhts/arborhts.html
Avocado Elementary School	http://avocado.dade.k12.fl.us
Cromwell Valley	http://www.clark.net/pub/cve
Desert View High School	http://wacky.ccit.arizona.edu/~susd/dvhome.html
Dodson Middle School Online	http://cyberfair.gsn.org/dodson/toc.htm
Duck Bay School	http://www.mbnet.mb.ca/~dfalk
Eldorado High School	http://coyote.accessnv.com/fmathews/index.html
Fahan School	http://www.tas.gov.au/fahan/
Fairbanks Alaska School	http://www2.northstar.k12.ak.us/schools/upk/upk.home.html
Fairland School	http://www.inform.umd.edu/UMS+State/UMD-Projects/MCTP/Technology/School_WWW_Pages/FairlandHomePage.html
Foothill High School	http://www.snowcrest.net/foothill/
Grandview Middle School	http://www.westonka.k12.mn.us/grandview.html
Henry M. Gunn Senior High School	http://www.gunn.palo-alto.ca.us/
Hillsdale School	http://hillside.coled.umn.edu/
Hoffer School	http://cmp1.ucr.edu/exhibitions/hoffer/hoffer.homepage.html
International School of Amsterdam	http://www.isa.nl/
Joe Nightingale's School's	http://www.sbceo.k12.ca.us/~eagles/
Kirby Hall School	http://www.bga.com/~kirby/index2.html
Lakeshore Elementary School	http://www.greeceny.com/ls/welcome.htm
Lewis Middle School	http://www.lewis.edu/
Meldreth Manor School	http://www.rmplc.co.uk/eduweb/sites/meldreth/index.html
Nagatsuka Elementary School	http://www.csi.ad.jp/school/project/nagatuka/indexe.html
Oakview Elementary School	http://oakview.fcps.edu:80
RESA's World	http://www.wcresa.k12.mi.us
Rising Stars	http://www.trc.org/risestar.htm
Springfield Estates Elementary School	http://www.fcps.k12.va.us/SpringfieldEstatesES/seesonian.html
Wangaratta Primary School	http://www.ozemail.com.au/~wprimary/
Wright Middle School	http://198.150.8.9/
Yamhill County EDS	http://198.237.200.47/ESDPage/index.html

List 1-2. School Web Pages.

Chapter 1: School District and Building Level Web Pages

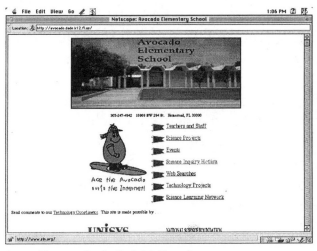

http://avocado.dade.k12.fl.us/

http://wacky.ccit.arizona.edu/~susd/dvhome.html

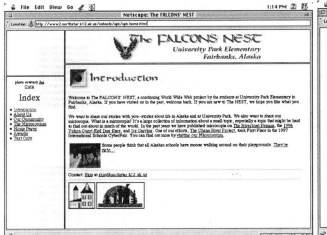

http://www2.northstar.k12.ak.us/schools/upk/upk.home.html

http://www.westonka.k12.mn.us/grandview.html

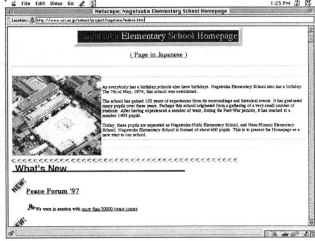

http://www.snowcrest.net/foothill/
Figure 1-2. School pages.

http://www.csi.ad.jp/school/project/nagatuka/indexe.html

Grandview Middle School is laid out slightly different from the others in Figure 1-2. It uses a table to present choices to users. Notice the emphasis on student projects.

Foothill High School (see Figure 1-e) is clearly proud of their football team. They even included the score board from their last game. They have also been successful in finding sponsorship for their site.

Schools from around the world can be found on the Internet. **Nagatsuka Elementary School** in Figure 1-2f is one of many Japanese schools on the web.

School Web Site Development

Developing a school web site is an important activity. Your site will be viewed by students, teachers, administrators, parents, members of the community, and people from around the world. It must provide accurate and timely information. For many people, it will be the first and only contact with your school. As a result, your site must reflect the personality and philosophy of your programs.

Explore the schools you attended.
Visit the other schools in your area.

Create two committees. One for idea generation. Another for writing.

Web Site Committee. Although most people hate projects that involve committee work, a committee is necessary. This committee will be developing policies, writing procedures, and making important decisions for the entire school. Your committee should include representatives from across the school. You need an administrator who can provide insights into current school policies and procedures. For example, what's the "official" name of the school, which logo should be used, and what information can legally be presented on the web page?

Teachers are an important part of the committee too. They can provide insights into what would be of interest to other teachers and how classroom information should be presented. Of course, the technology specialist, library media specialist, and other people involved with technology and computers should be part of your committee too. They can be helpful in

Chapter 1: School District and Building Level Web Pages

developing the technical side of the site and assist in the development of support areas such as lists of school links, copyright policies, and related educational technology issues.

It's also a good idea to involve students. What are their interests and needs regarding the web page? You might even be able to convince the high school computer club to maintain the web site! For example, the **Foothills High School** page in Figure 1-2e is maintained by a web development class.

Finally, involve parents, school board members, and community members in your initial planning phases. These people provide an "outsiders" look at your school and can help you provide parents and community connections within your site. They can also provide support. For example, you might be able to convince the local telephone company or radio station to support the cost of running your web server. You could then include their logo on your web page as advertising. Just as area business and industry advertise in school event programs and the yearbook, you may be able to persuade them to support your web site.

Look for local companies that already have web pages. Ask them for sponsorship.

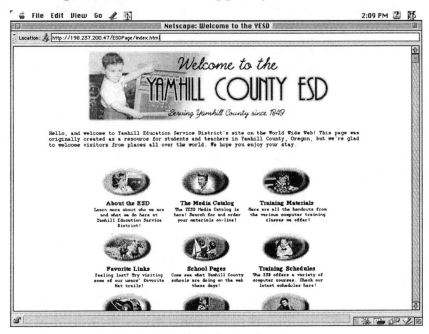

http://198.237.200.47/ESDPage/index.html
Figure 1-3. Yamhill County ESD

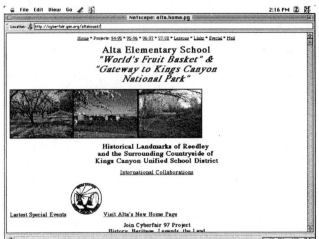

http://cyberfair.gsn.org/altakcusd/
Figure 1-4a. Alta Elementary School

http://www.zip.com.au/~elanora/
Figure 1-4b. Elanora Heights Primary School

If your school is very small or remote, consider working with the other schools in your county or region. Figure 1-3 shows the **Yamhill County ESD** pages that serve all the teachers and students in the county. This page then links to individual school pages.

Purpose of the Web Site. Once you've formed a committee, you're ready to tackle some important issues. Start with the purpose of your site. Why do you need a web site? The easy answer is: because all the cool schools have them. However, your reasons should go beyond the obvious and will help you develop the theme for your site. You may want to use your school web site as a public relations tool. For example, if a new family moves to your town, they might see your web site. Then, decide to send their children to your school because they like what they see.

Another purpose for your school web site might could be the global presence and interaction. Your school might develop a relationship with a series of schools in other countries and you could use the web site as the entry point for the activities. You could also use your page for sharing projects, research, and expertise.

Both schools in Figure 1-4 one from California and the other from Australia have a global community focus. They have worked together on projects as well as with other schools around the world. The mission statement from the primary school in Australia is similar to schools around the world: "Our mission is to develop in children attitudes, skills and knowledge so they achieve their full potential and realize self-worth in a harmonious environment." Their global focus fits perfectly with their mission.

Some schools use their web page for community outreach. For instance, you might have a "parent-school homework" connection web area where parents and students can find homework assistance. Some communities use the school page to post community event information or provide adult education resources. You might even start new programs that would use distance education materials to reach students and adults beyond the K-12 classroom. For example, some schools are providing alternative programs leading to a high school diploma through web-based courses.

Before creating a new policy, check the ones for old technology.

Policy Development. As you begin to develop your site, you'll find that there are many policies and procedures that must be generated for this new technology. For example, who will be responsible for checking to make certain that posted pages follow the school's copyright guidelines? Who will check the appropriateness of links? Who will be allowed to post individual pages? Will teachers have pages? What about personal pages for students?

Who decides what goes on the web site? Ask yourself: Is this information really needed online? Who will use it? How will it be used? Why will other people visit? Is the information available elsewhere? Is the entire document needed? Can you link to another site rather than create the document yourself from scratch?

Minneapolis schools (http://www.mpls.k12.mn.us/staffguidelines.html) have a set of guidelines for web development.

Webmaster Responsibilities. Committees are essential for making general web site decisions, but at some point you'll need to begin development of your web pages. This work needs to be left to a few competent web developers. These people will make recommendations regarding the general design of your site. Your web site should have a consistent look and feel. A standard background, graphics, icons, text, and formatting is important for a professional looking web site. Once a template is created that contains the standard layout, individuals can begin adding information.

Figure 1-5 shows consistency in layout. Notice the standard font sizes and graphic elements. Individual

http://www.amarillo.isd.tenet.edu/sleepyhollow/default.html
Figure 1-5. Sleepy Hollow Elementary School

teachers added their own quote and personal information within the template structure.

The webmaster will also need to develop timelines for updates and modification of the web pages. For example, when will sports scores be submitted and posted? Will the webmaster be responsible for checking the accuracy of information? Will they organize the information? Who will decide whether or not something gets posted? Who will monitor consistency? These are generally the responsibility of a web editor or webmaster. If students are involved with development of the web pages, then a teacher or administrator must act as a supervisor. Students should not be making decisions about building-level web page content, but they should be involved with the technical side of writing and creating the web pages.

Levels of Involvement. The webmaster may or may not be involved with the development of informational and instructional web pages. This depends on the web development skills of the teachers and students at your school. In some cases, teachers may provide the content to a webmaster who will then develop the pages from scratch. Projects can also be submitted as word processed documents and can be converted by the webmaster to HTML format. It's easy to use a WYSIWYG (what-you-see-is-what-you-get) web development tool such as **Claris Home Page**, **Microsoft FrontPage**, or **Adobe Pagemill** to create web documents.

The webmaster may wish to provide a template for people to fill in using a web development tool. Some students and teachers may decide to create their pages totally from scratch. In most school, you'll find a spectrum of ability levels and interests in web page development. Be flexible and get as many people as possible involved with the process. A teacher with few technology skills might be willing to "type up" a project on a word processor, but would be overwhelmed when confronted with a set of HTML guidelines.

Levels of Control. You'll need to decide on "levels of control" within the site. In other words, your webmaster may have control over the core or index page (first page people see) and the first level of administration, department, and policy pages. Their name and address will be used as the initial contact on each of these pages for updates and questions. Beyond that, individual students and teachers may have control over their own classroom and project pages.

In some cases, the webmaster will create password access areas on the web server. For example, a teacher would have a password to get into a particular classroom folder on the web server, but would not be able to make modifications to the main school pages. Given a password, a student could update the drama club page, but nothing else on the web server.

School Web Site Contents

What kinds of information should be contained in a school web page? There's no simple answer to this question. It depends. It depends on your purpose for having a page. It depends on your ability to quickly update and maintain your page. It depends on the level of support you have for your site. It depends on whether your site will be "adult" focused or "learner" focused. Let's explore some general characteristics of school pages.

School Information. Start your web page with something that represents the philosophy of your school. It could be a short mission statement, meaningful photograph, or lively logo. Make it professional, yet attractive and interesting. Many school pages start with a lifeless photograph of the school building. A school is about children and teachers not tables, chairs, and walls.

How can you convey your philosophy about your students in a short catchy motto, slogan, or statement? At first glimpse a user should be able to tell whether they are looking at an elementary, middle, or high

Contents:
    School Information
    People Information
    Resources

Chapter 1: School District and Building Level Web Pages

http://www.hipark.austin.isd.tenet.edu/home/main.html

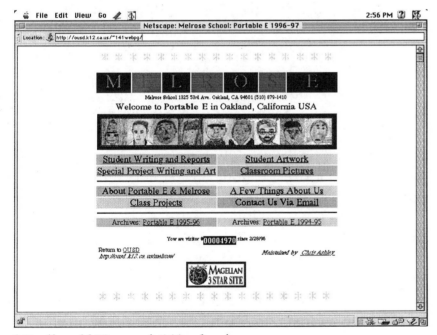

http://ousd.k12.ca.us/~141webpg/

Figure 1-6. Elementary School Pages.

http://www-tenet.cc.utexas.edu/Pub/barton_hills/tour.html
Figure 1-7. Barton Hills School Tour.

school page. They should also get the type of impression you're seeking. Are you looking for professional, interesting, fun, educational, insightful, or attractive? Examine (see Figure 1-6) the **Highland Park Elementary School** (http://www.hipark.austin.isd.tenet.edu/home/main.html) page and the **Melrose Elementary School** (http://ousd.k12.ca.us/~141webpg/) page. What impression do you get from the very first screen?

Most school web sites contain general school information. You'll find a school photograph, logo, contact information (address, phone, fax, email), and location (address, map, globe).

Be careful when including maps. Can users read the map? If not, it's useless. Be sure to include a context for your map. If the reader is from another country they may not recognize the name of your town or school. If you want to show users around your school consider developing a virtual tour of your school like the one shown in Figure 1-7.

You may wish to include a mission statement and background information about your school. Rather than a dry description from an outdated brochure, rewrite the text and add pictures. What makes your school unique and interesting? Have you won any special awards? Does your school have an interesting history?

Chapter 1: School District and Building Level Web Pages   17

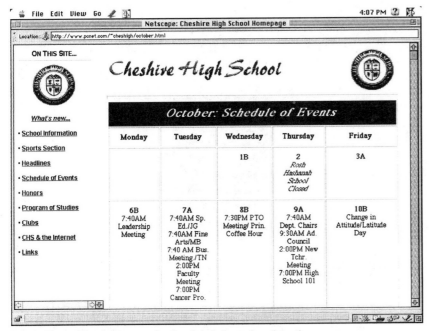

http://www.pcnet.com/~cheshigh/october.html
Figure 1-8. Cheshire High School Schedule.

Some schools include policies, procedures, handbooks, and other administrative materials. Although these can be useful in some cases, they are often left unread. Consider the value of putting the materials on the Internet. Who is the intended reader? If you do post policies and procedures, make certain that they are updated as new materials become available. Updating is critical in every area. Lunch menus, calendar of events, sports schedules, and other time-specific materials should be updated frequently or eliminated from the pages (see Figure 1-8).

People Information. What will be posted about people? Some schools post pictures and names of all the administrators, faculty, and staff. Other schools let individual teachers decide whether they wish to develop a page. Again, it depends on the purpose. Why is the information being posted? Some schools like to post the pictures of elementary teachers so that children can see a picture of their teacher before the first day of school. Some teachers even "introduce" them-

Keeping your site up to date is the most common problem schools face in developing web sites.

People often lose interest in the site once the novelty of having a web page wears off. Keep enthusiasm high.

http://www.uwf.edu/~stankuli/gbm/cparker/period2/caseyh.htm
Figure 1-9. Student Page.

selves to their students. Other schools see teacher pages as a way for faculty and staff to express their philosophies of teaching to parents and the community. Teacher pages may include all or part of the following information: name, photograph, classroom location and photo, phone, email, assignment, current projects, resume, interests, and favorite links.

Most schools don't have the storage space for all the students who would want to develop their own personal web pages. There are also concerns about monitoring the links that students might include. On the other hand, many teachers have developed projects where students work on web page development as part of a classroom activity as shown in Figure 1-9.

In this case you'll find some of the following information about students: name, picture, grade, family information, interests, hobbies, favorites (book, TV show, game, movies, sports), future plans, and favorite links. Students may also post autobiographies, term papers, class projects, writing samples, and other class assignments. Be careful when posting student information. Many schools require parents to give permission

Ask parents to sign permission forms.

Types of permission:
　Student Name
　Student Photos
　Student Info
　Classwork

Chapter 1: School District and Building Level Web Pages 19

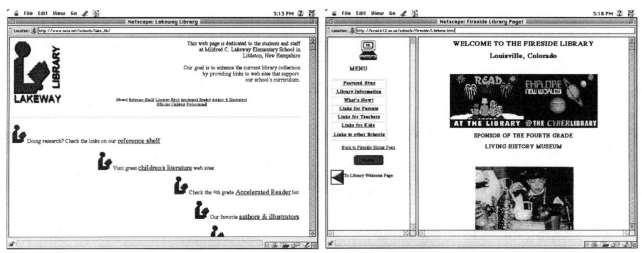

http://www.ncia.net/schools/lake_lib/   http://bvsd.k12.co.us/schools/fireside/LibHome.html
Figure 1-10. School Library Pages.

for their student's name and photograph to appear in any publication including the web. In many cases, schools use only the first name and last initial of students.

Resources. Many schools use the Internet as a way to distribute information. The core school page may contain links to many types of resources. An online school newspaper or yearbook is a popular high school project. Classroom pages and projects are also a great use for the school web server. Most schools encourage department, athletics, music, special centers, student clubs, student government, and grade level pages. For instance, many library media centers have web pages. Like the general school pages, they may post a logo, mission statement, policies, procedures, hours, calendar, activities, and service information. In addition, they may also provide resources unique to their area such as an equipment inventory, copyright information, book, video, and software review links, reading lists, and subject area research links. See Figure 1-10 for examples of school library pages.

Many schools provide starting point pages. In other words, there might be a page of popular links for students, teachers, parents, and the community. Student link pages might contain "child safe" fun links, subject area pages, homework pages, and other developmen-

Resources
   Newspapers
   Yearbook
   Class Page
   Projects
   Departments
   Student Groups

tally appropriate links. Teacher pages often contain links to professional organizations, lesson plans, and popular educational sites. The parent and community page might provide safety information, poison control facts, nutritional resources, and adult education programs.

Real World Considerations

You'll find some great school pages on the web. You'll also find some really ugly, useless school pages. Let's explore some of the most common errors schools make in designing their pages.

Yesterday's News. You need to keep your pages current. If your site posts the school lunch menu from last spring or the football schedule from the previous fall, it looks like you don't take the time to keep current. Outsiders might wonder if the rest of the school is also "behind."

Flashy, but Flat. Many schools invest lots of time in their core page and ignore the rest of the site assuming that teachers will add to it. In many cases this leads to page after page of "under construction" signs. Wait to make your links until after sections are completed.

Boring. Is your school page booooring? Does it lack pizzazz? Remember, your page is a reflection of your school. If your school is a lively place, then liven up your page with colorful photographs of students and highlights of important events. Brag about your school. Rave about your school. Bring your school alive for readers!

Tacky. Many school pages are just plain tacky. They're filled with tons of animations, meaningless clipart, java extras, wild backgrounds, and hard-to-read text. Don't over do it. Your site can be professional, yet fun without going overboard. Develop a consistent format. Use easy to read fonts against a muted background. Use animations to focus on particular areas of the screen without being distracting. For example Figure 1-11 uses an animated dog as the focal point of their page. In this case it works because the page isn't full of other distractions.

School Web Structures
Shallow
Deep
Balanced

Poorly organized. Some school web sites are poorly organized making it difficult to navigate, or move around the site. Sites that present all their options on the home page are too shallow. The first page is cluttered with long lists of unrelated topics. Other sites are too deep. In other words, users go through menu after menu without getting to useful information. A balanced web structure combines a logical main menu with quick access to information through submenus. See Chart 1-1 for examples.

Idea Exploration

Idea Exploration: School Exploration
Explore other schools around the world (see Chart 1-2). Identify five school sites that do a particularly good job with some aspect of their site. In other words, they may have a very effective index on the home page. Or, they may do an exceptional job describing their school's mission. Maybe they have a unique way to present sports scores.

Email the webmaster of the site and let them know they are doing a great job!

Summary
Many schools are on the web. With good planning and the involvement of students, teachers, administration, and community members, you can develop a site that reflects the excitement and enthusiasm of your building.

Unfortunately, after the initial site is posted, some people lose interest. Keep the momentum high by developing ongoing projects and involving a variety of people from across your school.

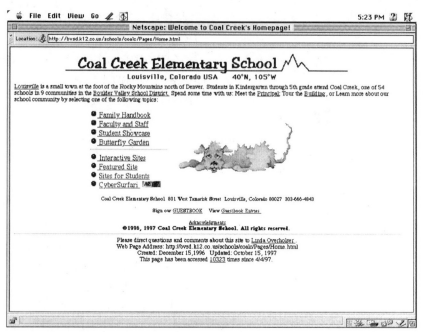

http://bvsd.k12.co.us/schools/coalc/Pages/Home.html
Figure 1-11. Animated dog.

School Web Sites Around the World

Web 66	http://web66.coled.umn.edu/schools.html
American School Directory	http://www.asd.com
Best of Online Schools	http://sln.fi.edu:80/qa96/caughtindex.html
British Columbia, Canada	http://www.etc.bc.ca/tdebhome/community/schools.html
Classroom Web	http://www.classroom.net/classweb/
High School Central	http://www.sftoday.com/enn2/hscentral.htm
Internet Home Pages	http://www.newlink.net/education/class/doe/examples.html
K-12 Schools on the Web & Texas	http://www.tenet.edu:80/education/main.html
Kids Did This! Hotlist	http://sln.fi.edu/tfi/hotlists/kids.html
Online Schools	http://sln.fi.edu:80/qa96/caughtindex.html
School Library Pages	http://www.cusd.chico.k12.ca.us/~pmilbury/lib.html
United Kingdom Schools	http://ifl.rmplc.co.uk/bin/$webdbc.exe/eduweb/qryeduweb/htx/&/eduweb/ewdir.htx

List 1-3. School Web Sites Around the World.

Chapter 1: School District and Building Level Web Pages

School Web Structure

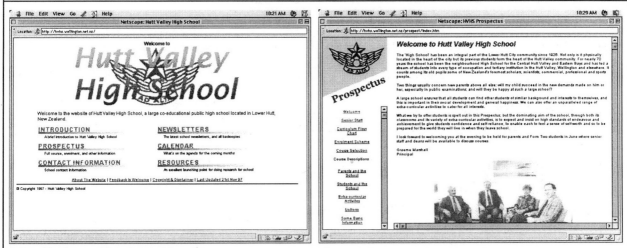

http://hvhs.wellington.net.nz/

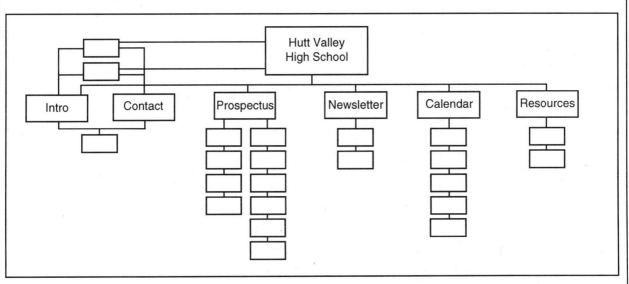

Explore the following sites and create diagrams of their web structure.

Miraloma Elementary School
  http://nisus.sfusd.k12.ca.us/schwww/sch722/miralomahome.html
Cupertino Junior High School
  http://www.cupertino.k12.ca.us/Cupertino.www/index.html
Woodlands Secondary School
  http://www.sd68.nanaimo.bc.ca/schools/wdls/woodland.htm

Chart 1-1. School Web Structure.

School Web Pages

Explore School Web Pages. Look for some of the following elements. Brainstorm things that you might include on your page.

Web Contents
   School Information
       Philosophy and Mission Statement
       Logo
       Address
       School Information
       Maps, Locations, Virtual Tours
       Policies, Procedures, Handbooks
       News and Current Events
   People Information
       Students
       Teachers
       Staff
       Administration
       Parents and Community
   Resources and Projects
       Online Newspapers
       Yearbook
       Class Pages
       Project Pages
       School Organizations (i.e., clubs, student government, sports)
       Informational Links
       Homework Links
       Parent and Community Links

Web Development
   Involvement
       Teacher Role
       Student Role
       Community Role

Web Structure

Chart 1-2. School Web Pages.

Chapter 2: Classroom, Course, and Unit Pages 25

Chapter 2: Classroom, Course, & Unit Pages

Is a classroom page appropriate for young students?
What goes into a class page?
Where can I get ideas?

In this chapter, you'll explore classroom, course, and unit web page projects found on the Internet. Some of these pages are created by teachers for their students. Others are created and maintained by students as they work through projects and activities within a class or unit of instruction. Class pages are great for all grade levels and all ages.

Functions of Classroom Web Pages

Classroom web pages can serve many functions. Explore **Peto's Class Student Projects** (http://www.owt.com/phs/classrooms/peto/stu.html) page (see Figure 2-1). Peto's page begins with a link that explains the importance of class projects. The page focuses on individual and small group informational, instructional, and communication projects with students around the world. What kinds of information does the page contain? Why? Who do you think will use the information? Is the page teacher, student, or parent "focused"?

Class Page Functions
Classroom Info
Assignments
Project Sharing
Instructional Content
Links

Class Information. Classroom rules, policies, guidelines, and other general class information may be

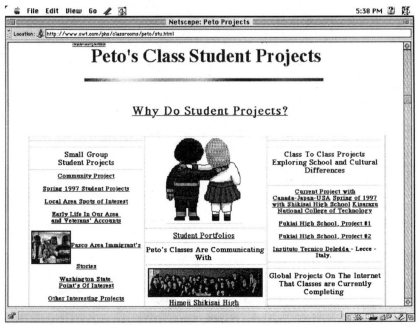

http://www.owt.com/phs/classrooms/peto/stu.html
Figure 2-1. Peto's Class Page.

posted on the classroom page. In many cases teachers will provide information of interest to parents and care givers. Upcoming events such as plays, open house, and field trips might also be listed. In the summer, teachers may list summer activities that students can do at home with their parents.

Assignments. Some teachers use the web to post homework assignments and criteria for projects. Rather than photocopying volumes of paper, teachers post the assignment on the web. This is helpful for students who can easily access computers, but it is problematic in schools where few students have home computers. Since not all students may have access, some teachers only use the web for challenge activities or supplemental work.

The ninth grade **Civil War** (http://www.rochester.k12.mn.us/john-marshall/overton/cwproj/main/civilwar.shtml) project incorporated student projects along with assignments, rubrics, and calls for participation of other classes. The projects even link to each other. For example, the Shiloh page links to the Grant page (see Figure 2-2).

Chapter 2: Classroom, Course, and Unit Pages

http://www.rochester.k12.mn.us/john-marshall/overton/cwproj/main/civilwar.shtml
Figure 2-2. Civil War Project.

http://www.greeceny.com/ls/grade4/
Figure 2-3. Animal Habitats Project.

Project Sharing. The Internet provides an audiences for children. Students can use the Internet to share ideas with other classrooms, collaborate on projects, and post their publications. They can ask other students for critiques and feedback or survey students from other countries around the world. Students might use the project sharing area to report on a field trip or share a classroom activity.

Some classes collaborate within their classroom, building, or around the world. The fourth grade classes at Lakeshore each explored a different animal habitat, then shared it on their **Animal Habitat** (http://www.greeceny.com/ls/grade4/) project page (see Figure 2-3).

Instructional Content. A growing number of teachers are developing original information for the Internet. Along with their students they are creating pages of original course content. For example, a school might post information about the Presidents of the United States or animals living in their region. This content can then be used by their class or other classes

Chapter 2: Classroom, Course, and Unit Pages

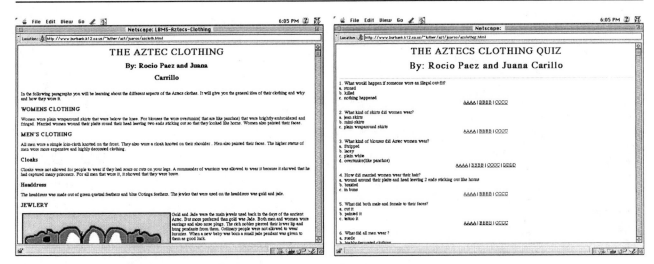

http://www.burbank.k12.ca.us/~luther/aztecs/aztec.html
Figure 2-4. Aztec Project.

as a regular part of classroom instruction. Some teachers have developed quizzes, test, simulations, and other types of activities to go with this course content. Others have developed Web Quests that link activities to specific Internet pages.

The **Aztec** (http://www.burbank.k12.ca.us/~luther/aztecs/aztec.html) page is a good example of a class unit page that is under development. It currently contains information, links, quizzes, pictures and other useful information for teaching this topic. See Figure 2-4 for a student project and quiz.

The **Civil Rights Movement** (http://www.fred.net/nhhs/project/civrts.htm) class page provides a list of all the different types of class projects and assignments, information, activities, and links:

A Photo Essay
Interview with Witness
Sketch timeline
Movie Review
Formal essay
Trivia Game or Quiz
On-line Newspaper
Poetry With illustrations
Maps of Historical Events
Letter to lawmaker

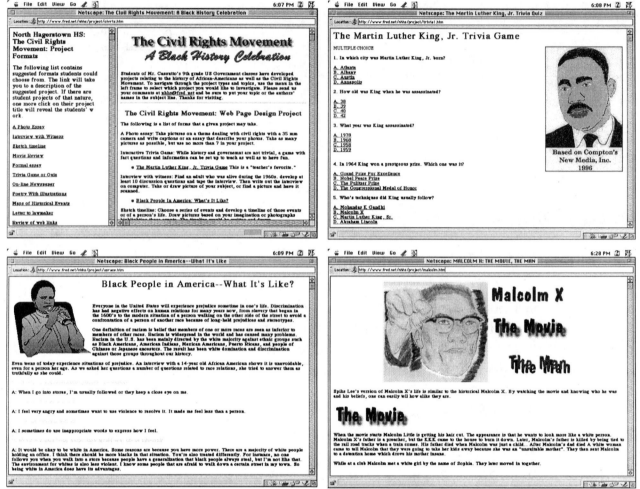

http://www.fred.net/nhhs/project/civrts.htm
Figure 2-5. Civil Rights Class Page.

Review of web links
Biographical sketch
Fictional short story
On-line Debate
Power Point presentation in HTML

Figure 2-5a shows the index page for the class. Figure 2-5b is a student produced quiz on Martin Luther King, Jr. In Figure 2-5c, the student developed a web-based interview. Figure 2-4d shows a movie review.

Links. Teachers often include hotlists on their classroom pages. These lists may relate to particular units of instruction, or they may simply be links students would enjoy for leisure browsing.

Chapter 2: Classroom, Course, and Unit Pages

Explore Class Pages

Thousands of teachers and their students around the world are developing pages for their classes. As you explore these pages consider their purpose and use. What do students and teachers learn from the experience of web page development? What unique perspectives and information does each classroom have to share with the world? What interesting experiences and activities could your class share with the world?

Prairie Chickens and the Prairie in Illinois (http://www.museum.state.il.us/mic_home/newton/project/): Third and fourth grade classes posted projects, activities, and links related to their study of the Illinois Prairie. This project is a good example of exploring a unique feature of a particular area, in this case prairie chickens. Students developed a virtual field trip and projects such as dioramas (see Figure 2-6) to share through the Internet. The teacher even posted lesson plans related to the unit.

Cotton Project (http://www.hipark.austin.isd.tenet.edu/home/projects/first/cotton/cotton.html): First Graders share what they've learned about cotton through KidPix pictures and writings (see Figure 2-7).

http://www.museum.state.il.us/mic_home/newton/project/
Figure 2-6. Prairie Chicken Project.

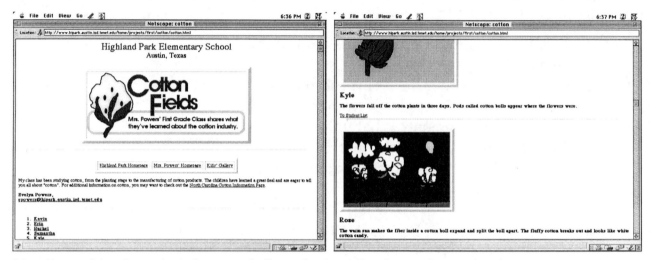

http://www.hipark.austin.isd.tenet.edu/home/projects/first/cotton/cotton.html
Figure 2-7. Cotton Projects.

Snow Depth (http://ffdlm1mac.uafsom.alaska.edu/snow/snow.html): Mrs. Gerke's First Grade Class at Pearl Creek School, Fairbanks, Alaska developed a science fair project involving measurement of snow depth.

Physics Page (http://www.iu13.k12.pa.us/lampstras/hschool/physics/home.html): A High School Physics Class shares their projects (see Figure 2-8a).

Insect Project (http://www.minnetonka.k12.mn.us/groveland/insect.proj/insects.html): A Third Grade Class at Groveland Elementary School in Minnetonka, Minnesota sponsors an annual insect project that involves insect research.

The Twin Cities (http://www.marin.k12.ca.us/~ncsweb/tchp.html): The Third Grade students in Room 22 at Neil Cummins School present information about their cities (see Figure 2-8b).

A Portrait of Houston (http://chico.rice.edu/armadillo/Rice/joelsclass/home.html): Seventh and eighth grade students developed a project focusing on the city of Houston.

Chapter 2: Classroom, Course, and Unit Pages

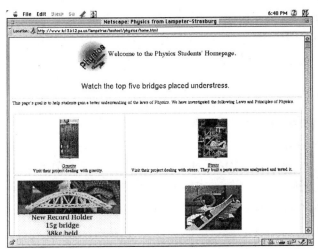

http://www.iu13.k12.pa.us/lampstras/hschool/
physics/home.html

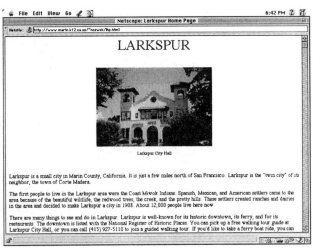

http://www.marin.k12.ca.us/~ncsweb/lhp.html

http://www.tas.gov.au/fahan/Compute/Flores/
pgone.html

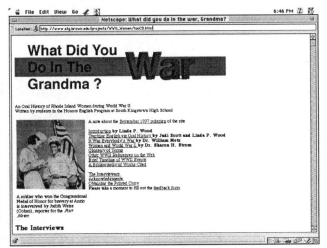

http://www.stg.brown.edu/projects/
WWII_Women/tocCS.html

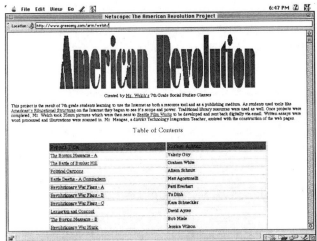

http://www.greeceny.com/arm/welch/
Figure 2-8. Class Project Pages.

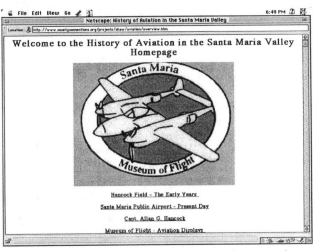

http://www.countyconnections.org/projects/
shaw/aviation/overview.htm

Folk Tales (http://www.tas.gov.au/fahan/Compute/Flores/pgone.html): Year Four students at Fahan School in Australia retell an Indonesian folk tale (see Figure 2-8c).

What did you do in the war, Grandma? (http://www.stg.brown.edu/projects/WWII_Women/tocCS.html): An oral history of Rhode Island women during World War II written by students in the Honors English Program at South Kingstown High School (see Figure 2-8d).

American Revolution (http://www.greeceny.com/arm/welch/): Mr. Welch's seventh grade social studies class studied the American Revolution (see Figure 2-8e).

Aviation Page (http://www.countyconnections.org/projects/shaw/aviation/overview.htm): Sixth graders created a web project to explore the history of aviation and a local airport (see Figure 2-8f).

Voices of the Timeliness Coast (http://www.countyconnections.org/projects/vistadlc/cruces/index.html): A sixth grade class collected these oral histories.

Biodiversity in San Diego (http://gsh.org/jeffweb/97/animate.html): A middle school class explores issues related to biodiversity in their area.

East Meets West: A Cultural Event (http://cyberfair.gsn.org/dodson/japan97/japan97.htm): Eighth graders developed a page to reflect what they learned about Japanese culture.

Calkanimal (http://www.huensd.k12.ca.us/beach/hbsrspcalka.html): Children in California and Kansas got together on email to write and draw picture of animals.

Chapter 2: Classroom, Course, and Unit Pages

Class Web Pages

Buchman's Class	http://buckman.pps.k12.or.us/room100/room100.html
Mrs. Burn's First Grade	http://home.pacbell.net/theburns/
Mr. Carle's Class	http://205.121.65.141/Millville/Teachers/Carles/carles.htm
Durand School	http://www.cyberenet.net/~durand
Elementary Resource Room	http://www.huensd.k12.ca.us/beach/hbsclassroomsrsp.html
Hazel's Home Page	http://www.geocities.com/Athens/5788/
Ms Hos-McGrane's Grade 6	http://www.xs4all.nl/~swanson/origins/intro.html
Ricki Peto's Class Page	http://www.owt.com/phs/classrooms/peto/peto.html
Room 2 Class Page	http://www.staffnet.com/hbogucki/aemes
Room 14A Page	http://www.cyberenet.net/~durand/index.html
Mrs. Silverman's Second Grade	http://www.classrooms.globalchalk.com/Clinton2nd/

List 2-1. Class Web Pages.

Idea Exploration: Class Web Page

Explore the class pages. Compare and contrast two class web pages. Use two from the list above or surf the web for a classroom page in your interest area. How are they alike and different? Were students involved in the development of the pages? Do you think this is important? Why? Share your analysis.

Idea Exploration

Designing Class Web Pages

As you design a class web page, consider the purpose. For some teachers, a class page is a way to reflect on classroom activities and forecast the future. It serves as a living classroom portfolio for both the teacher and the students. Consider the role that the teacher, students, and parents might play in the production and use of the pages.

In Figure 2-9 a kindergarten teacher has created an appealing web page for her class using teddy bears and crayon characters to talk about the daily schedule and class projects. There are also pages about the school and community. These pages were probably fun to create and are a great way to share class activities with parents who might visit the web page.

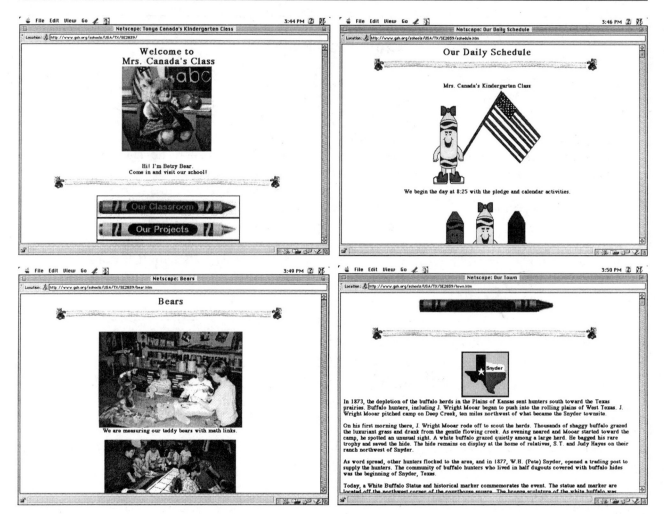

http://www.gsh.org/schools/USA/TX/SE2839/
Figure 2-9. Kindergarten class.

The middle school example in Figure 2-10 shows a number of classes working on various projects. There are individual student pages, class projects and activities, and well as teacher information. Students were involved in the activities and the teacher then posted the projects on the Internet.

Whenever possible, get students involved with the development of the class page. For example, you could assign small groups particular tasks or ongoing activities. Students could do their work in a word processor or graphics package, then you could put it together for the web page.

Chapter 2: Classroom, Course, and Unit Pages 37

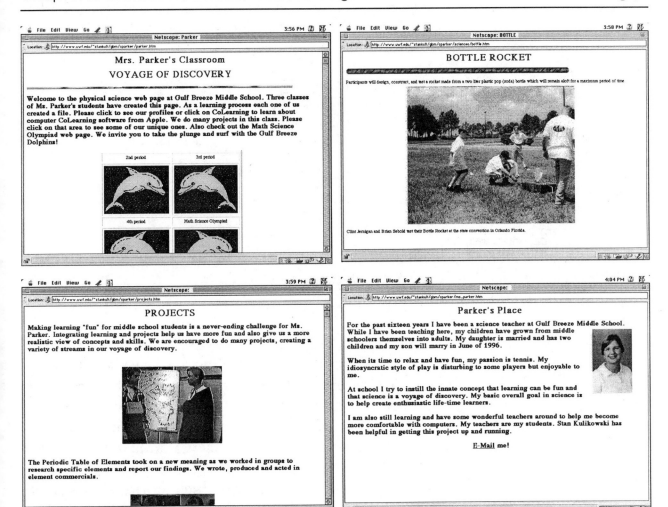

http://www.uwf.edu/~stankuli/gbm/cparker/parker.htm
Figure 2-10. Middle School science class.

Real World Considerations

Students love being involved with class web pages, but it takes planning to make a class page work. First, make students responsible for the page. Make specific assignments related to the page. Some students will be more interested than others, but everyone can participate at some level. Second, involve students in decision making matters. Let them choose the logo for the page and decide what types of projects are posted. Third, guide students in designing the pages, but give students final control. In other words, assist students in editing stories, but leave fragmented sentences and misspellings. You're the guide. See if these problems

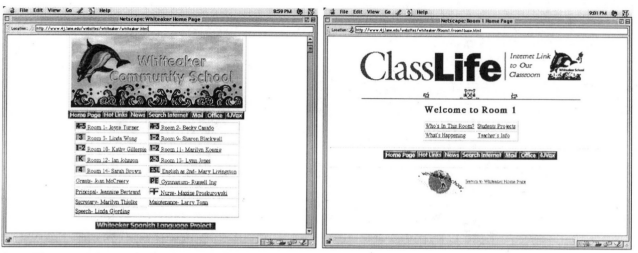

http://www.4j.lane.edu/websites/whiteaker/whiteaker.html
Figure 2-11. Whitaker Community School.

can be picked up with peer review. Fourth, use the web as a tool for portfolio publishing. Let students share their best work. Fifth, connect students with other children around the world using their page.

Getting students involved is exciting, but it's not always realistic. For example, it would take first graders hours to type entire stories on the computer. Get a parent involved with entering their stories after school. Sometimes the design decision students make interfere with the operation of a page. For example, they cram so many animations on the page it's hard to focus attention. Provide helpful revision suggestions to make the pages more readable.

Idea Exploration

Idea Exploration: Class Page
Explore different layouts for class pages. For example, **Whitaker Community School** has a simple, attractive layout for class pages as shown in Figure 2-11. Find a site that's similar to one you'd like to create. Write email to the developer (Webmaster) and ask how they got started.

Create a list of things that you'd like to put in your school, class, and personal home page.

Class Web Pages

Explore Class Web Pages. Look for some of the following elements. Brainstorm things that you might include on your page.

Web Contents
    Classroom Information
        Rules
        Policies
        Guidelines
        Teacher Information
        Student Information
        News
    Assignments
        Homework
        On computer activities
        Off computer activities
    Project Sharing
        Writing Projects
        Drawing Projects
        Multimedia Projects
        Communication Projects
        Collaborative Projects
    Instructional Content
        Information
        Tutorials
        Simulations
        Case Studies
        Tests
        Webquests
    Links

Web Development
    Involvement
        Teacher Role
        Student Role

Chart 2-1. Class Web Pages.

Summary

A class web page is a great way to bring a group of students together for a common cause. Start by exploring existing classes. Next, consider what your class has to bring to the Internet. Finally, design a plan that will get students involved with the project (see Chart 2-1).

Chapter 3: Online School Newspapers and Magazines

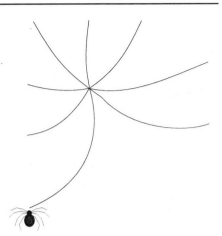

What's an ezine?
What goes into an online newspaper?
What's the difference between a traditional newspaper and an online newspaper?

In this chapter, you'll examine online newspapers and magazines. Schools have always been involved in the publication of newspapers, magazines, and yearbooks. In the past these projects were distributed on paper within the school or community. With the Internet, student publications can be shared with the world. This can be very motivating for the students involved in these activities. Think of the excitement among your students when they receive email praise from a class in Japan or an article contribution from a student in Canada.

Online Magazines for Kids and Teens

Some schools start their involvement with online publications by making use of private and commercial online projects. In other words, rather than producing your own school magazine, why not contribute to an ongoing ezine. There's no need to set up a web server or learn how to put together an entire web site. Students simply submit their work to the "ezine," as online magazines are called. For instance, **Freezone** (http://freezone.com/) posts student produced articles (see Figure 3-1). For other ezines, see List 3-1.

An **ezine** is an electronic magazine. Online publications are often called ezines.

Online Magazines

ABC Kids	http://www.eint.com/abagain/
Children's Art Gallery	http://redfrog.norconnect.no/~cag/
ClubZ	http://www.club-z.com/index.html
CyberKids - Elementary Students	http://www.cyberkids.com/
CyberTeens - Secondary Students	http://www.cyberteens.com/
Dragonfly	http://miavx1.muohio.edu/~dragonfly/
Freezone	http://freezone.com/home/index.html
Fresh Ink	http://www2.phillynews.com/online/fresh/
HyperStudio Projects	http://www.ladue.k12.mo.us/Wildwatch/hyper/project.html
Electronic Newsstand	http://www.enews.com/
Fishnet	http://www.jayi.com/jayi/
Global Show & Tell	http://www.telenaut.com/gst/
Kid Chronicles	http://www.gsn.org/kid/kc/index.html
Kid News	http://www.vsa.cape.com/~powens/Kidnews3.html
KidPub	http://www.kidpub.org/kidpub/
Kids Did This!	http://sln.fi.edu/tfi/hotlists/kids.html
Kid's World Online	http://www.kidsworld-online.com/
Kidz Magazine	http://www.thetemple.com/KidzMagazine/
Looking Glass Gazette	http://www.cowboy.net/~mharper/LGG.html
Natural Child	http://www.naturalchild.com/gallery/
Newwave	http://home.on.rogers.wave.ca/eliza/newswave/
MidLink Magazine - Middle School	http://longwood.cs.ucf.edu:80/~MidLink/
OwlKids	http://www.owl.on.ca/
Press Return	http://www.scholastic.com/public/Network/PressReturn/Press-Return.html
React - Secondary	http://www.react.com
Sources for Student Online Magazines	http://www.eduplace.com/kids/links/kids_4.html
Too Cool for Grownups	http://www.tcfg.com/
Yahooligans Guide to Magazines	http://www.yahooligans.com/Entertainment/Magazines/
Yahooligans Guide to Newspaper	http://www.yahooligans.com/School_Bell/Newspapers_and_Publications/
YesMag	http://www.islandnet.com/~yesmag/
ZuZu	http://www.zuzu.org/

List 3-1. *Online Magazines.*

Chapter 3: Online School Newspapers and Magazines

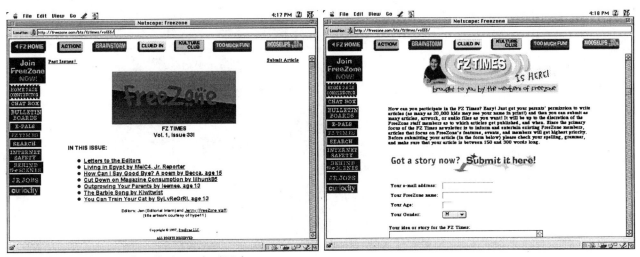

http://freezone.com/bts/fztimes/vol33/
Figure 3-1. Freezone.

Many ezines publish student articles. Explore some of the publications, pages, and projects that are by and for kids!

Idea Exploration: Ezines
Explore online magazines.
　Write a review of the ezine. What do you like and dislike about the magazine? What do they need to add or change? Would you recommend it? Why or why not?
　Create a web page that provides a summary of the magazine, a link the site, and a review. Email your ideas to the Webmaster of the magazine.

Idea Exploration

School Newspapers and Magazines

Hundreds of schools from around the world already have online school publications such as magazines or newspapers. Some are developed in conjunction with a print publication, while others are newly created projects. Let's explore some of the features to look for in student publications.

　Professional Look. Students can create very professional looking web-based publications. The **Horace**

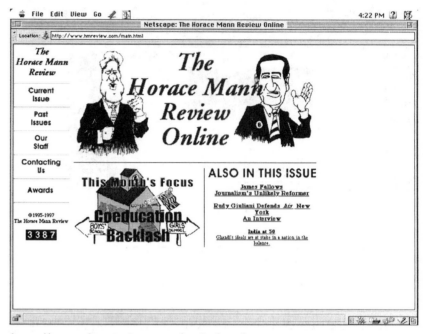

http://www.hmreview.com/main.html
Figure 3-2. Horace Mann Review Online.

Look For:
   Professional look
   Logical layout
   Publishing guidelines
   Text
   Columns
   Audience
   Updates
   Topical Focus
   Student Involvement
   Special Features
   Advertising
   Download Options

Mann Review (http://www.hmreview.com/) is an excellent example of a very professional and commercial student newspaper (see Figure 3-2). It is available in both a print and paper version. Explore their editorial staff, read their articles, and notice their layout.

Examine **NandoNext** (http://www.nando.net/links/nandonext/next.html) as a high school example. It contains high quality articles, columns, and cartoons aimed at the high school student population. **Crest Chronicle** (http://170.177.2.3/hillcrest/chron/chron.html) is a middle school newspaper produced by and for middle school students. The **Junior Seahawk** (http://www.halcyon.com/arborhts/jrseahaw.html) is an elementary example. The key to an effective newspaper is keeping it current and up-to-date. The Junior Seahawk comes out regularly. In addition, past issues are available (see Figure 3-3).

Logical Layout. Be sure that people can easily find the information in your newspaper. Explore a variety of newspapers. How are they organized? **Mountain View Black and Silver** (http://www.isdnet.com/

Chapter 3: Online School Newspapers and Magazines

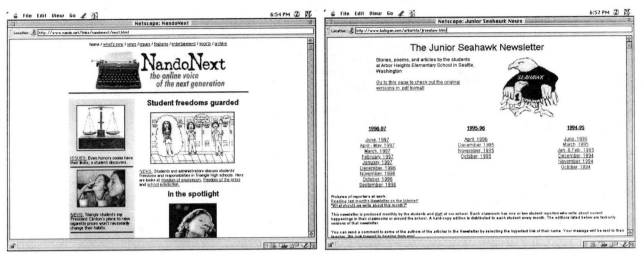

http://www.nando.net/links/nandonext/next.html http://www.halcyon.com/arborhts/jrseahaw.html
Figure 3-3. School Newspapers.

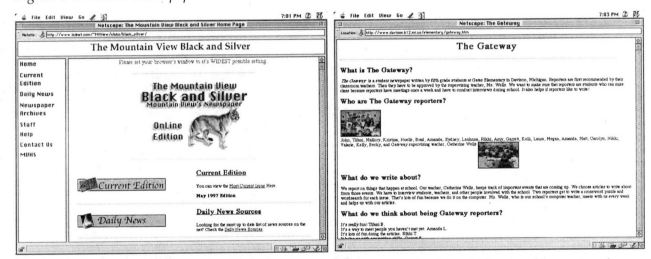

http://www.isdnet.com/~MtView/clubs/
black_silver/
Figure 3-4. Newspaper Layout.

http://www.davison.k12.mi.us/elementary/
gateway.htm

~MtView/clubs/black_silver/) uses frames. It also provides a graphical and text description of each section of the paper. Your newspaper doesn't need to contain more than one page. The **Gateway** (http://www.davison.k12.mi.us/elementary/gateway.htm) is a fifth grade project that contains interesting articles and only a few pictures. As a result, an issue is a single web page (see Figure 3-4).

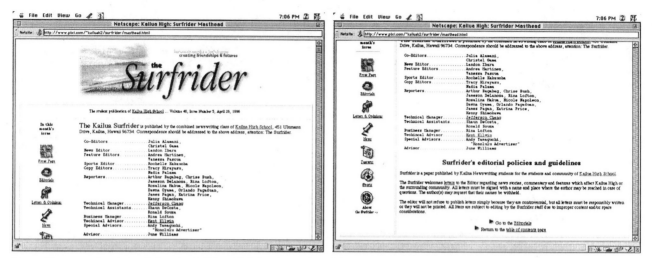

http://www.pixi.com/~kailuah2/surfrider/masthead.html
Figure 3-5. Editorial Guidelines

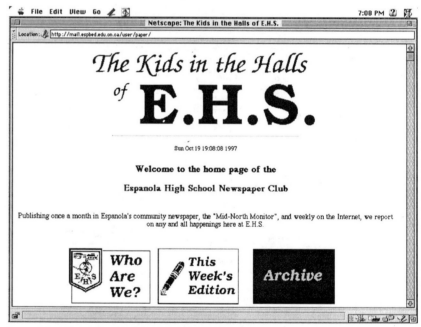

http://mail.espbed.edu.on.ca/user/paper/
Figure 3-6. Text.

Publishing Guidelines. Who is involved in the writing process? How do they decide what to publish? Many newspapers provide a page that lists the editorial board and explains their policies. Check out **The Surf Rider's** (http://www.pixi.com/~kailuah2/surfrider/masthead.html) masthead page in Figure 3-5.

Chapter 3: Online School Newspapers and Magazines   47

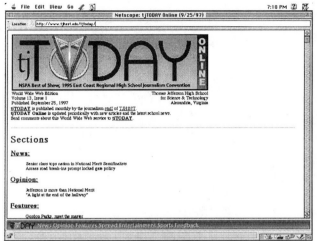 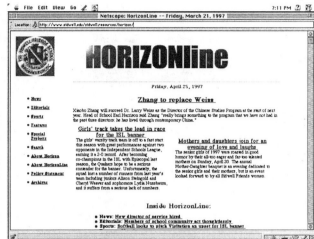

http://www.tjhsst.edu/tjtoday/   http://www.sidwell.edu/sidwell.resources/horizon/
Figure 3-7. Columns.

Text. Consider the size and color of the text presented. The text should be large enough so the reader doesn't tire from reading off the screen. The font and style should also be easy to read. For example, **The Kids in the Halls of EHS** (http://mail.espbed.edu.on.ca/user/paper/) uses green text to match their green school colors. This font is large and easy to read on most pages (see Figure 3-6).

Columns. Many school newspapers are organized into regular sections or columns. Examine the **TJToday** (http://www.tjhsst.edu/tjtoday/) and **HORIZONline** (http://www.sidwell.edu/sidwell.resources/horizon/) (see Figure 3-7). Their categories include news, opinion, features, entertainment, special projects, and sports. What topics might be included in your school newspaper? Examine the print edition. Are there other columns that could be added? Which are the most popular columns? Why? Could they be expanded in an online version? Can you find other categories in other publications?

Audience. Who is the audience of the publication? Is the newspaper developed by and for the students at the schools or is it part of an outreach program?

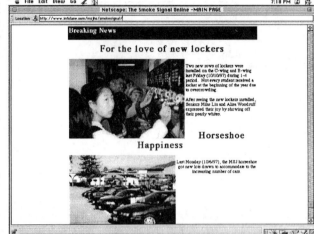

http://www.infolane.com/msjhs/smokesignal/
Figure 3-8. Audience.

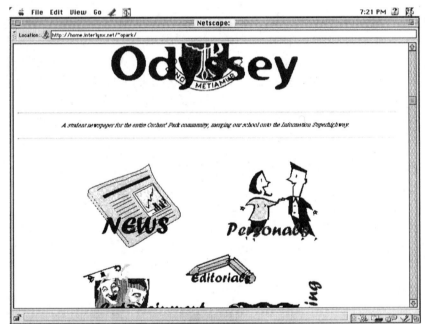

http://home.interlynx.net/~opark/
Figure 3-9. Community and School Audience.

Smoke Signal (http://www.infolane.com/msjhs/smokesignal/) is a high school newspaper that focuses on local events and news (see Figure 3-8). It includes student surveys and highlights exceptional students. It also includes photos and descriptions of current local events. **The Orchard Park Odyssey** (http://home.interlynx.net/~opark/) was developed for their entire community (see Figure 3-9).

Chapter 3: Online School Newspapers and Magazines

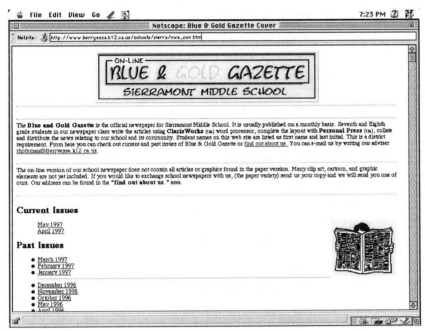

http://www.berryessa.k12.ca.us/schools/sierra/nws_cov.htm
Figure 3-10. Updates.

Update. Keep your newspaper up to date. Notice that the **Blue and Gold Gazette** (http://www.berryessa.k12.ca.us/schools/sierra/nws_cov.htm) provides the most recent issue first on the list, then presents back issues (see Figure 3-10).

Topic Focus. Many high school classes have begun creating newspapers and magazines in particular content areas. **Xenophile Internet Science Magazine** (http://lams.losalamos.k12.nm.us/~doe/Xenophile/) is a good example of a subject-area school magazine in the science area (see Figure 3-11a). The **Camden Kids Literary Magazine** (http://homer.louisville.edu:80/~mfpetr01/litmag/litmag.html) focuses on literary work of children (see Figure 3-11b). **Elevator Ride to the Write** (http://www.geocities.com/SoHo/Lofts/9781/) is a creative writing publication involving students from five high schools (see Figure 3-11c). **The Vocal Point** (http://bvsd.k12.co.us/schools/cent/Newspaper/Newspaper.html) uses significant local or global topics as the basis for each issue. They also call for students outside their school to submit articles for publication (see Figure 3-11d).

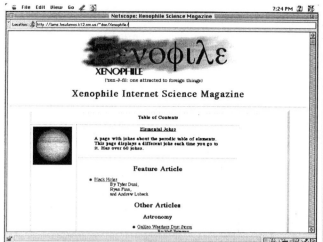

http://lams.losalamos.k12.nm.us/~doe/Xenophile/

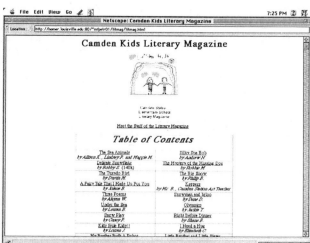

http://homer.louisville.edu:80/~mfpetr01/litmag/litmag.html

http://www.geocities.com/SoHo/Lofts/9781/
Figure 3-11. Topical Focus.

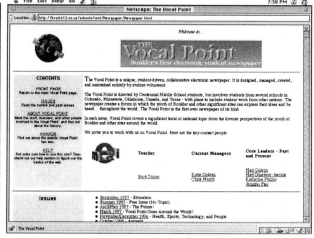

http://bvsd.k12.co.us/schools/cent/Newspaper/Newspaper.html

Student Involvement. Online school newspapers and magazines may be developed by a club or a class. **Adrian's Wall** (http://www.island.net/~aburrus/awall/index2.html) is a class publication by a high school computer class and contains articles on a range of subjects (see Figure 3-12).

Special Features. Some newspapers and magazines include graphics, photographs, animation, sound, and interaction on their pages. **Slummit** (http://spider.netropolis.net/slummit/photo/photmenu.htm)

Chapter 3: Online School Newspapers and Magazines 51

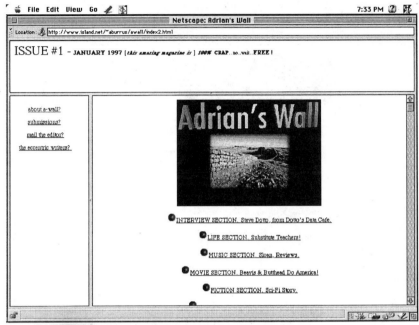

http://www.island.net/~aburrus/awall/index2.html
Figure 3-12. Student Involvement.

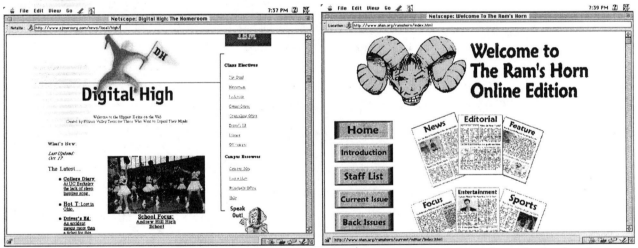

http://www.sjmercury.com/news/local/high/
Figure 3-13. Special Features.

http://www.chsn.org/ramshorn/index.html

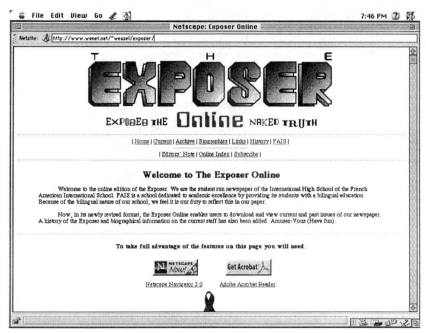

http://www.wenet.net/~weasel/exposer/
Figure 3-14. Download Options.

has a photography section in their online magazine. The **Digital High** (http://www.sjmercury.com/news/local/high/) ezine contains a forum for discussions. The **Ram's Horn Online Edition** (http://www.chsn.org/ramshorn/index.html) contains a simple animation in the ram logo (see Figure 3-13).

Advertising. Advertising is used in some newspapers and not in others. Check out the **Taton** (http://www.best.com/~latalon/). They are looking for advertisers.

Download Options. Some newspapers are built in a format that requires downloading. **The Exposer** (http://www.wenet.net/~weasel/exposer/) is an example (see Figure 3-14). They even provide the links for downloading the required **Adobe Acrobat** (http://www.adobe.com/prodindex/acrobat/readstep.html) software. The **Inklings** (http://204.249.212.251/Inks.html) is a print-based newspaper that is scanned and placed on the web. Rather than downloading software for viewing, the graphics are viewed on the web.

Chapter 3: Online School Newspapers and Magazines 53

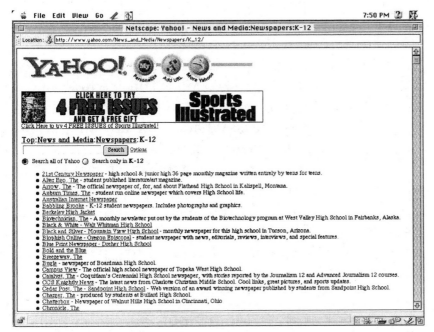

http://www.yahoo.com/News_and_Media/Newspapers/K_12/
Figure 3-15. Yahoo list.

Explore School Magazines and Newspapers

Explore some **Yahooligans School Newspapers** (http://www.yahooligans.com/School_Bell/Newspapers), **Yahoo School Newspapers** (http://www.yahoo.com/News_and_Media/Newspapers/K_12/) (see Figure 3-15), and **Kids Did This** (http://sln.fi.edu/tfi/hotlists/kid-news.html). You may also want to explore **College Campus Newspapers Online** (http://beacon-www.asa.utk.edu/resources/papers.html).

Idea Exploration: Acrobat
Download **Adobe Acrobat** (http://www.adobe.com/prodindex/acrobat/readstep.html). Explore some of the online newspapers and magazines that are available only in the Acrobat format.

Compare and contrast the web-based format and the Acrobat format for viewing and reading newspapers.

Idea Exploration

Idea Exploration

Idea Exploration: Newspapers

Explore lots of school newspaper and magazine pages. Use **Eddie Blick's** (http://eb.journ.latech.edu/Schol_journ/HS_pub_web.html) pages for more High School Newspaper ideas. What are the most important elements? What draws interest (see List 3-2)?

Design the core page of a school newspaper for your school or classroom. You don't need to develop the content for the entire newspaper, just the first page as an example. You could even make up fictitious article titles and columns. Design the first page anticipating the types of links you might wish to include.

School Newspapers and Magazines

The Arrow Online	http://www.netrix.net/fhspub/
The Black and Gold	http://tiger.chuh.cleveland-heights.k12.oh.us/BlackGold/BlackGold.html
Blue and Gold Gazette	http://www.berryessa.k12.ca.us/schools/sierra/nws_cov.htm
Cougar Times	http://www.centennial.k12.mn.us/cjhs/newspaper/index.html
Crest Chronicle	http://170.177.2.3/hillcrest/chron/chron.html
Hanabi	http://www.asij.ac.jp/journalism/hanabi.html
Horace Mann Review	http://www.hmreview.com/
Hornet Herald	http://www.elk-grove.k12.il.us/schoolweb/highland/highland.news.html
Inklings	http://204.249.212.251/Inks.html
Junior Seahawk	http://www.halcyon.com/arborhts/jrseahaw.html
Kidzette	http://www.pbpost.com/kidzette/
KIDS Report	http://wwwscout.cs.wisc.edu/scout/KIDS/index.html
Meadow News	http://www.lbe.edu.on.ca/bonavent/newsontario/mnmain.htm
Miller Post	http://riceinfo.rice.edu/armadillo/Rice/Miller/
Mountain View Bla	http://www.isdnet.com/~MtView/clubs/black_silver/
NandoNext	http://www.nando.net/links/nandonext/next.html
Patriot Press	http://www.chesapeake.net/patpress/
Smoke Signal	http://www.infolane.com/msjhs/smokesignal/
Spokesman	http://spokesman.pds.k12.nj.us/page2.html
Summit	http://spider.netropolis.net/slummit/
The Surf Rider	http://www.pixi.com/~kailuah2/surfrider/
TJ Today	http://www.tjhsst.edu/tjtoday/

List 3-2. School Newspapers and Magazines

Chapter 3: Online School Newspapers and Magazines

Newspaper Web Pages

Explore Online Newspaper Web Pages. Look for some of the following elements. Brainstorm things that you might include on your page.

Web Periodical Options
- Newspapers
- Ezines
- Yearbooks

Web Newspaper Contents
- Professional look
- Logical layout
- Publishing guidelines
- Text
- Columns
- Audience
- Updates
- Topical Focus
- Student Involvement
- Special Features
- Advertising
- Download Options

Web Newspaper Development
- Involvement
    - Teacher Role
    - Student Role

Online Newspapers vs Print Newspapers
- Advantages

- Disadvantages

- Keeping Both

Chart 3-1. Newspaper Web Pages.

Real World Considerations

Many schools already have paper-based schools newspapers. Are online newspapers really necessary? Is there really a need for students to publish in an ezine? What's the difference between a traditional newspaper and an online newspaper?

The advantage of an online newspaper is its flexibility. Unlike a school newspaper which is restricted to exactly 8, 12, or 16 pages, the length of a web newspaper is without limit. In addition, online newspapers can be constantly updated. They aren't restricted to a duplication deadline like traditional newspapers. Rather than a full edition, some schools continuously add to their web newspapers. For example, sports scores are integrated the day after the game rather than appearing in the weekly newspaper. Another advantage of an online newspaper is the cost savings if the print version is eliminated. Finally, an online newspaper can easily incorporate multimedia elements such as audio, video, graphics, and other enhanced features.

Online newspapers also have some major drawbacks. For example, you can't carry an ezine to lunch or share parts of the newspaper between classes. An online newspaper requires a computer and Internet access.

Summary

School newspapers are a popular new trend. Rather than eliminating their print newspaper, many schools are adding an online version of their newspaper thereby incorporating the best of both worlds. The online version contains up-to-date information and an archive of older articles, while the paper version is still available for leisure reading.

Chapter 4: Project Pages

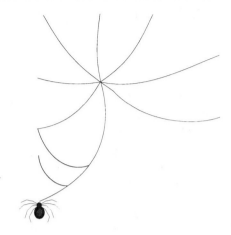

Are there projects in all content areas?
How can I involve students in a web-based project?
Where can I find ideas?

In this chapter, you'll find examples of great Internet-based projects in every content area. Let's explore each of the following content areas and examine some sample projects.

Art
Music
Social Studies
Math/Science
Literacy

Art Projects

Art is a popular topic for Internet projects. You'll find lots of examples of student art work. In some cases, the artwork was done in pencil, marker, or paints, then scanned into the computer. Sculptures, puppets, paper folding, dioramas, and other three dimensional projects can be shown by using a digital camera picture or digitizing a still picture from a videotape. It's a good idea to include a small thumbnail picture on an index page. Then interested users can click on the thumbnail for an enlarged picture. Student might also wish to include descriptions with their projects. It's also fun for

Art Projects
   Scanned pictures
   Step-by-step
      directions
   Research
   Critiques
   Sharing
   Ask an artist
   Access art
   Showcase art
   Art contests

students to collaborate on art projects over the Internet. For example, one class could draw pictures and post them on the Internet. Another class could then write a story to go with the picture.

The Internet is also a great way for students to demonstrate their art skills. For example, a student could write step-by-step instructions for creating a tie dyed shirt or batik wall hanging. The instructions could be illustrated with digital photographs or illustrations.

Combine student projects with links. For example, ask students to write about an artist, style, or piece of artwork, then link to a site or sites for additional information. There are many museum sites that contain famous works of art and information about popular artists. You might have students critique a piece of artwork found on the web, then share their critique with others. Students could create and share their rating system with students at another school.

Claude Monet Project (http://www.greeceny.com/lr/monet/monet.htm): Elementary students studied the artist Monet, developed a biography and drew pictures.

Greece Schools Artwork (http://greeceny.com/artshow/saw.htm): This K-12 site provides examples of artwork from all grade levels (see Figure 4-1a).

Art Space (http://www.uni.uiuc.edu/uniartspace.html): Since 1994, this high school art gallery has posted great examples of teen art.

Peace In Pictures Project (http://www.macom.co.il/peace/): Children from around the world are invited to submit their artwork to this project sponsored by a group in Jerusalem.

Chapter 4: Project Pages

http://greeceny.com/artshow/saw.htm
Figure 4-1. Art Projects.

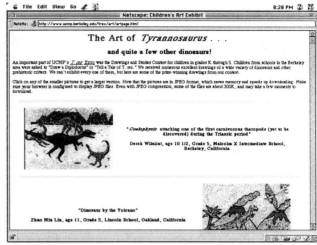

http://www.ucmp.berkeley.edu/trex/art/artpage.html

The Art of Tyrannosaurus (http://www.ucmp.berkeley.edu/trex/art/artpage.html): Students submit dinosaur art to this art museum project (see Figure 4-1b).

Magazine Collage (http://cmp1.ucr.edu/exhibitions/hoffer/collage/collage.html): This class developed desert collages from magazine pictures.

Storyteller Dolls (http://www.inform.umd.edu/UMS+State/UMD-Projects/MCTP/Technology/School_WWW_Pages/Storytellers/TitlePage.html): Students learn about storytellers and develop art projects.

Music Projects

There's nothing parents love more than to hear their child play the trumpet in the band or sing a solo in chorus. It's easy to digitize short audio clips from a concert to include on your web site. For example, you might have the school song playing when you open your music page. On the other hand, you need to be careful about the music you select. Check the copyright guidelines before posting music of any kind.

Get your students involved with developing original musical compositions. These can be posted on the

Music Projects
  Sound clips
  Concert pictures
  Critiques
  Research
  Reviews
  Music scores
  Access Music
  Pair artists
  Cultural study

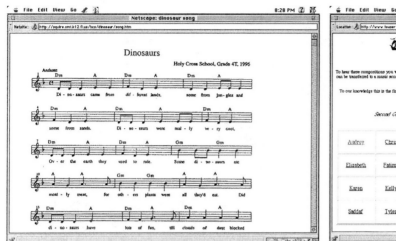

http://squire.cmi.k12.il.us/hcs/dinosaur/song.htm *http://www.teaser.fr/~lforish/mids00.html*
Figure 4-2. Music Projects.

Internet and shared with students at other schools. Students can also work on informational projects related to types of music or composers. They can incorporate links to dozens of great music sites. Ask students to review popular music and share their critiques on the Internet.

Web Music Files
MIDI
au
aiff

Dinosaur Song (http://squire.cmi.k12.il.us/hcs/dinosaur/song.htm): This fourth grade class wrote a dinosaur song and have the music available for other classes. The students made instruments (http://squire.cmi.k12.il.us/hcs/dinosaur/tyrrano.htm) to go with their project (see Figure 4-2a).

Musical Composition (http://www.teaser.fr/~lforish/mids00.html): Students at the American School in Paris share their musical compositions. You can listen to their compositions (see Figure 4-2b).

Diablo Valley Music Page (http://cyberfair.gsn.org/woodside/). Student shares experiences with music.

Social Studies Projects

Social studies topics are a natural for Internet projects. With up-to-the minute data and reports, students can easily keep on top of popular issues and topics. Consider developing a current events pages that students keep updated with popular, timely topics. Internet is also a super way to get students to share their concerns and ideas regarding current events and issues on a global level. Use the many chats and forums for social issues discussions and debates. Join with other schools in the development of a project that might have a significant social impact.

Use Internet as a way to share information collected from interviews. For example, oral history projects are currently a popular social studies activity. Post the text along with photographs on a web page. Experts are another good resource for interviews. Local officials and politicians are always happy to provide information for this type of project.

Involve students in real-world issues and topics. Ask them to develop a research question and create a survey or poll. The students can post their results on the Internet. These results can be shared and combined with the data from other schools. Topics such as political campaigns, environmental issues, and global events are good for this type of project.

Traditional reports can be brought alive through the use of the Internet. Ask students to link their reports to existing web resources or combine their projects with students from other sites. Develop pages that use a museum floorplan, timeline, or map as an organizational structure.

Explore geography by participating in worldwide projects. Learn more about the participating countries.

> Social Studies Projects
>   Research
>   Reports
>   Data sharing
>   Oral histories
>   Interviews
>   Polls & Surveys
>   Timelines
>   History chains
>   Maps
>   Virtual field trips
>   Newsletters
>   Investigations
>   Culture comparisons
>   Problem solving
>   Access information
>   Investigate bias
>   Editorialize
>   Take social action
>   Chart a journey
>   Debate an issue
>   Virtual elections

President's Page (http://www.peoples.net/~southbd/). Children post information about US Presidents (see Figure 4-3a).

62 Spinnin' the Web

http://www.peoples.net/~southbd/

http://www.adventureonline.com/pca/

http://www.ozemail.com.au/~wprimary/acts.htm

http://www.rmplc.co.uk/eduweb/sites/chatback/memories.html

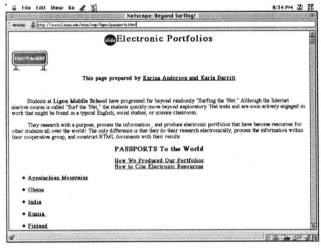
http://www2.ncsu.edu/ncsu/cep/ligon/passports.html

Figure 4-3. Social Studies Examples.

http://neptune.esc.k12.in.us/commnet/wabash1/wabash.html

Chapter 4: Project Pages

63

Project Central America (http://www.adventureonline.com/pca/): Students from around the world participated in this project which explores the history, culture, and people of Central America (see Figure 4-3b).

Australia (http://www.ozemail.com.au/~wprimary/acts.htm): Children at Wangaratta Primary School developed activities about their country to share around the world (see Figure 4-3c).

Memories of the 1940's (http://www.rmplc.co.uk/eduweb/sites/chatback/memories.html): The extraordinary stories of ordinary people are shared in this memory collection project involving people from around the world (see Figure 4-3d).

Revolutionary War (http://www.rbs.edu/history/rbs/rbspage.html): Students share information about the revolutionary war.

Layfayette History (http://wildcats.lafsd.k12.ca.us/happy_valley/lafayette_history/index.html): This project was developed by third graders to share historical information about the area where they live.

Passports to the World (http://www2.ncsu.edu/ncsu/cep/ligon/passports.html): Student share their projects related to regions and countries of the world (see Figure 4-3e).

Welcome to Wabash (http://neptune.esc.k12.in.us/commnet/wabash1/wabash.html): Students share information about the history of their local community (see Figure 4-3f).

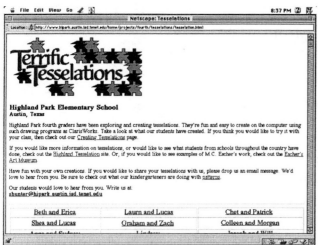

http://www.hipark.austin.isd.tenet.edu/home/projects/fourth/tesselations/tesselation.html

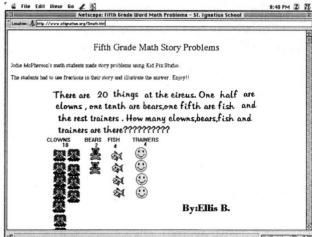

http://www.stignatius.org/5math.htm

http://www.li.net/~stmarya/stm/home.htm

http://met.open.ac.uk/heronsgate/projects/IntoSpace/IntoSpace.html

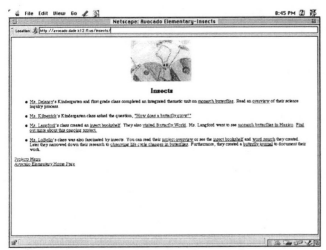

http://avocado.dade.k12.fl.us/insects/
Figure 4-4. Math and Science Projects.

http://www.sci.mus.mn.us/sln/monarchs/

Chapter 4: Project Pages

Math/Science Projects

Sharing is the key to effective math and science projects on the Internet. Have your children develop story problems for other students to solve. Develop a project that involves data collection around the world. As a global group, come up with conclusions and make recommendations. Post the results of science projects and lab experiments.

Get students involved with accessing and analyzing information they find on the Internet. Ask them to compare and contrast information and resources and draw conclusions based on their findings. This is a great way to bring math alive for students. Analyze baseball statistics, stock market data, or interest rates. Explore shifts in world population data, endangered species populations, or global warming.

Many colleges, universities, and research institutions sponsor exciting Internet projects. Join with other schools in developing projects and post the results on the Internet. Explore the following examples.

Math/Science Projects
　Data analysis
　Problem solving
　Inquiry
　Experimentation
　Info Sharing
　Research
　Reports
　Animations
　Simulations
　Demonstrations
　Data comparison
　Ask an expert
　Inverview
　Debate issues
　Info Access
　Track data
　Polls & Surveys
　Identify problems
　Share results

Terrific Tesselations (http://www.hipark.austin.isd.tenet.edu/home/projects/fourth/tesselations/tesselation.html): This project involved fourth graders in the development of tesselations using Clarisworks (see Figure 4-4a).

Fifth Grade Math Story Problems (http://www.stignatius.org/5math.htm): Students published story problems using Kid Pixs (see Figure 4-4b).

Making Waves (http://www.li.net/~stmarya/stm/home.htm): An online guide to sound and electromagnetic radiation by a high school physics class (see Figure 4-4c).

Into Space (http://met.open.ac.uk/heronsgate/projects/IntoSpace/IntoSpace.html): Students share their simulated space exploration using video clips of their lego project (see Figure 4-4d).

Insect Projects (http://avocado.dade.k12.fl.us/insects/): Elementary classes share what they've learned about insects (see Figure 4-4e).

Fractal and Tessellation Projects (http://www.granite.k12.ut.us/Jefferson/studentw.htm): Students at Thomas Jefferson Junior High posted their tesselations.

Patterns (http://www.hipark.austin.isd.tenet.edu/home/projects/kinder/patterns/patterns.html): A kindergarten class discovers patterns and shares their exploration through drawings.

Monarchs and Migration (http://www.sci.mus.mn.us/sln/monarchs/): Teachers and students from around the world are studying Monarch butterflies in this multischool project (see Figure 4-4f).

Environment (http://cissus.mobot.org/MBGnet/): The Missouri Botanical Garden sponsors lots of great projects and contests related to the environment.

Noon Observation Project (http://www.ed.uiuc.edu/coe/projects/noon-project/): In this project, students work together to accurately estimate the circumference of the earth.

Power River Coal Company (http://web.ccsd.k12.wy.us/mines/PR/pr.html): This online report provides information and links regarding coal mining and processing.

Butterflies Take Wing (http://www.greeceny.com/wr/jones/btrfly.html): A second grade class raised butterflies and share what they learned.

Chapter 4: Project Pages

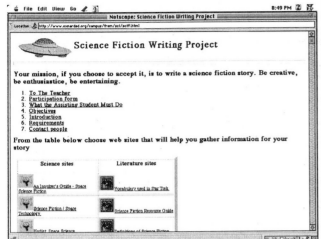

http://www.oxnardsd.org/campus/frem/sci/scifi.html

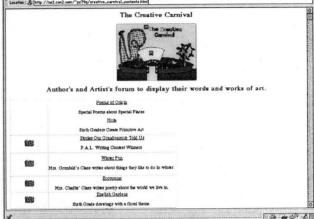

http://ns2.con2.com/~ps79q/creative_carnival_contents.html

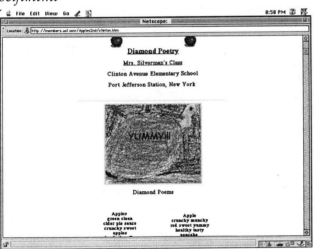

http://members.aol.com/Apples2nd/index.html

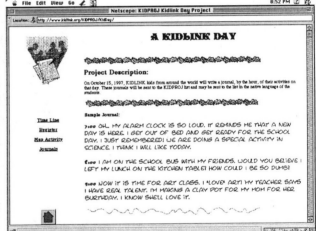

http://www.kidlink.org/KIDPROJ/KidDay/

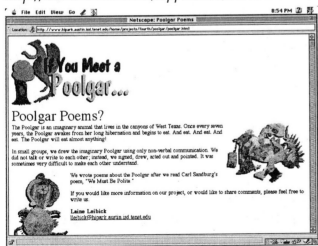

http://www.hipark.austin.isd.tenet.edu/home/projects/fourth/poolgar/poolgar.html

Figure 4-5. Literacy.

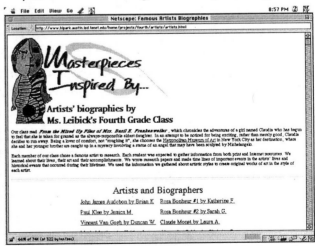

http://www.hipark.austin.isd.tenet.edu/home/projects/fourth/artists/artists.html

Literacy Projects

English, literature, reading, and writing are all areas of literacy that can be enhanced through the development of Internet projects. Use the Internet to explore information about authors, then ask students to share their favorite book or new book idea by emailing an author.

Develop a book buddy activity where students across the country pair with other students to read and share books, develop critical reviews, or write poetry.

Use the Internet to post creative writing projects, investigations, journals, articles, and other original writing.

Science Fiction Writing Project (http://www.oxnardsd.org/campus/frem/sci/scifi.html): Students learn about science fiction writing and write their own stories (see Figure 4-5a).

The Creative Carnival (http://ns2.con2.com/~ps79q/creative_carnival_contents.html): This page contains elementary school writing and art projects (see Figure 4-5b).

Collection of Poetry (http://members.aol.com/Apples2nd/index.html): This site is used to share poetry from classes around the world (see Figure 4-5c).

KidDay (http://www.kidlink.org/KIDPROJ/KidDay/): This global project involves students sharing a day in their lives through journal writing (see Figure 4-5d).

ReadIn (http://www.readin.org/): Students get involved with reading at the Read In project.

If you meet a poolgar... (http://www.hipark.austin.isd.tenet.edu/home/projects/fourth/poolgar/poolgar.html): This creative project involved students in both drawing and poetry (see Figure 4-5e).

Literacy Projects
- Literature study
- Write letters/email
- Role play characters
- Peer Editing
- Culture study
- News reporting
- News access
- Journalism
- Opinion/Editorials
- Biographies
- Book reviews
- Author studies
- Original prose
- Original Poetry
- Sharing
- Technical writing
- Peer writing
- Web publishing
- Foreign language connections

Chapter 4: Project Pages

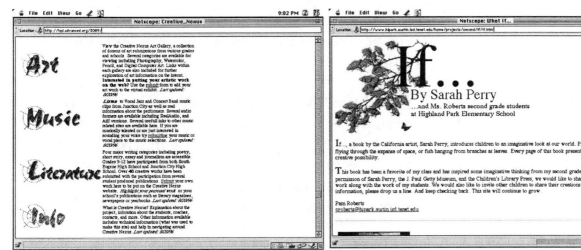

http://tqd.advanced.org/3089/
Figure 4-6. Interdisciplinary.

http://www.hipark.austin.isd.tenet.edu/home/projects/second/if/if.html

Masterpieces (http://www.hipark.austin.isd.tenet.edu/home/projects/fourth/artists/artists.html): Students read the book **From the Mixed Up Files of Mrs. Basil E. Frankenweiler**, learned about art museums, then created their own masterpieces (see Figure 4-5f).

Interdisciplinary Projects

Cross-discipline projects are easy with the Internet. Focus on popular topics in the news or world events such as the WWII Commemorations or the Olympics. Ask students to share unique experiences such as life after a natural disaster or living with war.

Share your local area with other classrooms through the creation of virtual field trips and pen pal projects. As you design projects, think about the multiple intelligences. Are you reaching the interests and needs of all children?

Creative Nexus (http://tqd.advanced.org/3089/): In this project, students can share their art, music, and writing projects (see Figure 4-6a).

Barney Bear's Travels (http://members.aol.com/nkoeh48321/barney.html): In this project a stuffed bear

Multiple Intelligences
Verbal/Linguistic
Visual/Spacial
Mathematical/Logical
Bodily/Kinesthetic
Interpersonal
Intrapersonal

is traveling around the world collecting and sharing information about geography, writing, and other activities.

If.. (http://www.hipark.austin.isd.tenet.edu/home/projects/second/if/if.html): This second grade project combines a picture book with writing and drawing activities. Notice that the author of the picture book was contacted to get permission for use of the illustrations (see Figure 4-6b).

Loteria Cards (http://www.hipark.austin.isd.tenet.edu/home/latino/latino.html): Students combined art, games, and the study of culture in this project.

Castle Creations (http://www.hipark.austin.isd.tenet.edu/home/projects/third/castles/castles.html): Students wrote and drew about castles in this third grade project.

Idea Exploration

Idea Exploration: Project Pages
Explore web projects. Use the list shown in List 4-1 to identify some online projects.

Examine the topic of the project. Does it reflect objectives that you teach? What computer and Internet access is required for the project? How does this compare to your access? What about the duration of the project? Would a project of this type take too much time in your classroom? How would you fit it into your curriculum? Consider how you would redesign the project.

Project Web Pages

List the units you teach each year. Explore the Internet for project ideas to go with each unit.

Unit	Project Idea

Chart 4-1. Project Web Pages.

Project Idea Pages

Canada's SchoolNet	http://schoolnet2.carleton.ca/
Electronic Elementary Magazine	http://www.inform.umd.edu/MDK-12/homepers/emag/
ExploraNet	http://www.exploratorium.edu/media_projects.html
Global Heinemann	http://www.reedbooks.com.au/heinemann/global/project.html
Global Schoolnet Network	http://www.gsn.org/
Kidlink	http://www.kidlink.org/KIDPROJ/
NickNacks Telecommunicate	http://www1.minn.net:80/~schubert/NickNacks.html
Pitsco's Launch: Projects	http://www.pitsco.com/p/collab.html
Project Center	http://www.hmco.com/hmco/school/projects/index.html
Project Watch	http://www.eduplace.com/hmco/school/projects/online.html

List 4-1 Project Idea Pages.

Ideas
  Be realistic
  Start small
  Duplicate
  Expand

Real World Considerations

Projects can be fun, but they can also be frustrating and time consuming. Before you jump in, plan.

Be realistic. Although the Internet is simple to use, there are lots of potential frustrations. Your students will read slower than you anticipated, sites will take longer to load than you planned, and group projects may lead to conflict rather than collaboration. As you explore projects, look for suggestions from experienced teachers.

Start small. Rather than asking 20 schools to participate, start with two. Instead of having each student create a page, work in small groups. Start with a two-week project rather than a semester commitment.

Duplicate an existing project. Try replicating a project that another teacher has just completed. Email the teacher for suggestions.

Expand an existing project. Take a project that has just been completed and go one step further. Build on the web pages that another class started.

Summary

Web projects are a great way to reach outside your classroom. Begin by exploring the possibilities in each content area and unit you teach. Then jump right in!

Chapter 5: Student Pages

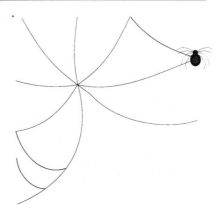

Are student pages realistic?
What should be included on student pages?
Who monitors what students post?

In this chapter, you'll explore pages developed by students. Students are creating web pages at school and at home. Some are created for fun and others are developed as part of a formal class. Regardless of the reason, students seem to love web page development.

Take the **Weird Guys Who Write Poems** (http://www.geocities.com/SoHo/Lofts/8981/) site for example. This project is sponsored by a small group of middle school guys who like to write poetry (see Figure 5-1).

Idea Exploration: Student Page Exploration
Let's examine some of the common elements of student web pages (see List 5-1). As you explore, examine the role of the child, teacher, and parent. Are students really developing the pages or simply providing input? Are all students involved in web development or just a few? Are students working individually or in small groups?

Idea Exploration

Student Pages

Berit's Best Sites for Kids	http://db.cochran.com/li_showElems:theoPage:theo:4006:0.db
K-12 CyberTrail	http://www.wmht.org/trail/trail.htm
Kids Space - Kid's Village	http://www.kids-space.org
By Kids For Kids	http://www.cyberkids.com/Launchpad/BannerPages/Kids.html

List 5-1. Student Pages.

Student Page Elements
About me
Topics
Sharing

Elements of Student Pages

You'll find lots of great student pages on the Internet. Explore some student pages (see Figure 5-2).

About Me

Many students are developing autobiographical-type pages. They provide information about their interests, backgrounds, hobbies, and favorite things. Links to favorite sites are often a focal point of the page.

Jessica's Page (http://www.itp.tsoa.nyu.edu/~student/mags/jessy/index.html): Explore information, artwork, and writing by Jessy (see Figure 5-2a).

http://www.geocities.com/SoHo/Lofts/8981/
Figure 5-1. The Weird Guy Who Write Poems.

Chapter 5: Student Pages

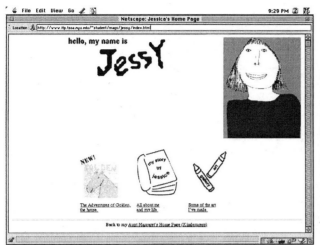

http://www.itp.tsoa.nyu.edu/~student/mags/
jessy/index.html

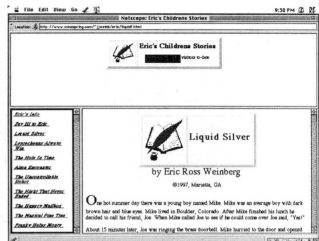

http://www.mindspring.com/~jjweinb/eric/
eric.html

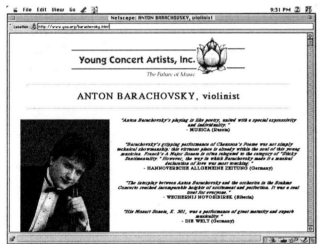

http://www.yca.org/barachovsky.html
Figure 5-2. About Me Sites.

http://www.asiaonline.net.hk/lilywong/kids/
ivan.htm

Eric's Page (http://www.mindspring.com/~jjweinb/eric/eric.html): Eric's page provides information about this child and his writings (see Figure 5-2b).

Young Concert Artists (http://www.yca.org/barachovsky.html): Find out about concert violinist Anton Barachovsky (see Figure 5-2c).

Original Artwork by Ivan (http://www.asiaonline.net.hk/lilywong/kids/ivan.htm): Learn about this six year old world traveler who displays his photographs and artwork (see Figure 5-2d).

http://www.humboldt1.com/~gralsto/einstein/einstein.html

http://www.netlink.co.uk/users/itcentre/hilton/christopher/

Figure 5-3. Topical Pages.

Topics

Some students are really involved in a particular sport, music, hobby, collection, or issue. These students sometimes create a web site that focuses on their favorite thing. They often include pictures from their collection and information about it (see Figure 5-3).

Jesse's Albert Einstein Project (http://www.humboldt1.com/~gralsto/einstein/einstein.html): Jesse likes Albert Einstein and developed this web project based on his life and works (see Figure 5-3a).

Christopher's Guide to Newcastle (http://www.netlink.co.uk/users/itcentre/hilton/christopher/): This project is a student's guide to a city in the United Kingdom (see Figure 5-3b).

Lorinda's Art Gallery (http://www.mitchellware.com/mitchell/home/lorinda/): This child loves art, particularly computer art. Check out her work.

Chapter 5: Student Pages

77

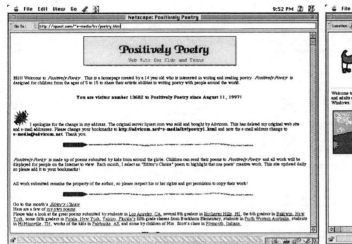 

http://iquest.com/~e-media/kv/poetry.html *http://www.cvns.net/~pfd/kids/*
Figure 5-4. Sharing Pages.

Sharing

One of the most popular web projects for students involves sharing. Students often collect the writings of other students and post them on their page or share their own work. Some examples of sharing pages are shown below (see Figure 5-4):

   Positively Poetry (http://iquest.com/~e-media/kv/poetry.html): This teenager developed a page for poetry sharing around the world (see Figure 5-4a).

   Dempsey Kids Art Gallery (http://www.cvns.net/~pfd/kids/): This page shows the artwork developed in KixPix by Katie (10) and Mike (7 (see Figure 5-4b).

   Poetry Project (http://www.isa.nl/student/Saney/wallflo.htm): Teenagers posted their web poetry. One student used **Sunflowers** (http://www.isa.nl/student/Saney/wallflo.htm) as a theme. Another used **Boy Meets World** (http://www.isa.nl/student/margevich/home1.htm).

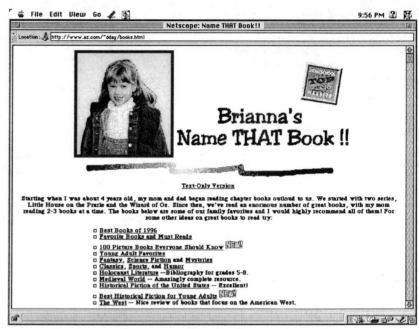

http://www.az.com/~dday/books.html
Figure 5-5. Brianna's page.

Designing Student Pages

The key to successful student pages is the level of involvement of learners. Get them excited about web page development by showing them lots of models. Then, give them a specific assignment, but let them have free rein within the parameters of the project. Although you might choose different colors, graphics, or fonts, let students explore and try out their ideas. Once they feel comfortable developing and maintaining a page, review design guidelines and provide specific ideas for improving the content and design of the pages.

Rather than making web development a one-shot project, make it a regular part of what your children do in the classroom or at home. For example, Brianna maintains her own web page (see Figure 5-5) related to books. It even contains book reviews and trivia games.

Chapter 5: Student Pages 79

Student Web Pages

Student Web Pages at School
   Explore how schools handle web page postings. Some provide all students with access, while others only provide space for specific classes.

Student Web Page Purpose
   Students post information for many different reasons. Some students do it for fun, others for a class assignment, and some are reaching out for others with similar interests. Explore student sites and discuss the purpose of each page.

Student Web Development
   Explore the involvement of teachers. Can you tell the assignment? Do you think teachers are editing student work before it's posted?

Chart 5-1. Student Web Pages.

Real World Considerations

Student pages can be lots of work. If the school is sponsoring the student pages, someone must monitor student content and links.

If you're planning a classroom activity, consider your access to computers. Students type very slowly. Think about starting with group pages rather than individual pages.

Keep in mind that a student-produced page is a learner developed product. Be careful when you give suggestions. Although you might not select a black background, red letters, and links to popular music groups, it's their choice within the parameters of the assignment you provided. Misspellings and ugly background are up to the student to revise, not the teacher.

Kids love graphics. If your student pages are content specific, be sure to make students responsible for the text first. Otherwise they may never get to the written portion by the time they scan pictures, select GIF animations, lines, and other multimedia elements.

Idea Exploration

Idea Exploration: Student Page

Work with a child or teenager who is interested in developing their own web page. Teach them the basics and let them develop it on their own. Post their page on your web server! Start with your own children or siblings.

Summary

For young children, student web page development is a great way to begin their involvement with technology. For teenagers, it's a fun way to share ideas with other students around the world and help students who often feel alone and isolated.

Part II: Selecting Powerful Projects

Do you sometimes feel like you're brain dead? Do you lack creativity? Or, are you just having trouble thinking of a topic for your project? The following chapters will provide lots of ideas for developing powerful Internet-based projects.

In this section, you'll examine large-scale, ongoing projects and small-scale, short-term projects. Which kind of project best fits your needs? How do you select a project for your classroom?

Projects

Large-Scale, Ongoing

Small-Scale, Short-Term

This section is divided into two chapters.

Large-Scale, Ongoing Projects
Small-Scale, Short-Term Projects

Large-Scale, Ongoing Projects. Explore web initiatives that take a long time to plan and implement. Students may collect data throughout the year or build on concepts taught during a semester. Although these projects can be time-consuming, they can also be very rewarding.

Small-Scale, Short-Term Projects. Examine small, focused projects that take a day or week to implement. These projects may involve a single classroom or reach out to other students around the world. While small projects are easy to plan and don't require the long-term commitment of a bigger project, they can be just as effective.

Once you've explored the two chapters in this section, you'll be ready to plan, develop, and implement your project.

Chapter 6: Large-Scale, Ongoing Projects

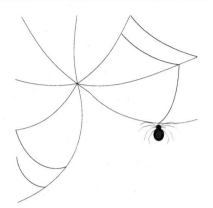

What's involved in a large scale project?
Is it a good idea to get involved in a year-long project?
What are the characteristics of a good project?

In this chapter, you'll explore large-scale, ongoing projects. Large scale projects are demanding and time consuming, but also rewarding and worthwhile.

Explore Large-Scale, Ongoing Projects

Large-Scale, Ongoing Projects are a way to immerse you and/or your class into a long-term activity such as professional or student portfolios, school web pages, class web pages, or an online newspaper, magazine, or yearbook. These types of projects may require coordination over years as in the case of a student portfolio or several semesters in the case of a yearbook.

Although you may begin a large-scale project on your own, many ongoing projects are sponsored by organizations or funded through grants. It's a good idea to gain support before committing to a large project. For example, can you enlist the help of some other teachers? Can you depend on a small group of technology literate students? Maybe you could tap the high school computer class for assistance.

Large Scale Projects
  Professional Portfolio
  Student Portfolio
  School Web Page
  Class Web Page
  Classroom
    Yearbook
    Newspaper
    Magazine
  Topical/Unit Projects

http://www.miamisci.org/hurricane/hurricane0.html
Figure 6-1. Hurricane Project.

Idea Exploration

Idea Exploration: Large Scale
The **Hurricane Project** (http://www.miamisci.org/hurricane/hurricane0.html) does an excellent job combining teacher and student resources, information, instruction, and communications (see Figure 6-1).

Explore the hurricane project and list the different aspects of the project. What kinds of student and teacher resources are included? What kinds of activities are involved? How do learners participate? Are the activities high level or low level? Is the Internet an important part of this project or could it have been done with paper and pencil?

Chapter 6: Large-Scale, Ongoing Projects 85

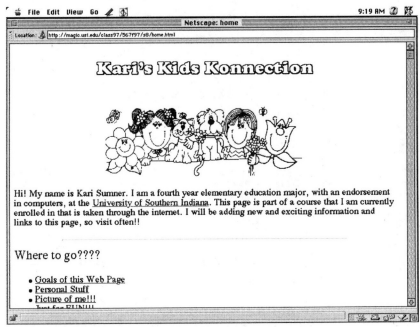

http://magic.usi.edu/class97/567f97/s8/home.html
Figure 6-2. Professional Portfolio.

Explore each of the following large-scale projects.

Professional Portfolio
Student Portfolio
School Web Page
Class Web Page
Classroom Yearbook, Newspaper, or Magazine
Topical and Unit Projects

Professional Portfolio
Learn by doing. Rather than a project that involves students, you may wish to start by getting yourself organized and learning the tools. Create a web page(s) that provides information about yourself and your career. You might include evidence of writing skills, creativity, knowledge base, organization, curriculum integration, inclusion, enthusiasm, teaming, self-evaluation, technology, leadership, achievement, initiative, or innovation as a teacher.

Examples might include units of instruction, lessons, planning materials, teaching strategies, assessment instruments, student work, writing samples,

Professional Portfolios

Impress a prospective employer, your principals, and your students.

Do it for yourself.

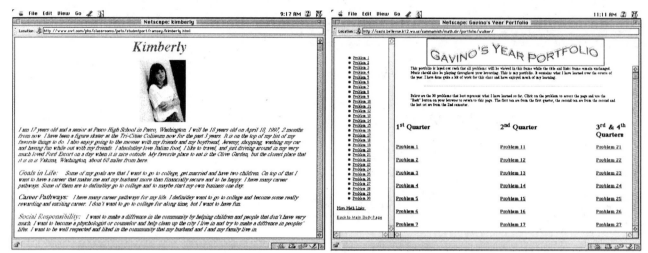

http://www.owt.com/phs/classrooms/peto/
studentport/ramsey/kimberly.html
Figure 6-3. Student Portfolio.

http://oasis.bellevue.k12.wa.us/sammamish/
math.dir/portfolio/walker/

teaching philosophy, personal statements, teacher journal, summative appraisals, classroom photographs, and a resume. In addition, you could include other autobiographical information such as education, interests, hobbies, and family information (see Figure 6-2).

Related Projects: Develop a short version of your portfolio to share on the first day of school. It could even be on the web for students before school starts. The autobiography would help students get to know you and your interests.

Consider developing a web-based resume or vita to share with the world. You never know, you might get a call from a rich potential employer!

Student Portfolio

Wouldn't it be great for students to be able to trace their development in reading, writing, mathematics, social studies, science, music, art, and physical education all the way through school? With writing, reading, and project samples, students can build a priceless chronicle of their learning. Use the web as a tool for organizing this information. With password access, students could even update their projects from home and share their learning with their parents.

Student Portfolios:
   Multimedia Elements

   Scan handwriting
   Digitize voice
   Videotape demo
   Photograph projects

Chapter 6: Large-Scale, Ongoing Projects

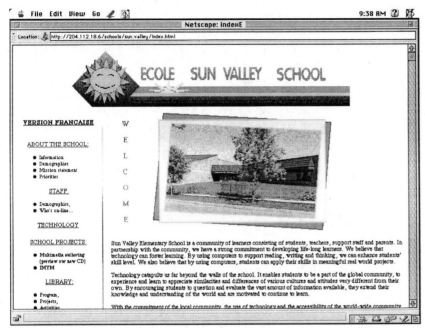

http://204.112.18.6/schools/sun.valley/Index.html
Figure 6-4. School Web Page.

Related Projects: Ask students to develop an extensive autobiography (see Figure 6-3a). In addition to personal information, it might also include a study of their family tree, interviews with family members, photographs through the generations, and home videos. Figure 6-3b shows a high school student's math portfolio.

School Web Page
Create a web project that provides information about your school. Figure 6-4 shows an elementary school in Manitoba Canada that participates in lots of cool projects.
 Identify the purpose of the page. Are you selling your school to outsiders or providing a service for your students, parents, and the community? Since this will be the starting point for all building level links, design the home page carefully. The first page should be an index with lots of links to other pages.
 For traditional school pages include school logo, address, and location, mission statement, history, academic departments, groups (athletics, special centers,

School Web Pages

Actively involve students in the planning and development of your school web site.

A computer class may even be able to maintain the site!

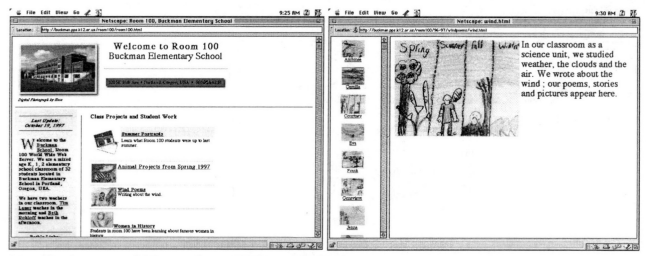

http://buckman.pps.k12.or.us/room100/room100.html
Figure 6-5. Class Web Page.

clubs, grade levels), school activities, projects, policies and procedures, map, floorplans, facilities, personnel, student population, demographics, school calendar, recent events, school news, favorite links, classroom links, access by surface mail, phone, email, and fax.

Related Projects: Design a web project for a particular department (science, social studies), center (library/media center), club (astronomy, chess, band), or organization (Band Boosters, 4H).

Class Web Page

Create a web page(s) for a particular class, course, or unit. This page could be available on the Internet or it could run off the hard drive in your classroom. Your class page would become the default home page on your web browser. Unit and activity links could be presented on the page. Or, the page could contain a list of class teams or particular students with individualized assignments. Figure 6-5 shows a primary class web page.

Your class page could contain information that is normally distributed in class such as the course description, goals and objectives, materials, requirements, grading, timeline, lecture notes, homework assignments, and readings. Provide links to online course

Class Web Pages

You don't need a webserver to use a page in your classroom. You can run your page locally off your hard drive.

Chapter 6: Large-Scale, Ongoing Projects

http://www.smplanet.com/imperialism/teacher.html

http://tqd.advanced.org/3310/higraphics/index.html

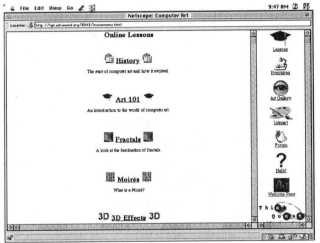

http://tqd.advanced.org/3543/
Figure 6-6. Class Pages.

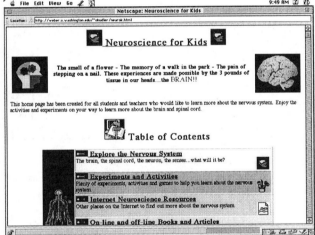

http://weber.u.washington.edu/~chudler/neurok.html

resources and develop matching questions or activities. Include instructional materials such as step-by-step instructions, anticipation guides, vocabulary guides, study materials, graphic organizers, reading guides, research/search strategies, writing journal guidelines, and thinking/listening protocols. Post student projects, experiments, prose, or other student-produced materials. Ask for interaction such as adding to a list, sharing experiences, trying story problems, or answering a question.

Explore some classroom pages:

Age of Imperialism (http://www.smplanet.com/imperialism/teacher.html). This project includes lesson plans, activities, and links. Rather than being produced by a teacher in a classroom, these units are being produced by a company called Small Planet Communications (see Figure 6-6a).

Chem101 (http://tqd.advanced.org/3310/). An online textbook, experiments, and video clips are included. In addition, students can communicate through discussion groups or a chat page (see Figure 6-6b).

Civil War (http://www.smplanet.com/civilwar/civilwar.html). This page contains links and lessons related to the Civil War.

Computer Art (http://tqd.advanced.org/3543/). This project contains lessons, an art gallery, and a forum for interaction (see Figure 6-6c).

Fractals (http://cml.rice.edu:80/~lanius/frac/). Learn about fractals through this web page.

Neuroscience of Kids (http://weber.u.washington.edu/~chudler/neurok.html). This page provides a table of contents to resources for this unit (see Figure 6-6d).

Solar System (http://www.smplanet.com/science/SL9.html). This activity page provides the resources for a solar system unit.

Chapter 6: Large-Scale, Ongoing Projects

http://www.newreach.net/people/hnoden/
Figure 6-7. Newspapers.

Classroom Yearbook, Newspaper, Magazines

Create a web page(s) that provides information about your classroom this year. An interactive yearbook could include school pictures, biographical sketches about children, reflections about thematic units, large-scale projects, or year-long activities, recorded information provided by children, favorite prose, artwork, or other materials by children.

The project could be used during an open-house, parent night, or year-end party. Or, focus on a particular child in your class. How have they evolved over the past year? Also consider the production of a class newspaper or magazine. **MiddleZine Magazine** (http://www.newreach.net/people/hnoden/) is a student-published, middle school magazine and includes a variety of articles (see Figure 6-7).

Related Projects: Coordinate production of a school or class online newspaper or ezine.

Parent Newsletters

Keep parents up to date with a class newsletter.

Include pictures of students and highlight the activities for each week.

Spinnin' the Web

http://www.omsi.edu/sln/air/

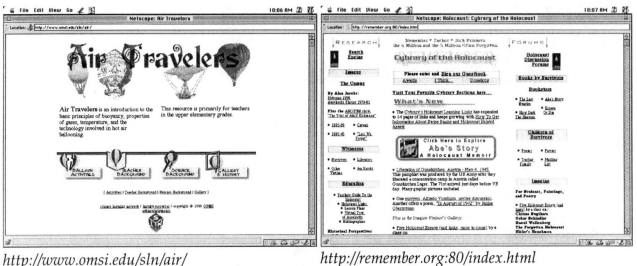
http://remember.org:80/index.html

http://www.kids-commons.net/geotouch/
GeoTouch.html

http://www.gsn.org/project/zoo/index.html

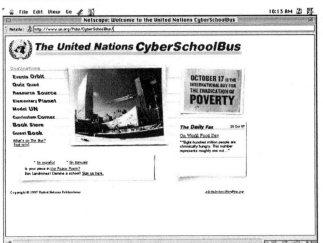
http://www.un.org/Pubs/CyberSchoolBus/
Figure 6-8. Topical Projects.

http://pen1.pen.k12.va.us/Anthology/Div/
Albemarle/Schools/Crozet/ClassPages/
Woodward/weather/weatherhome.html

Chapter 6: Large-Scale, Ongoing Projects 93

Topical and Unit Project Projects

Large-scale topical and unit projects may be developed by a classroom teacher or a group of educators. In some cases, these projects have funding from outside sources. Sometimes they are developed by a dedicated teacher, media specialist, or technology coordinator. These projects often include a number of related small-scale projects. Explore the projects below and examine the different types of activities embedded in the large scale project.

Unit Projects

Develop a web page for each unit you teach. Include activities to accompany the unit that students can work on at home.

Ask students to add their home projects to the web page as they are completed.

Air Travelers (http://www.omsi.edu/sln/air/) are student and teacher activities related to basic principles of buoyancy, properties of gases, temperature, and the technology involved in hot air ballooning (see Figure 6-a).

CyberSpace Middle School (http://www.scri.fsu.edu/~dennisl/CMS.html) is designed to help students with their science projects.

Cybrary of the Holocaust (http://remember.org:80/index.html) explores information and resources related to the Holocaust. Includes student activities and teacher resources (see Figure 6-8b).

GeoTouch (http://www.kids-commons.net/geotouch/GeoTouch.html) is a world-wide environmental education project. Students from around the world explore and analyze their environment and report to the group. This project involved writing, drawing, discussing, and sharing (see Figure 6-8c).

The **Global Zoo** (http://www.gsn.org/project/zoo/index.html) project involves students in the study of wildlife (see Figure 6-8d).

The **Living School Book** (http://lsb.syr.edu/) contains a textbook of the future.

OutPost 101: Space Station (http://library.advanced.org/11356/) contains information and links related to learning about space.

The **Student Ambassadors** (http://www.gsn.org/kid/sa/index.html) project gets students involved with Internet leadership activities.

United Nations CyberSchoolBus (http://www.un.org/Pubs/CyberSchoolBus/) page contains lots of projects for students (see Figure 6-8e).

Weather Wizards (http://pen1.pen.k12.va.us/Anthology/Div/Albemarle/Schools/Crozet/ClassPages/Woodward/weather/weatherhome.html) contains information and activities related to the weather. It also includes teacher resources (see Figure 6-8f).

Related Projects: Develop entire thematic units on the web, or use the Internet to trace special events such as a hurricane, the Olympics, or an Election.

Idea Exploration

Idea Exploration: Building Large Scale Projects
Examine some large scale projects. Where do they get their sponsorship? Who is involved? Are they individual schools working together or is a large organization involved? How are students and teachers involved? Where and how are materials posted on the Internet?

Select one of the large scale projects to evaluate. What is the purpose of the project? Is it just "fun" or does it meet an instructional need? Is the project focused toward teachers or students? Would it be a realistic project for a classroom with limited access to the Internet?

What are the advantages and disadvantages of a large scale project over a series of smaller scale projects?

Chapter 6: Large-Scale, Ongoing Projects

Large Scale, Ongoing Projects

Explore Large Scale-Onging Projects.
Brainstorm ideas for each of the following areas:

Professional Portfolio

Student Portfolio

School Web Page

Class Web Page

Classroom Yearbook, Newspaper, or Magazine

Topical and Unit Projects

Chart 6-1. Large-Scale Projects.

Real World Considerations

Large scale projects are very rewarding, but they are also a drain on energy. Don't start a project unless you're willing to complete it.

Project Selection. Pick your project carefully. Chart 6-1 gives you a chance to explore each type of project before making a decision.

Time. Projects take time. How will you adjust your schedule and life to accommodate a large scale project? If your life is already full, something will need to be streamlined, eliminated or changed.

Technology Resources. If students will be making web pages, using email, and accessing Internet information, you'll need lots of technology in your room. Consider writing a grant for your project to fund additional Internet connections, hardware, or software.

People Power. Large projects take lots of people power. Start recruiting the help of students, other teachers, and Internet contacts. Share the workload. Develop a partnership with a university or local business.

Summary

There are many types of large-scale projects. As you explore the possibilities, consider the purpose of the project. What are the advantages of an Internet environment over a traditional classroom environment for the project? Where will you get the resources necessary to coordinate a large project? If you're not ready for a big project, consider trying a small project first.

Chapter 7: Small-Scale, Short-Term Projects

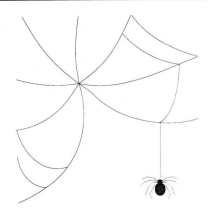

What can I do that won't take much time out of class?
We only have one Internet connection, what can I do?
I want to start out simple, where do I begin?

In this chapter, you'll examine small-scale, short-term projects. There are dozens of different kinds of small-scale projects that beginners can try.

Small-Scale, Short-Term Projects

Small-Scale, Short-Term Projects are a great way to get started with Internet-based projects. Rather than commit yourself to a years worth of activities, design projects that take a couple days or weeks. With some experience you may dive into a semester long project. Consider small scale projects such as hot lists, treasure hunts, sharing, and informational projects first. Then, work on developing instructional materials, webquests, case studies and other projects that involve lots of planning and development.

Explore a short term project such as the **Everglades Project** (http://www.miamisci.org/ecolinks/everglades/). What's the purpose of the project? How were students involved? Is this a good use of the Internet. Why or why not (see Figure 7-1a)?

Small-Scale,
   Short Term Projects

Informational
Instructional
Communication/
   Collaboration
Publishing

http://www.miamisci.org/ecolinks/everglades/
Figure 7-1. Small Scale Projects.

http://met.open.ac.uk/heronsgate/projects/index.html

Explore **Our Class Projects** (http://www.geocities.com/Athens/5788/projects.html) and **Heronsgate** (http://met.open.ac.uk/heronsgate/projects/index.html) to get a glimpse of the diverse projects of this classroom. How were the children involved in these projects? Did they require students to have access to Internet? What role did the teacher play in the projects (see Figure 7-1b)?

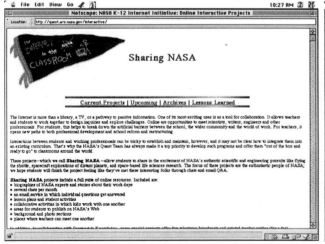

http://quest.arc.nasa.gov/interactive/
Figure 7-2. Small Scale Projects to Explore.

http://www.onlineclass.com/

Chapter 7: Small-Scale, Short-Term Projects 99

Idea Exploration: Small-Scale
Explore **NASA's Online Project** (http://quest.arc.nasa.gov/interactive/) and **Online Class** (http://www.onlineclass.com/) to see how many different kinds of projects are available from these groups (see Figure 7-2). Compare and contrast the projects. What is involved? What is the length of the project? How do students participate? Are there costs associated with the projects?

Idea Exploration

There are many different types of small-scale projects. We'll explore each of the following areas:

Informational Projects
Instructional Projects
Communication/Collaboration Projects
Publishing Projects

Informational Projects
Teachers Develop, Students Use

Many teachers begin with informational projects. You can use a single site or a hot list of popular sites related to the topic.

http://advweb.cocomm.utexas.edu/world/   http://lcweb2.loc.gov/ammem/
Figure 7-3. Single Site Projects.

http://www.mapquest.com
http://nutribase.com/
Figure 7-4. Single Site Tools.

```
 ┌─────────────────────────────┐
 │   Informational Projects    │
 │                             │
 │       Single Sites          │
 │       Hot Lists             │
 │       Activity Projects     │
 │       Hunts                 │
 │       Web Quests            │
 └─────────────────────────────┘
```

Single Site Projects

An easy way to start a project is by using a single page as the basis for a project. For example, you might start with a good "starting point" site that provides lots of links related to the topic. For example, **University of Texas' Advertising World** (http://advweb.cocomm.utexas.edu/world/) provides links to all kinds of information about advertising and marketing. Students could find lots of resources without having to link to search engines (see Figure 7-3a). Another single page project may revolve around a large information site such as **Library of Congress' American Memories** (http://lcweb2.loc.gov/ammem/) pages (see Figure 7-3b). This site contains dozens of pages of information about American History. You could do the same thing with **Abridged History of the United States** (http://www.us-history.com/) or **History Net** (http://www.TheHistoryNet.com/). Consider which of these sites would contain the best information and resources for the grade, interest, and ability level of your students.

Use sites that contain tools such as **Mapquest** (http://www.mapquest.com). This site lets students develop trips, explore places, and print maps (see

Chapter 7: Small-Scale, Short-Term Projects 101

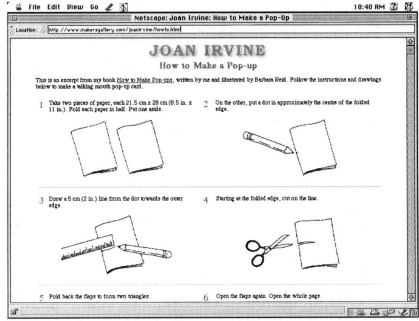

http://www.makersgallery.com/joanirvine/howto.html
Figure 7-5. Single Site Activities.

Figure 7-4). **Nutribase** (http://nutribase.com/) is another good example. It's a database that students can use as a tool to identify nutrient information about food products (see Figure 7-4). The **Food Finder** (http://www.olen.com/food/) is very similar.

A single page site doesn't have to contain facts and statistics. For example, the **How To Make a Pop Up Book** (http://www.makersgallery.com/joanirvine/howto.html) page would be a fun way to teach students how to make a popup book for their project rather than write a paper or draw a picture (see Figure 7-5).

Pick projects that it would be difficult to implement using the resources you have available in your classroom or school library. For example, if you wanted to explore the sports of different countries, Internet would be a logical tool. Each small group could concentrate on a particular page such as the **Australian Sport WWW** (http://www.ausport.gov.au/).

Single Site Projects

Try choosing a site that's likely to be available when you need it. Focus on large, sponsored sites.

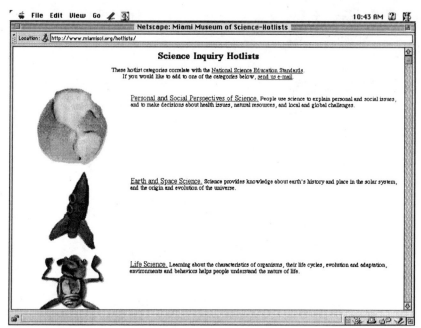

http://www.miamisci.org/hotlists/
Figure 7-6. Hot Lists Projects.

Idea Exploration

Idea Exploration: Site Activity Page
Create a web page that focuses on a particular topic and specific web site. The page should provide very specific guidelines, activities, and assignments for students. For example, there might be a series of discussion questions, criteria for writing a paper, standards for a video production, or guidelines for developing a poster based on the information found.

Hot Lists Projects
Rather than just providing one site, you may wish to provide a series of sites for a particular project. For example, check out the **Science Inquiry Hotlists** (http://www.miamisci.org/hotlists/).

Some projects involve collecting and evaluating web sites related to a particular topic. This can save endless hours searching through notes and bookmarks. Some people call them Hot Lists, Hot Points, Lists of Links, Resource Lists, or Starting Points. Read about **Hot Lists** (http://www.kn.pacbell.com/wired/fil/formats.html#Hotlist) and **Scrapbooks** (http://www.kn.pacbell.com/wired/fil/

Chapter 7: Small-Scale, Short-Term Projects 103

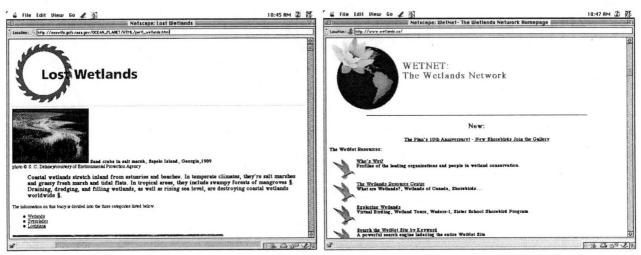

http://seawifs.gsfc.nasa.gov/OCEAN_PLANET/HTML/peril_wetlands.html

http://www.wetlands.ca/

Figure 7-7. Wetlands Projects.

formats.html#Scrapbook). Be sure to explore examples.

Carefully select sites that provide insights into particular aspects of the project, then develop activities to go with each site. It's also a good idea to provide a brief description of each site along with the activity so students know what to look for in the site. For example, let's say you're studying the Wetlands. The following five sites provide information: **Wetlands** (http://seawifs.gsfc.nasa.gov/OCEAN_PLANET/HTML/peril_wetlands.html), **WetNet** (http://www.wetlands.ca/), **Run the Wetlands** (http://dino.ils.nwu.edu/wetlands/index.html), **Restoring Iowa's Agricultural Wetlands** (http://www.ia.nrcs.usda.gov/wet_restore.html), and **National Wetlands Inventory** (http://www.nwi.fws.gov/) (see Figure 7-7). Each site provides different kinds of information and links. How would you organize the information? What kinds of activities would be interesting and involving for students?

Consider whether the sites you choose will be broadly focused. For instance, the **Biography** (http://www.biography.com/) site is a great way for students to find information for a project relating to a famous person, but it can also be overwhelming (see Figure 7-8). Will students be using the site to browse through

Hot Lists

Think "higher order thinking skills". Don't just ask students to go to the site and write down facts. Design activities that ask students to analyze information and make decisions.

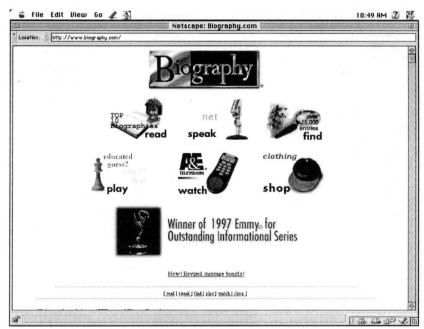

http://www.biography.com/
Figure 7-8. Biography Site.

options for their project or as an important resource for information about a person they've already selected? Browsing can be fun, but it can also be time consuming. Rather than providing a broad site, you may provide starting points on each of the historical figures your students will be studying. For example, **Albert Einstein Revealed** (http://www.pbs.org/wgbh/pages/nova/einstein/) provides information based on the PBS series. The **Einstein** (http://www-groups.dcs.st-and.ac.uk/~history/Mathematicians/Einstein.html) page provides great biographical information. **Einstein Online** (http://www.sas.upenn.edu/~smfriedm/einstein.html) contains lots of links and is a good place for a student to start exploring this individual. These three sites would provide enough information to get the student started. It's a good idea to have at least three sites related to your topic in case one or even two aren't functioning on the day they are needed.

You'll find many hotlist type sites. Explore three.

Chapter 7: Small-Scale, Short-Term Projects 105

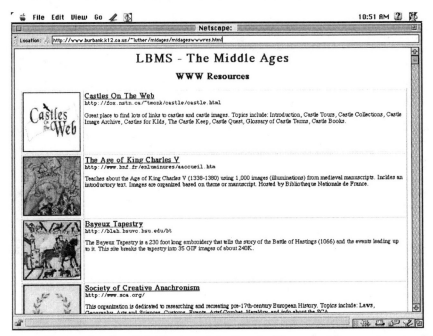

http://www.burbank.k12.ca.us/~luther/midages/midageswwwres.html
Figure 7-9. Hotlist Project.

LBMS - The Middle Ages (http://www.burbank.k12.ca.us/~luther/midages/midageswwwres.html). Contains a picture representing the site, a link, and a description (see Figure 7-9).

Let's Keep it Clean (http://www.kn.pacbell.com/wired/filamentality/ex.hotlist.html). Contains links and annotations to sites related to water pollution.

Math Links (http://forum.swarthmore.edu/students/). Contains links and descriptions for math projects.

Idea Exploration: Hot List Page
Explore Hot List Pages. Create a list of those elements you like on particular pages. Consider the way the list was constructed and presented on the page. Was the name and the address provided? Was a logo or graphic included? What about an annotation, outline, or overview of the site?

Create your own Hot List Page. Rather than just listing sites, provide an annotation for each link. Consider using a logo to identify particular types of pages. You may also wish to rate the quality and contents.

Idea Exploration

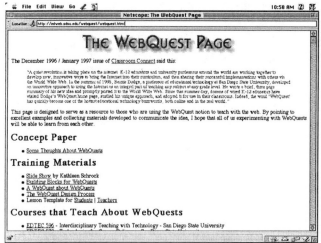

http://edweb.sdsu.edu/webquest/webquest.html
Figure 7-10. WebQuests.

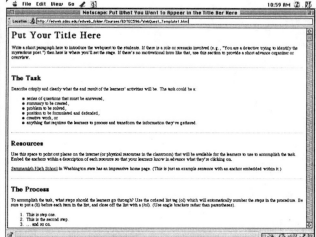

http://edweb.sdsu.edu/edweb_folder/Courses/
EDTEC596/WebQuest_Template1.html

WebQuests

Task
Process
Resources
Learning Advice
Conclusion
Hypertext Dictionary

Activity Projects

Treasure Hunts (http://www.kn.pacbell.com/wired/fil/formats.html#Hunt), **Subject Samplers** (http://www.kn.pacbell.com/wired/fil/formats.html#Sampler), and **WebQuests** (http://www.kn.pacbell.com/wired/fil/formats.html#WebQuest) get students involved with information they find on the Internet. Treasure Hunts and Scavenger Hunts focus on using specific sites to answer questions. In some cases, they ask students to search the Internet to answer questions on a particular topic or range of topics rather than providing specific sites.

Read more about **WebQuests** (http://edweb.sdsu.edu/webquest/webquest.html) (see Figure 7-10). These projects require more planning, but also involve students in the highest levels of thinking. The project could include an overview, guidelines, questions, links, and a chance to write, create a product, or answer questions.

Explore lots of **webquests** (http://www.kn.pacbell.com/wired/bluewebn/apptypes.html) for ideas. You can even use a **template** (http://edweb.sdsu.edu/edweb_folder/Courses/EDTEC596/WebQuest_Template1.html) for a webquest (see Figure 7-10b). Go to **Example**

Chapter 7: Small-Scale, Short-Term Projects 107

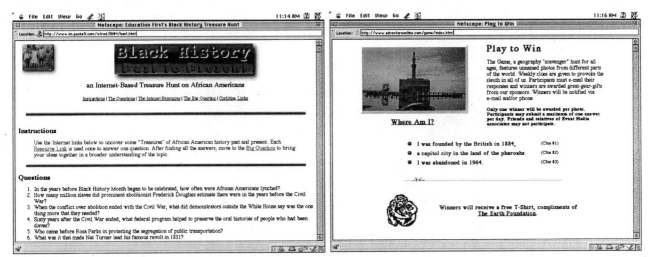

http://www.kn.pacbell.com/wired/BHM/hunt.html

http://www.adventureonline.com/game/index.html

Figure 7-11. Treasure Hunts.

WebQuests page (http://edweb.sdsu.edu/webquest/matrix.html) for more great webquest examples.

African American Treasure Hunt (http://www.kn.pacbell.com/wired/BHM/hunt.html). Includes information, questions, and links associated with African American studies (see Figure 7-11a).

Indian Hill Treasure Hunt (http://www.ih.k12.oh.us/treasure/). A school sponsored treasure hunt.

Way Cool Science Scavenger Hunt (http://www.ced.appstate.edu/whs/goals2000/projects/97/karla/karla.htm). This site provides links and questions for a number of science topics.

Geography Scavenger Hunt (http://www.adventureonline.com/game/index.html). This site contains geography scavenger hunt questions (see Figure 7-11b).

Question of the Week (http://www.louverture.com/question.html). This page pro-

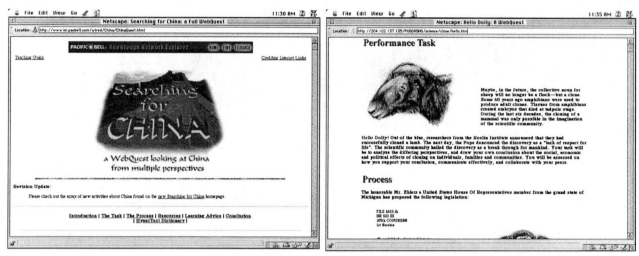

http://www.kn.pacbell.com/wired/China/
ChinaQuest.html
Figure 7-12. WebQuests.

http://204.102.137.135/PUSDRBHS/science/
clone/hello.htm

vides a question of the week for students to investigate.

Searching for China WebQuest (http://www.kn.pacbell.com/wired/China/ChinaQuest.html). This project helps students understand life in China. The web page contains an introduction, task, process, resources, learning advice, conclusion, and a hypertext dictionary (see Figure 7-12a).

Archaeotype (http://edweb.sdsu.edu/Courses/EDTEC596/WebQuest1.html). This webquest involves students in an archaeological dig.

Hello Dolly (http://204.102.137.135/PUSDRBHS/science/clone/hello.htm). This webquest focuses on the issue of cloning. It provides a task, describes the process, and links to a wealth of resources.

Chapter 7: Small-Scale, Short-Term Projects 109

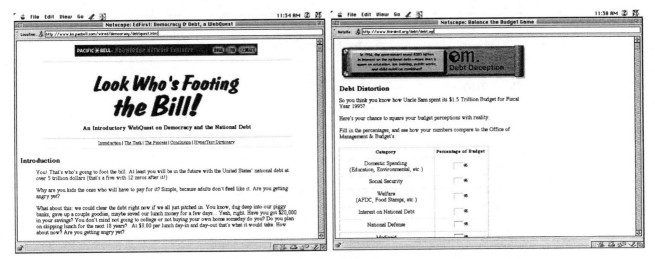

http://www.kn.pacbell.com/wired/democracy/
debtquest.html

http://www.thirdmil.org/debt/
debt.cgi

Figure 7-13. WebQuest.

Idea Exploration: WebQuest Analysis

Explore the WebQuest called **Who's Footing the Bill** (http://www.kn.pacbell.com/wired/democracy/debtquest.html) shown in Figure 7-13. You can get students involved with democracy and issues related to the national debt with this webquest. Students link to sites around the country to locate and analyze information about the national debt. Be sure to examine all the activities and links (see Figure 7-13b). Examine the format of the web page including the introduction, task, process, resources, learning advice, conclusion, and a hypertext dictionary. Would you use the same categories? Are there other ways the activity could be organized?

Idea Exploration

Idea Exploration: WebQuest Exploration

Use the **WebQuest** (http://edweb.sdsu.edu/webquest/webquest.html) page to identify a web quest. Go through the entire webquest from the student perspective. Do you think students would like or dislike this project? Why? What are the advantages and disadvantages of using this web quest rather than a traditional textbook-type activity or term paper.

Idea Exploration

Hot Lists

Create a hot list page.

Describe a topic that you enjoy teaching.

List three cool web sites that contain information about this topic and write a short description.

1.

2.

3.

Create a list of low level questions that could be answered at each site.

Transform the low level questions into higher level thinking skills questions that require students to apply, synthesize, formulate, and create.

Chart 7-1. Hot Lists

Web Activities

Create an activity page.

Introduction. Select a topic and write a short paragraph that would get students interested in learning more about the subject, theme, or issue.

Task. Describe a situation or problem that could be addressed or solved using web-based information.

Process. List the steps that students would follow in the activity.

Resources. Create a list of at least three web sites that students would use in the project.

Helpers. Create a list of help for learners.

Conclusion. Write a short paragraph that would bring the project together and help students transfer what they've learned.

Chart 7-2. Web Activities

Instructional Projects
Teachers Develop, Students Use

You may wish to create instructional pages that make use of Internet sites. Explore each of these instructional project formats.

Case Studies
Virtual Field Trips
Practice and Testing
Simulations
Tutorial

Case Studies

Create a case study project. For example, the user could be presented with a single or series of problems, incidents, or situations. They would explore information in the web, link to other sites, and make recommendations or solve the problem. Ask students to pretend they are buying a new car. They can use the web to price the car, hunt for good financing rates, and

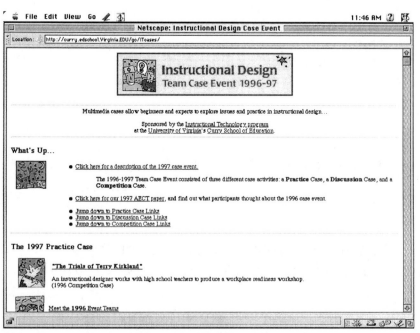

http://curry.edschool.Virginia.EDU/go/ITcases/
Figure 7-14. Case Studies.

Chapter 7: Small-Scale, Short-Term Projects 113

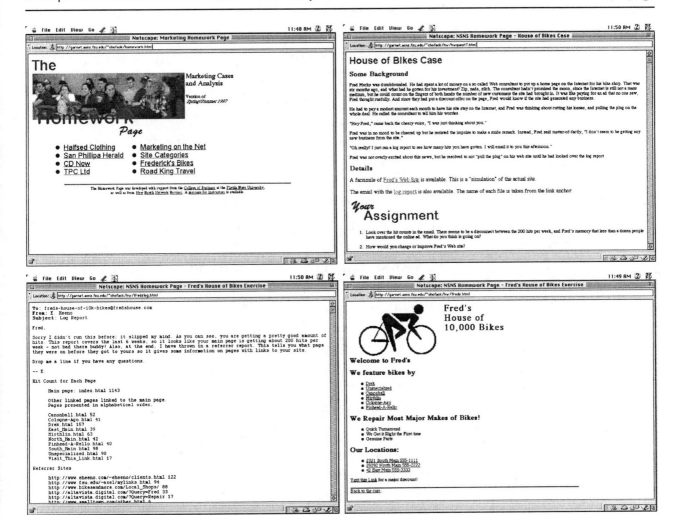

http://garnet.acns.fsu.edu/~chofack/homework.html
Figure 7-15. Case Studies.

compare insurance coverage. Explore **Case Studies Online** (http://curry.edschool.Virginia.EDU/go/ITcases/) for ideas (see Figure 7-14).

The **Marketing Homework Page** (http://garnet.acns.fsu.edu/~chofack/homework.html) involves marketing students in various case studies and online activities. Examine the **House of Bikes** example. A problem is clearly presented along with a series of questions. In addition, links to real and fictional sites provide information and data for analysis as shown in Figure 7-15. In this case, a simulated web page for a Bike company along with web use data is provided. Explore some of the other cases: **CD-NOW Analysis** (http://garnet.acns.fsu.edu/~chofack/hw/

hwquest6.html), **Halfsed Clothing** (http://garnet.acns.fsu.edu/~chofack/hw/hwquest1.html) and **San Phillipa Herald** (http://garnet.acns.fsu.edu/~chofack/hw/hwquest4.html). Does the instructor provide enough information for the student to complete the assignment? Why is the Internet used for this activity?

Idea Exploration

Idea Exploration: Case Studies
Case Studies are a great way to make use of real world information found on the web. Can you make your classroom activities more interesting through the use of authentic information and resources? Brainstorm sites that contain data that could be used in a case study. For example, your students might use the baseball statistics from ESPN or government resources from the C-SPAN site.

Virtual Field Trips
Virtual Field Trips can take people to places they couldn't otherwise visit. Sometimes visits are real-time, live interactive experiences, other trips are recordings from past trips or simulated field trips such as trips to the moon. For example, the **Break the Cycle** (http://boe.cabe.k12.wv.us/jefferso/habitat/breakthe.html) project is a live project. This Habitat for Humanity project involves a country-wide cycling trip to raise money and awareness. **The Heart: An Online Exploration** (http://sln.fi.edu/biosci/heart.html) is an example of a simulated field trip. This trip takes students through the heart. You may have seen simulated trips through the solar system or to the center of a volcano.

In most cases these field trips are designed to teach specific learning outcomes in a very interactive way. You can find many **links** (http://www.adventureonline.com/other/index.html) to virtual field trips.

Explore some of the following well-known virtual field trips.

Chapter 7: Small-Scale, Short-Term Projects 115

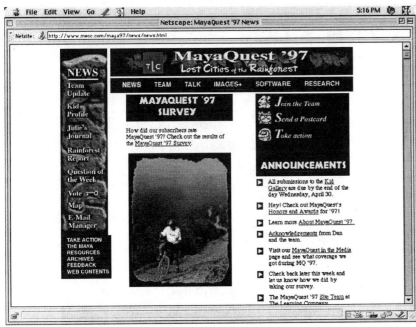

http://www.mecc.com/mayaquest.html
Figure 7-16. Virtual Field Trips.

MayaQuest (http://www.mecc.com/mayaquest.html). Students go on a virtual trip to Central America to visit the Maya Ruins (see Figure 7-16).

Global Learn (http://www.globallearn.com). Students follow groups as they travel around the world (see Figure 7-17).

Ocean Expo (http://www.bwsailing.com/SOC.html). Students take a virtual world trip on the ocean celebrating 500 years of Portuguese exploration and discovery.

Solar System Tour (http://inspire.ospi.wednet.edu:8001/curric/space/planets/sstour.html). Explore the solar system. There are many solar system projects. Look for a project that contains content appropriate for your grade level interest.

Case Study

Create a case study.

Overview. Create a case or setting for students to explore. Include the people, places, and things that are involved. Be sure to include a problem to solve.

Process. List the steps that students would follow in the activity. Diagram options and paths that might be presented to students.

Resources. Create a list of at least three web sites that students would use in the project.

Reflection. How will the case end? Is there a particular ending or alternatives? Present the options as part of a reflection activity.

Chart 7-3. Case Study.

Virtual Field Trip

Create a virtual field trip.

Who? Who will be involved with the real field trip and the virtual field trip? Will a student or character guide users through the trip?

What? What form will the virtual field trip take? Will there be text, graphics, audio, video, and other elements?

When? When will the field trip take place?

Where? Where are you going on the field trip?

Why? What's the purpose of the field trip? Are there particular outcomes users will learn using the virtual field trip?

Chart 7-4. Virtual Field Trip.

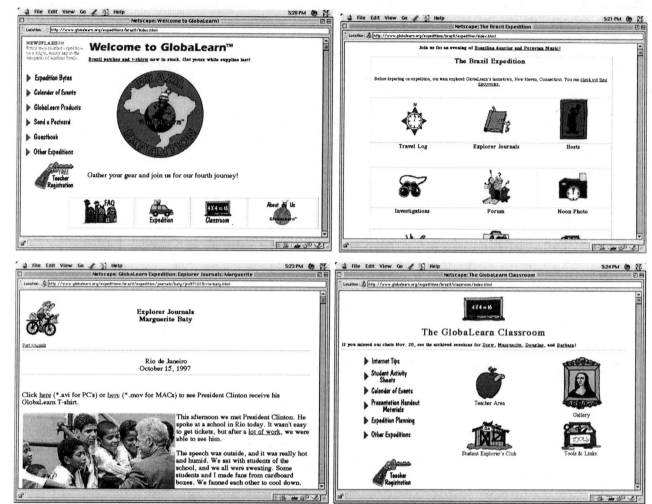

http://www.globallearn.org
Figure 7-17. Global Learn: Brazil

Tidal Passages (http://www.tidalpassages.com/). This trip takes students on an exciting virtual field trip on an ocean voyage.

Where on the Globe is Roger? (http://www.gsn.org/roger/index.html) Follow a person who is traveling around the world while teaching about geography and social studies. A student teacher wanted to try a project, so I suggested that she contact Roger who had just returned to the United States. The student never imaged that a "big-time" world traveler would come to Southern Indiana, but the elementary children were thrilled when Roger came to their school. It's like the lottery, you can't win if you don't

Chapter 7: Small-Scale, Short-Term Projects 119

buy a ticket. You won't be involved in neat projects, if you aren't willing to make a call or send an email request!

Yukon Quest (http://www.yesnet.yk.ca/schools/projects/quest/). Each year this Alaska project is held in conjunction with an International Sled Dog Race.

Practice and Testing

Internet provides many ways for students to practice new concepts. There are also opportunities for testing. For example, the **Biology Page** (http://www.execulink.com/~ekimmel/) contains quizzes. Many web pages provide game formats for learning. For example, the **GeoNet Game** (http://www.eduplace.com/geo/indexhi.html) is an online game related to geography. You could develop a standardized test practice page for your students.

Art Museum (http://www.uampfa.berkeley.edu/exhibits/newchild/famguide5.html). Learn about art through a virtual museum. Explore questions related to specific paintings.

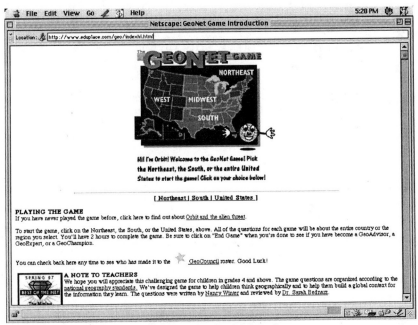

http://www.eduplace.com/geo/indexhi.html
Figure 7-18. GeoNet Game.

Simulations

Simulations help students apply their skills to "real life" situations by providing an environment to manipulate variables, examine relationships, and make decisions. They may be used to prepare students for a field trip or real experiment. For example, frog dissection simulations are commonly used in biology. While some simulations have a particular mission to accomplish, others are intended to help students explore a particular situation or environment. In most cases, simulations should be used as a culminating activity after students have basic skills in the concepts being addressed in the web site. Without the background skills, the simulation may become a game rather than a meaningful learning experience.

Explore the **Volcano Simulation** (http://hobbes.unitecnology.ac.nz/volcano/home.html). It's simple but effective. Students are given a real-world problem to solve related to volcanoes in New Zealand (see Figure 7-19). Examine other **Educational Simulations** (http://www.simulations.com/index5.htm). Then explore some of the following examples.

Anatomy of a Murder: A Trip Through Our Nation's Legal Justice System (http://tqd.advanced.org/2760/). This project takes learners through the justice system.

http://hobbes.unitecnology.ac.nz/volcano/home.html
Figure 7-19. Volcano simulation.

Chapter 7: Small-Scale, Short-Term Projects

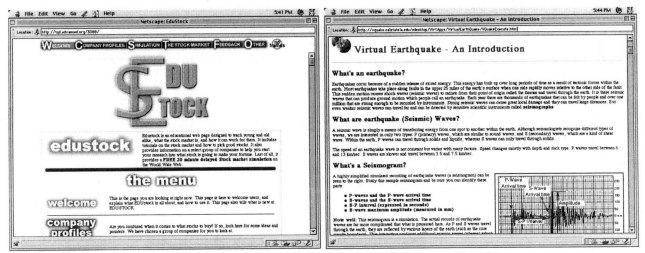

http://tqd.advanced.org/3088/   http://vquake.calstatela.edu

Figure 7-20. EduStock and Virtual Earthquake simulations.

Design Paradise (http://tqd.advanced.org/2111/). This simulation explores the interrelationships among industry, environment, and population.

EduStock (http://tqd.advanced.org/3088/). This stock market simulation allows users to play a stockmarket game online (see Figure 7-20a).

The Mysteries of Caminos Reales (http://tqd.advanced.org/2832/). Explore this area of Texas.

Presidential Strategy (http://www1.minn.net:80/~schubert/President.html). Explore presidential speeches and strategies.

Raiders of the Lost Art (http://tqd.advanced.org/3708/). This simulation lets users go on an archeological dig.

Virtual Fly Lab (http://vflylab.calstatela.edu/edesktop/VirtApps/VflyLab/Design.html). Conduct virtual genetics testing at the Virtual Fly Lab.

Virtual Earthquake (http://vquake.calstatela.edu). Explore virtual earthquakes (see Figure 7-20b).

Simulation

Create a simulation.

Overview. Create a simulated environment for students to explore.

Process. Create a chart or diagram showing the major choices and results.

Resources. Create a list of at least three web sites that students would use in the project.

Reflection. Describe how you will debrief simulation users.

Chart 7-5. Simulation.

Tutorial

Create a tutorial.

Outcome. What do you want students to be able to do or talk about after completing the tutorial?

New Information. Describe the information that will be presented to the learners including definitions, models, examples, and nonexamples.

Practice and Feedback. Provide sample practice problems and feedback for learners.

Remediation. Discuss how you will help students who need additional help.

Challenge. What challenge or transfer activities will you provide?

Chart 7-6. Tutorial.

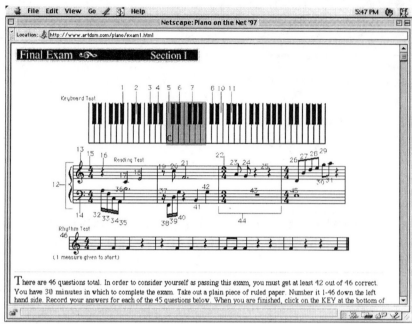

http://www.artdsm.com/piano/exam1.html
Figure 7-21. Piano tutorial.

World War II (http://www.gi.esu10.k12.ne.us/SDGI/Walnut/Japan/j1.html). Students explore a simulation related to Japan and World War II.

Tutorial

Create a web project that teaches an important skill. The tutorial should address a specific objective and provide new information including lots of examples and nonexamples. It should have an introduction and option for help. You'll want to provide opportunities for students to practice. Feedback should be provided by the program (for example, you could link to an answer page). Include an assessment at the end of the tutorial. Consider the development of a homework help page.

Music Theory (http://www.mibac.com/NN_Theory.html). Learn basic music theory.

Piano on the Net (http://www.artdsm.com/piano/exam1.html). This tutorial teaches users to play the piano (see Figure 7-21).

Chapter 7: Small-Scale, Short-Term Projects

Communication/Collaboration Projects
Teachers and Students Work Together

The Internet is a great tool for communication and collaboration. **Communication** projects involve students sharing information with others. In addition to sharing, **collaboration** projects ask students to work together with students at remote sites to reach a common goal. NickNacks has some excellent suggestions for **designing a collaborative project** (http://www1.minn.net:80/~schubert/LeadNet.html). Use NickNack's **checklist** (http://www1.minn.net:80/~schubert/NNreschek.html) to inventory the resources you have available. Use the planner page as a **template** (http://www1.minn.net:80/~schubert/NNplanner.html) for your project. Read a **Call for Collaboration** (http://www.gsn.org/project/newsday/callspring.htm View **The Evolution of a Classroom Telecomputing Project** (http://168.216.210.13/mjhs/integrat/pevolut/sld001.htm). Explore the ideas in List 7-1.

Communication Projects
Collaborations
Teacher Starters
Interactive Projects
Ask the Expert
Data Collection
Joint Ventures
Contests/Challenges

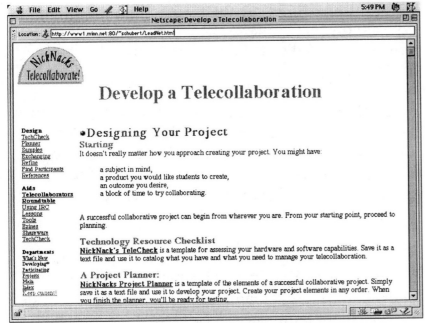

http://www1.minn.net:80/~schubert/LeadNet.html
Figure 7-22. NickNacks site.

Communication Projects

NickNack's	http://www1.minn.net:80/~schubert/exchange.html
Bill Burrall's Ideas	http://www.bell-atl.com/wschool/html/whatsnew/seminar.htm
Successful Projects	http://www.ala.org/ICONN/cur_key.html

List 7-1. Collaborative Projects.

Collaborative Activities

Consider a project that involves students in a forum or other type of collaboration. For example, the **Children's Book Forum** (http://faldo.atmos.uiuc.edu/BOOKREVIEW/welcome.html) is just getting started. It asks students and teachers to submit their book reviews. It's a great alternative to the traditional book report. Students can even add their ideas to the reviews that other people have submitted.

Most of the following projects use a combination of technologies including email, forums, chats, video conferencing, surface mail, and web pages to share their ideas and work on joint projects.

Building Bridges through CyberSpace (http://www.knownet.net/users/venturer/bridges.htm). This page discusses the email projects undertaken by a middle school.

Critical Issues Forum (http://education.lanl.gov/resources/cif/Education.html). This project was designed to focus on current, global oriented topics crucial to the security of interest to all nations. Students collaborate through email and other telecommunications systems.

Family History Project (http://www.kidlink.org/KIDPROJ/FamHistory/). This project involves students in the study of family history and sharing information about family across cultures.

Chapter 7: Small-Scale, Short-Term Projects

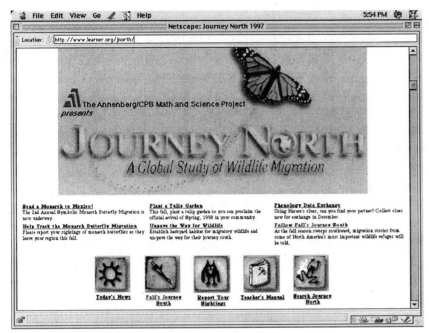

http://www.learner.org/jnorth/
Figure 7-23. Journey North Project.

Guess Who? (http://www.corona.bell.k12.ca.us/teach/swa/guess.html). Developed by fifth graders, this page asks users to guess who the famous people are based on a picture and hints.

I Have A Dream, Too (http://www.inform.umd.edu/UMS+State/MDK12_Stuff/homepers/emag/dream.html). Children share their dreams.

Inmates and Alternatives: The Prison Project (http://168.216.210.13/mjhs/pproject/pproject.htm). Students connect with inmates.

Journey North (http://www.learner.org/jnorth/). This project follows the migration of the Monarch butterfly (see Figure 7-23).

Monster Project (http://www.csnet.net/minds-eye/home.html). Students exchange email descriptions of monsters in this fun K-9 email project.

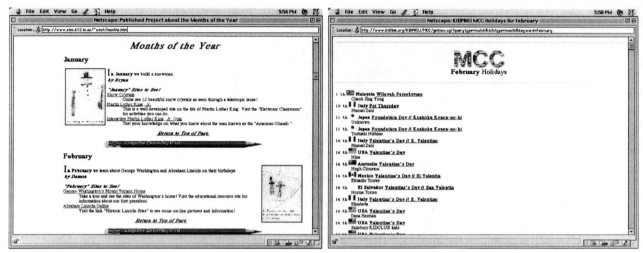

http://www.siec.k12.in.us/~west/months.htm
http://www.kidlink.org/KIDPROJ/MCC/
Figure 7-24. Months of the Year and Multicultural Calendar Projects.

Months of the Year (http://www.siec.k12.in.us/~west/months.htm). Students in Loogootee, Indiana originate the months of the year project based on a popular children's book (see Figure 7-24a).

Multicultural Calendar (http://www.kidlink.org/KIDPROJ/MCC/). Students submit information about important events and traditions (see Figure 7-24b).

Signs of Spring (http://www1.minn.net:80/~schubert/spring.html). Involves students in the northern and southern hemispheres sharing information about springtime.

Travel Buddies (http://owl.qut.edu.au/oz-teachernet/projects/travel-buddies/travel-buddies.html). Students follow the travels of a stuffed animal.

Where Are We? (http://wacky.ccit.arizona.edu/~susd/chall1.html). This project involves students in answering challenging questions and sharing postcards through the mail.

Chapter 7: Small-Scale, Short-Term Projects   129

Teacher Starters

Create a story starter web page system that gets students started, then encourages them to add or expand the project. Think big. Maybe you could have story starters or activities for each theme of the semester or each person you study. You could use paragraphs, pictures, and photographs for starting discussions, stories, or writing assignments. Users could copy and paste the information into a word processor. Participants could use snail mail, email, or the web to submit additions to your project.

Interactive Projects

Start a unit, experiment, or contest and ask others to join. Post proposed lessons, results of science experiments, or scanned pictures of woodworking projects. Summarize a book, link to an article or piece of artwork, then ask for critiques or reviews. Develop a peer development project for collaborative online creative writing, musical composing, or scientific inquiry. Hold online debates on topics of interests and archive the results.

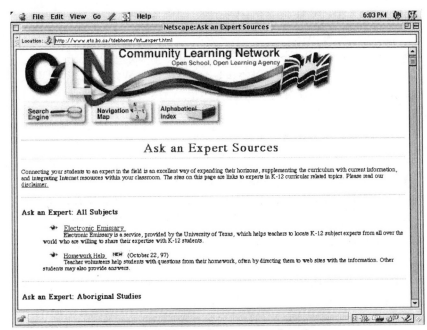

http://www.etc.bc.ca/tdebhome/int_expert.html
Figure 7-25. Ask the Expert Page.

Get parents involved in your classroom by acting as experts online.

Ask the Expert

Get involved with interacting with experts (see Figure 7-25). Look for contacts at the **Ask An Expert Pages** (http://www.etc.bc.ca/tdebhome/int_expert.html). Use the following pages for additional ideas: **National Science & Technology Week Pages** (http://www.nsf.gov/od/lpa/nstw/start.htm) and **Social Studies Topics** (http://www.socialstudies.com/).

Find experts and mentors to help your class answer specific questions. For example, you might email an office worker about the use of spreadsheets in the real world. You might get a firefighter, doctor, or scientist to answer questions that could be posted on your web page.

Data Collection

Polls, surveys, experiments, and other data collection activities are a great way to actively involve students from around the world in a wonderful learning experience. Post the goal of the activity, task, procedures, and timeline well ahead of the project to recruit participants. Involve all the sites in data collection and sharing. Look for activities that are unique to different geographic areas. For example, ask students along a river to conduct water experiments. Or, conduct a pricing survey in different parts of the world. Be sure to post a map and list of participants on the web project page.

Joint Venture

There are endless opportunities for classes to work together toward a common goal. Look for projects that involve interaction and collaboration rather than just sharing. In other words, develop a peer writing activity, combine information to create a single document, or ask each site to add to a collage. Select projects that encourage students to take action.

Chapter 7: Small-Scale, Short-Term Projects

Contests and Challenge

Students sometimes work harder when they have a challenge, but don't let competition get in the way of learning. Start with a positive collaboration and move into an activity where students work together to solve a problem or come up with solutions. Hold contests where projects are peer reviewed basic on specific criteria.

Idea Exploration: Collaboration

Integrate video conferencing projects into your classroom. Read **Collaboration in the Classroom and Over the Internet** (http://www.gsn.org/gsn/articles/article.collaboration.html) and **Elements of an Effective CU-SeeMe Video Conference** (http://www.gsn.org/gsn/articles/article.videoconf.html) by Yvonne Marie Andres and **NickNacks** (http://www1.minn.net:80/~schubert/NickNacks.html).

Create a list of before, during, and after reminders that you will need for collaborating over the Internet. Or, create a list of reminders for children and adults who will be using the distance learning resources.

Idea Exploration

Publishing Projects
Teachers Guide, Students Develop

Publishing projects involve students in posting information about what they are doing at their schools. Although some projects ask for critiques or feedback, most publishing projects are intended as final products to be shared with the world. Here's a list of some popular things to publish. Explore each area.

Writings, Artwork, Music, & Multimedia Creations
Experiences
Inquiry
Action
Research
Information Resource
Demonstrations
Alternative Products

Publishing Projects

Writings,
   Artwork,
   Music, &
    Multimedia Creations
Experiences
Inquiry
Action
Research
Information Resource
Demonstrations
Alternative Products

Communication & Collaboration Projects

Create a communication and collaboration project.
Brainstorm ideas for projects in each of the following areas.

Collaborations

Teacher Starters

Interactive Projects

Ask the Expert

Data Collection

Joint Ventures

Contests/Challenges

Chart 7-7. Communication & Collaboration Projects.

Publishing Projects

Create a publishing project.
Brainstorm ideas for projects in each of the following areas.

Writings, Artwork, Music, & Multimedia Creations

Experiences

Inquiry

Action

Research

Information Resource

Demonstrations

Alternative Products

Chart 7-8. Publishing Projects

Students love to share their work. The Internet is the world's biggest audience for your classroom projects.

Writings, Artwork, Music, Multimedia Creations

Students can create a web project that represents a fiction and/or nonfiction original work. It could be an interactive work of fiction, a nonfiction exploration of a topic or issue, or a musical composition. Consider alternative presentation formats. For example, use a "choose your own adventure" format or use a linear fictional story with nonfiction links on each page. Create a historical fiction story that links to facts about the time period on a timeline. Consider something unique (information about your town or state, interesting people in your community).

Students can share their word processed creative writing, poems, articles, and critiques. They can share their artwork including photographs, scans of artwork, digitized pictures of sculptures, masks, and other 3D art. Finally, they can share their Hyperstudio projects, and desktop presentations. Explore the following examples.

Henderson's Multimedia (http://www.glenbrook.k12.il.us/gbssci/phys/THender/HCardInf.html). Provides a page of sample HyperCard and HyperStudio stacks.

Modigliani Project (http://met.open.ac.uk/heronsgate/projects/modigliani/modi.html). This page describes the projects and the student creations (see Figure 7-25a).

Poems and Portraits (http://www.greeceny.com/ev/frames38.htm). Students write poems and write an autobiography.

Puppets from Around the World (http://www.xs4all.nl/~swanson/origins/puppetmenu.html). Sixth grade students share their puppets (see Figure 7-25b).

Chapter 7: Small-Scale, Short-Term Projects   135

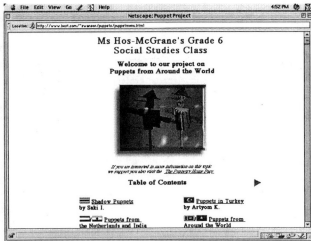

http://met.open.ac.uk/heronsgate/projects/modig
liani/modi.html

http://www.xs4all.nl/~swanson/origins/
puppetmenu.html

Figure 7-25. Modigliani Art Project and Puppets from Around the World.

Winter Wonderland (http://members.aol.com/Winter2nd/index.html). Collection of children's writing projects.

Experiences

Students have many exciting experiences at school. Classrooms are starting to share their experiments through the development of virtual field trips, reflection pages, and other experience-based web pages. Ask students to think about their audience. What would other people like to know about their experience? How could they help others who might suffer through a similar experience?

Children who experience a traumatic event such as a natural disaster are sharing their feelings through web pages. Many children who lived through the **Japanese earthquake** (http://www.city.kobe.jp/kobe-city/cityoffice/57/050/kec/200d-e.html) shared experiences on the Internet. Students in England shared their feeling after the death of Princess Diana. Figure 7-26 shows the **Grand Forks** school page. Their page provides information about how they dealt with the Flood of 1997 (http://www2.grand-forks.k12.nd.us/).

Use real-world experiences to bring the outside world closer to your students.

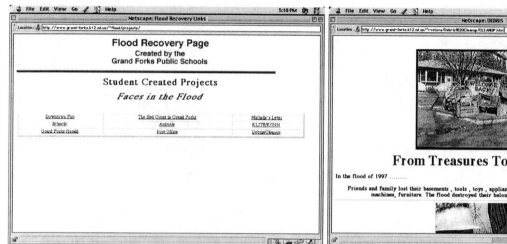
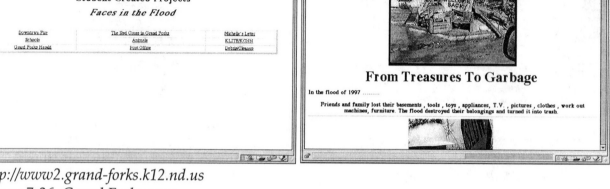

http://www2.grand-forks.k12.nd.us
Figure 7-26. Grand Forks page.

Diablo Valley Music Page (http://cyberfair.gsn.org/woodside/). Student share experiences with music.

Electronic Field Trips (http://www.fcps.k12.va.us/SpringfieldEstatesES/fieldtrips/fieldtrips.html). A set of field trips from an elementary school (see Figure 7-27a).

Maple Sugaring Field Trip (http://www.greeceny.com/pl/esl/maple/index.htm). A virtual field trip based on a class trip to learn about maple sugaring (see Figure 7-27b).

Virtual Canoe Trip (http://www.oxbow.anoka.k12.mn.us/e2/e2quest.htm). Students worked to create a virtual field trip around their Great Lakes region.

Inquiry

Learning involves exploration and discovery. Inquiry projects ask students to reflect on their knowledge, ask questions, and seek answers. For example, in the **Pigeon Inquiry** (http://www.miamisci.org/pigeons) students share their experiences learning about pi-

Let students be the explorers in an inquiry project. Encourage students to discovery and share using the Internet.

Chapter 7: Small-Scale, Short-Term Projects 137

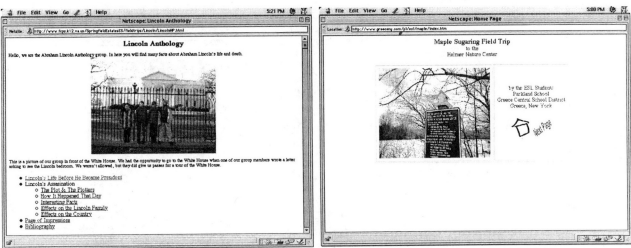

http://www.fcps.k12.va.us/SpringfieldEstatesES/fieldtrips/fieldtrips.html
http://www.greeceny.com/pl/esl/maple/index.htm
Figure 7-27. Virtual field trips.

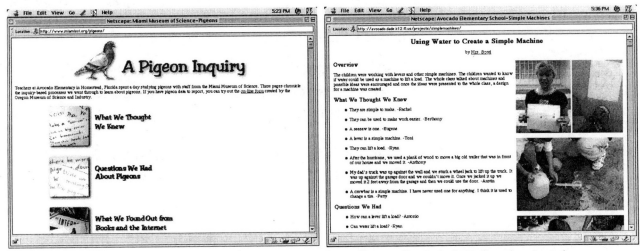

http://www.miamisci.org/pigeons/
Figure 7-28. Inquiry projects.

http://avocado.dade.k12.fl.us/projects/simplemachines/

geons (see Figure 7-28a). Many inquiry pages are set up with the following categories: What We Thought We Knew, What Questions We Had, What We Found in Books and on the Internet, Our Data, and Our Conclusions. Inquiry projects can be developed for all subject areas.

After Andrew (http://avocado.dade.k12.fl.us/afterandrew/). Chronicles an inquiry project where students investigated the effect of exotic Australian Pine needles on the germination of native finger grass.

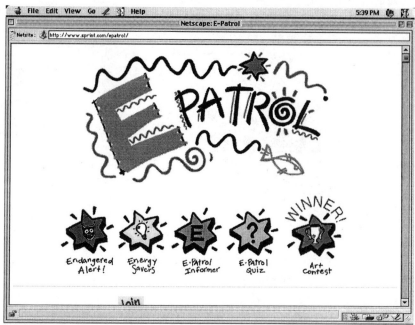

http://www.sprint.com/epatrol/
Figure 7-29. Action projects.

Simple Machines (http://avocado.dade.k12.fl.us/projects/simplemachines/). Students share their inquiry into simple machines (see Figure 7-28b).

Egypt (http://avocado.dade.k12.fl.us/egypt/). Learners share what they have learned about Egypt.

Action

Start an issues forum. Take a stand on an important social issue or discuss an environmental concern. Focus on local social activism, but link to national and international resources. Post your local projects. For example, show pictures before and after a local park clean-up effort. When you plan action projects, be sure that students act, not just write about the project.

Increasingly, students are taking action on topics and issues where they have exhibited great concern. For example, **Epatrol** (http://www.sprint.com/epatrol/) is a large-scale project that asks students to share their artwork and opinions related to ecology and the environment (see Figure 7-29).

Let students take the lead in an action project. They need to believe in the issue and act on the concern themselves.

Chapter 7: Small-Scale, Short-Term Projects 139

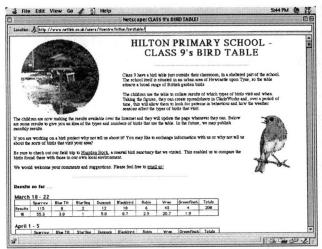
http://www.netlink.co.uk/users/itcentre/hilton/birdtable/

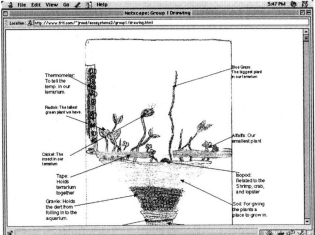
http://www.frii.com/~jreed/ecosystems2/index.htm

Figure 7-30. Research projects.

Community Leadership (http://cspace.unb.ca/nbco/pigs/croft/index.html). This project involves students in community leadership roles.

War Eyes (http://tqd.advanced.org/2636/page.html). Contains information about encounters with war. Actual accounts, photographs, and chat rooms bring war alive for users.

Research

Students have always done book reports and term papers. Today, an increasing number of students are publishing their work on the Internet. These research projects have expanded to include oral histories, community projects, and lab experiments. Be creative! You might use a metaphor such as a museum, book, or a time machine to present your information. Consider a character that could lead you through information or a theme that could be followed throughout the project. Explore some examples.

Hilton Primary School's Bird Table (http://www.netlink.co.uk/users/itcentre/hilton/birdtable/). Students build a bird table and post information about the birds who visit (see Figure 7-30a).

Bring research alive on the Internet, but don't forget the library. Books, videos, maps, and globes are still important tools in web development projects.

Our Ecosystems (http://www.frii.com/~jreed/ecosystems2/index.html). Each group cultivated a terrarium and designed an aquarium. The results are being posted on the Internet (see Figure 7-30b).

Maryland County Quilt (http://www.worldweb.net/~cesmith/quilt/quilt.htm). Students explored information about Maryland and developed a computer graphic quilt.

Virginia Indians (http://oakview.fcps.edu:80/~cassella/virginia/history/indians/). Students provide information about Native Americans and write about a day in the life of an Indian.

Information Resource

Start an information resource that might be used by others. For example, design a region page, lizard page, or limerick page. It could have existing links as well as lots of original information. Include bibliographies and reviews of materials. Ask other people to provide input and ideas. Career information and contact center, hobbies pages, and collection pages are other possibilities. Explore some examples.

Ancient History Project Pages (http://www.xs4all.nl/~swanson/origins/eg_history_intro.html). Sixth graders share information and links regarding ancient history (see Figure 7-31a).

Hollister's Third Grade Weather (http://www.hollister.goleta.k12.ca.us/weatherwatch/wwhome.html). The page contains everything you need to know about weather.

States Pages (http://www2.northstar.k12.ak.us/schools/and/statesproject/statesproject.html). Elementary students in Alaska post information about states and other topics. Two 10-year olds served as the web project managers (see Figure 7-31b).

Put your students in charge. From locating information to making the pages, even young students can be leaders on the Internet.

Chapter 7: Small-Scale, Short-Term Projects

141

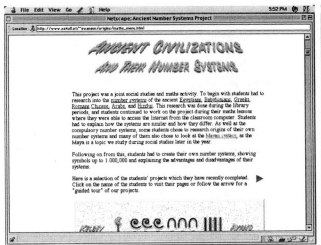
http://www.xs4all.nl/~swanson/origins/eg_history_intro.html

http://www2.northstar.k12.ak.us/schools/and/statesproject/statesproject.html

Figure 7-31. Student information resources

Demonstrations

Create a demonstration project. It could teach a skill, describe an experiment, or illustrate the correct/incorrect procedure for an activity. This type of project would be highly visual and contain graphics, photographs, or movies that would help a user understand the concept.

Some students want to share their understanding of a particular skill or demonstrate how to make something so others could make it themselves. **Castle Attacking Weapons** (http://met.open.ac.uk/heronsgate/projects/Mangonel/mangonel.html) is a student project developed in lego. The web page is used to demonstrate the functioning of the model using text, still pictures, and short video clips. Explore another example.

Mars Buggy (http://met.open.ac.uk/heronsgate/projects/mars/buggy.html): Students worked with a model of the rover and developed a page to show how it operates.

Use a digital camera to take pictures for demonstrations.

http://met.open.ac.uk/heronsgate/projects/Mangonel/mangonel.html
Figure 7-32. Demonstrations.

Alternative Products

Develop a model that could be used by students to learn about a topic or gain ideas for their own product. For example, create an interactive travel brochure including clickable maps, a greeting in the country's native language, and lists of destinations and activities. Or, create an interactive timeline that would provide information about major historical events and biographical sketches of historic figures.

Idea Exploration

Idea Exploration: Publishing

Explore student work that has been published on the web. What projects are your students doing that might be shared?

Publish some writing, artwork, or other projects that your students have done on a web page.

Small-Scale, Short Term Projects

Choose a project in each of the following three areas.

Informational

Instructional

Communication/Collaboration

Publishing

Chart 7-9. Small-Scale, Short-Term Projects

Real World Considerations
Small scale projects are a realistic way to begin spinning the web. Start by examining the projects you already do in your classroom. Could these be adapted or expanded for the Internet environment?

Team. Think about teaming with another teacher in your building on your first project. You might collaborate with a teacher of the same subject or try an interdisciplinary project. For example, the history and computer teacher might work together.

Limit Pages. Resist the urge to develop volumes of original information. Your first web project may only involve one page. Rather than emailing dozens of experts, start with a single expert or online connection.

Local Pages. You don't need a web server to get started on a small scale. Try running the pages locally on your classroom computer.

Summary
Informational, instructional, communication, and publishing projects are all a super way to get your students started with the Internet. Get your students involved with the project from the beginning. Give learners ownership and leadership roles and they've excel.

Part III: Planning & Implementing Internet-based Projects

Loosely organized, poorly managed projects can be a time-consuming disaster. Projects that are well-planned run smoothly and are an exciting addition to an Information Age classroom.

In this section, you'll design, develop, implement, and evaluate web-based projects. Along with project planning, you'll learn to create effective, efficient, and appealing web pages.

This section is divided into five chapters.

Planning Web-based Learning Environments
Designing Web Pages
Creating Web Pages
Designing and Developing School Web Sites
Implementing and Evaluating Web Projects

Planning
Planning Web-based Learning Environments
Designing Web Pages
Creating Web Pages
Designing/Developing School Web Sites
Implementing and Evaluating Projects

Planning Web-based Learning Environments. A successful web project takes planning. In this chapter, readers will explore tips for planning and creating effective projects, pages, and web sites.

Designing Web Pages. Learn to design and develop the individual pages that go into a web-based project. This chapter will help you plan and organize your project pages.

Creating Web Pages. Learn how to create web pages using a variety of web development tools.

Designing and Developing School Web Sites. Now that you've explored schools sites, you're ready to design your own. Examine the elements that go into an effective school site.

Implementing and Evaluating Web Projects. Classroom, time, and project management skills are essential to a successful project. In addition, you need opportunities for evaluation, reflection, and revision. The chapter will discuss the nuts and bolts of making your project work.

Chapter 8: Planning Web-Based Learning Environments

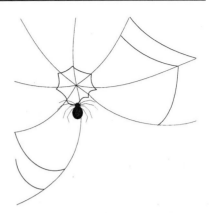

Where do I start?
What will my students and I be doing?
Is planning really worthwhile?

In this chapter, you'll learn to plan web-based learning environments. First, you'll explore the roles that students and teachers take in a web project. Next, you'll analyze the materials, resources, and activities that might go into the project. Finally, you'll plan the project.

Roles in Project Development and Use

Students can play different roles in web projects. What role do you want your students to play in project development?

Explorer. Students explore information on the Internet. They may use search engines or they may be provided with starting points, but the purpose is to use the Internet as an information resource.

Learner. Learner is a logical role for students. In this case, the Internet provides the resources and tools students need to learn. An easy way to set up this environment is the development of webquests or activity pages (see Chart 8-1). A web activity page should be a mini lesson that starts with an **Introduction** that is motivating and informs the learners about the pur-

Student Roles
Explorer
Learner
Teacher
Publisher
Participant

Web Project Planning

How to Design a Successful Project
http://www.gsn.org/teach/articles/design.project.html
Designing Resource-Based Projects that Use the Internet
http://www.ncsa.uiuc.edu:80/edu/RSE/RSEviolet/RSEviolet.html
Telecomputing for Teaching and Learning
http://www.ed.gov/Technology/TeleComp/
Learn Why and How to Join a Project
http://www.indirect.com/www/dhixson/why.html
Internet Project Design Template
http://www.indirect.com/www/dhixson/project.html

List 8-1. Web Project Planning.

pose of the activity. **Starters** are links that provide background information. **Investigations** are activities, experiments, interactions, or other active learning materials that get students involved in learning the concepts. **Extensions** are links that help students apply their new skills or share their learning with others. Finally, **Challenges** are activities that go beyond the scope of the lesson. They may be links to related content areas or thought provoking questions.

Teacher. Students may teach others through the Internet. Many sites include questions and activities that students have designed for other students. Learners enjoy the role of teacher. They like the idea of teaching children around the world what they have learned.

Publisher. Some teachers post pictures on bulletin boards or share their projects at a science fair. Use the Internet to publish student work. Students can design and publish their own web pages. Or, the teacher may develop the pages and use student work on the pages. Figure 8-1 shows a class that published their project on **Abraham Lincoln** (http://www.nh.ultranet.com/~wendyh/lincoln/lincoln.htm).

Mini Lesson

Design a simple mini lesson. Incorporate at least one web site into each of the following levels of the activity.

Lesson Background
    Topic
    Learners
    Expected Outcomes
    Materials Needed
    Classroom Management Plan

Mini Lesson Format
    Introduction

    Starters

    Investigations

    Extensions

    Challenges

Chart 8-1. Mini Lesson Format.

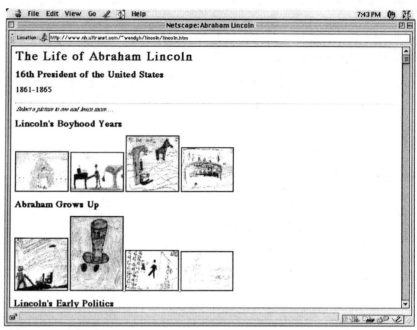

http://www.nh.ultranet.com/~wendyh/lincoln/lincoln.htm
Figure 8-1. Student as publisher.

Participant. You may ask students at remote sites to participate in your project or you may choose to contribute to a project at another school. Share ideas, information, writings, artwork, and scientific data. The **Reading Rainbow** (http://gpn.unl.edu/Writers/Writers.html) sponsors a contest shown in Figure 8-2a. In Figure 8-2, students become involved in an **Endangered Animals** (http://www1.tip.nl/~t232053) project.

With so many potential projects and student roles, it's sometimes hard to know where to begin planning. It may be easiest to follow some guidelines and ideas that have been generated by groups with lots of Internet project experience. There are many groups worldwide who are coordinating collaborative projects and contests for kids. See List 8-2.

Chapter 8: Planning Web-Based Learning Environments   151

http://gpn.unl.edu/Writers/Writers.html
Figure 8-2. Student participants.

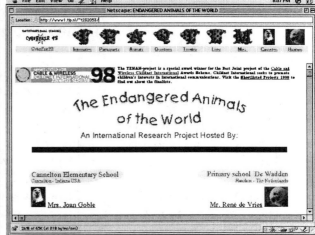

http://www1.tip.nl/~t232053/

Idea Exploration: Internet Integration
Pitsco's Launch to On-Line Collaborative Projects (http://www.pitsco.inter.net/p/collab.html), **NickNack's Projects** (http://www1.minn.net:80/~schubert/EdHelpers.html), **Project Center** (http://www.hmco.com/hmco/school/projects/index.html), and **Judi Harris' Network-Based Educational Activity Collection** (http://lrs.ed.uiuc.edu/Activity-Structures/) are great starting places to explore online collaborative projects. **European Schools Projects** (http://www.esp.educ.uva.nl/) is a site containing links to projects from Europe. Explore the projects.

   Select a project that you find interesting. Explore a project, summarize a specific activity within the project, and discuss how you might expand the project.

Idea Exploration

Getting Started with Planning

Start your project by collecting web sites related to your topic or theme. What have other people done already? What links might be useful? Can you find puzzles, games, simulations, virtual field trips, or activities that are already posted? What clip art, gif animations, sounds, and movies can you find that might be useful?

Internet Integration Projects

Australian Project Registry	http://owl.qut.edu.au/registry/
Curriculum Projects	http://edweb.sdsu.edu/triton/curriculum.html
Join An Online Project	http://www.siec.k12.in.us/~west/online/join.htm
Global SchoolNet Projects	http://www.gsn.org/pr/index.html
Global Schoolnet Network	http://www.gsn.org/
Global Heinemann	http://www.reedbooks.com.au/heinemann/global/project.html
Integrating Internet	http://www.unm.edu/~jeffryes/units.html
Integrating the Internet	http://www.indirect.com/www/dhixson/index5.html
Internet Projects	http://www.etc.bc.ca/tdebhome/int_projects.html
Lesson Plans	http://www.libertynet.org/~lion/lessons.html
NickNacks	http://www1.minn.net/~schubert/NickProjects.html
Blue WebN Applications	http://www.kn.pacbell.com/wired/bluewebn/
Pitsco's Launch to Projects	http://www.pitsco.com/p/collab.html
Project Center	http://www.hmco.com/hmco/school/projects/index.html
Project Zone	http://www.cccnet.com/success
Science Integration	http://kendaco.telebyte.com:80/billband/Possibilities.html
ThinkQuest	http://io.advanced.org/ThinkQuest/index.html
Web Page Design	http://edweb.sdsu.edu/edfirst/appcamp/web/thinking.html
World Lecture Hall	http://www.utexas.edu/world/lecture/index.html

List 8-2. Internet Integration Projects.

Explore projects at your grade level. How do they present information? Notice the length of pages and the presentation of activities. How are graphics integrated? What would be useful and appealing for your learners?

Explore projects that contain the technology elements you wish to use. For example, if you're considering a project that involves email, explore email projects in your grade level and content area. Try lurking at a desktop video conference or a chat and see what students and teachers do.

Evaluate the interactions and look for things that you might do differently. What technology do they use? How are students grouped? Will each student develop their own page? An example of individual student pages is shown in the **Fifty States** (http://

Chapter 8: Planning Web-Based Learning Environments

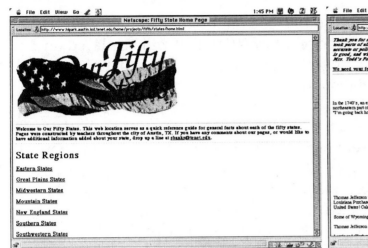

http://www.hipark.austin.isd.tenet.edu/home/
projects/fifth/states/home.htm

http://web.ccsd.k12.wy.us/sunflower/toddmm.htm

Figure 8-3. Our Fifty States and Mountain Men.

www.hipark.austin.isd.tenet.edu/home/projects/fifth/states/home.html) project (see Figure 8-3a). Will students work in small groups or will the entire class work together on the page? What works best? Some fourth graders in Wyoming (see Figure 8-3b) combined information they learned and pictures they drew on a single web page on **Mountain Men** (http://web.ccsd.k12.wy.us/sunflower/toddmm.html).

Planning Internet Learning Environments

Students play many roles in the distance learning environment. They may be consumers, contributors, and/or creators. Before you can begin designing your learning environment, you need to determine what role students and teachers will take.

Levels of Student Involvement

Consumers. Who will use the web pages that you and your students create? Will the pages be used within your classroom or will they be placed on the web server and available for the world to explore? Who is the audience for the pages; you and your students or other teachers, students, and members of the global community?

Student Involvement
Consumers
Contributors
Creators

Remember that grade level designations and ages vary around the world.

Your consumers are important and they will determine the type of information that will be placed on the pages. For example, if the pages will only be used within the building you may wish to identify each child with their picture and name. On the other hand, you may just use the first name on a child's work if it will be sent out over the Internet. If your consumers are young children, you'll need to consider reading and interest level. When sharing projects across the globe, it's essential to describe your children, school, and the purpose of the page very clearly so that the project is meaningful to the viewers.

How do you decide who your consumers will be? Consider interest. Is there a reason that people outside your classroom should be aware of your project? Are you doing something that might be of interest to the parents of your children or members of the local community? If your students are doing a project related to a social issue, they might be interested in the reactions of people in other parts of the world. Students developing a science page might wish to share their data with students at another school. The stories that your students begin could be expanded by a sister school in another part of the country.

As you can see, the look, feel, and content of the pages will be determined by who you envision being

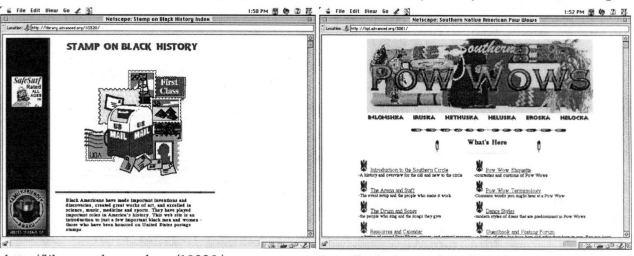

http://library.advanced.org/10320/   http://tqd.advanced.org/3081/

Figure 8-4. Stamps on Black History and Southern PowWows.

Chapter 8: Planning Web-Based Learning Environments

the consumer of the page. Remember; however, that once you place your page on the web without restrictions, anyone can access your pages regardless of whether they are your intended audience.

Examine some informational pages (see Figure 8-4). Black history is explored through postal stamps at the **Stamp On Black History** (http://library.advanced.org/10320/) site. **Southern PowWows** (http://tqd.advanced.org/3081/) contains information about the Native American PowWow and **An Amazon Adventure** (http://168.216.210.13/amazon/index.htm) explores reports and information about the Amazon.

Contributors. Who will contribute to the web project? Will the information come from you and your students, or will you invite students in other schools or the community to contribute? If you have an online newspaper, will you solicit editorials and articles from the outside world? For example, the **Vocal Point** (http://bvsd.k12.co.us/schools/cent/Newspaper/Newspaper.html) is an issues based school newspaper that requests contributions from students in other parts of the world (see Figure 8-5a). The **Oceans** (http://

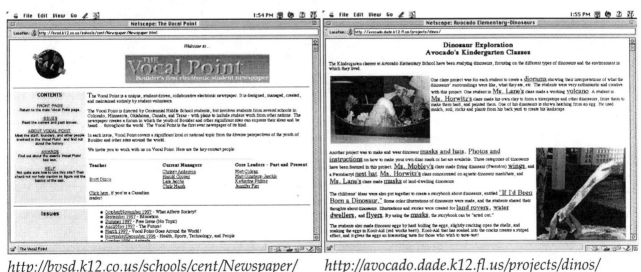

http://bvsd.k12.co.us/schools/cent/Newspaper/Newspaper.html

http://avocado.dade.k12.fl.us/projects/dinos/

Figure 8-5. The Vocal Point and Dinosaur Exploration.

bird.miamisci.org/oceans/) project from Avocado Elementary requests teachers to contribute to their thematic unit.

In the **Spiders** (http://avocado.dade.k12.fl.us/projects/spiders/) project, students became scientists by observing, collecting data, and reporting results on the Internet. Students contributed their ideas to the **Dogs of the North** (http://avocado.dade.k12.fl.us/projects/northerndogs/) project and even added links at the end. In the **Dinosaurs** (http://avocado.dade.k12.fl.us/projects/dinos/) project, students contributed pictures, artwork, and dioramas, that were posted on the web by their teacher (see Figure 8-5b).

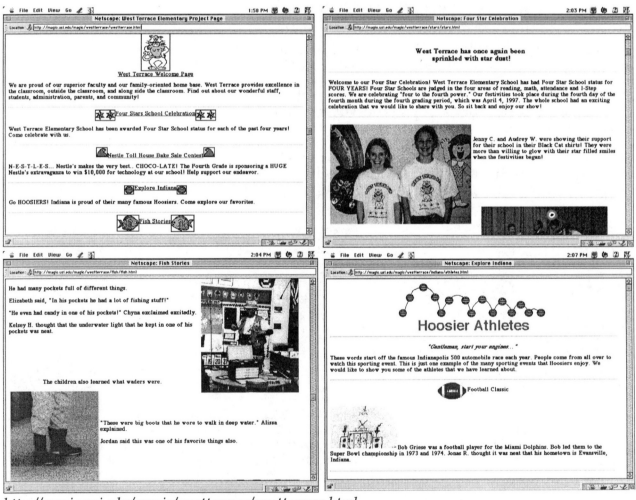

http://magic.usi.edu/magic/westterrace/westterrace.html
Figure 8-6. West Terrace Elementary School.

Creators. Who will produce the web pages? In some cases, schools have hired outside consultants or found volunteer parents to develop their school web pages. In other cases the high school computer club is in charge of the school web site. Teachers, students, community members, and others may all be involved in the development of web pages. We even get student teachers involved with helping area schools take their first steps into web development. A student teacher at **West Terrace Elementary** (http://magic.usi.edu/magic/westterrace/westterrace.html) school designed some projects to get their school site started. The projects represent different levels of student and teacher involvement. The Five Stars school project (see Figure 8-6b) was developed by a teacher to review a school event. In Fish Stories (see Figure 8-6c), students contributed comments and chose the pictures that would be included. The Explore Indiana project in Figure 8-6d combined on and off computer activities. The students created their drawings on paper and entered the text into the web page.

Help your students become creators! Get students involved with the development of web pages. In the **Zoo** (http://avocado.dade.k12.fl.us/projects/zoo/) project, second and third grades developed web pages based on information they learned on a zoo field trip.

There are many ways that even young children can get involved with the development of web pages. Let's say your class is studying whales. Your students could become creators by doing any of the following:

1. The teacher writes about the project and students draw a picture with paper and markers. The teacher scans the pictures and places them on the web.
2. Students draw a picture in Kidpix. The teacher copies the picture into the web page.
3. The students draw with Kidpix and copy the picture into a web page template.
4. The student designs the web page and inserts their own picture.

Which project is best? That depends on your goal, time available, technology, and skills. Are you interested in a teacher or learner centered web page. Students who design and develop their own pages are at the center of the activity rather than onlookers. They have power over the technology tools and learning experience. However this situation is not always possible. For example, consider the amount of time you have for the project and the available technology. Do your students have skills in scanning or using web development tools? Could students work in teams? Does every student project need to be included? Could you work with small groups throughout the semester on different elements of a large project? As you can see there are many options.

We've found that it works well to move slowly from teacher to student produced projects. For example, you may first involve students in the decision making process, but create the pages yourself. Your second project may involve students using the word processor to create the text files, but you may design the web pages. Another project might involve small groups working as a team to create a single page that will be linked to a core class page. Select the right project for the purpose, content, and time available. Compare this to class research projects. There are times when you provide students with the books and other resources they need to complete a project. On other occasions, you let students browse the library and select their own books. It depends on the objective and the time available.

Idea Exploration

Idea Exploration: Levels of Involvement
Explore the different levels of student and teacher project involvement. Will your students be passive observers or active participants in learning? Who will be producing the project, the student or the teacher? Complete Chart 8-2 to explore project options.

Chapter 8: Planning Web-Based Learning Environments

Levels of Involvement

Select a Topic
    Current Events
    World Monetary System
    Global Warming
    US History
    Author Studies

Levels of Involvement
Brainstorm ways that an activity could be modified for each of the following levels of involvement. Describe the pros and cons of implementing the activity at each level.

Students as Consumers Activity	Pros	Cons

Students as Contributers Activity	Pros	Cons

Students as Creators Activity	Pros	Cons

Chart 8-2. Levels of Involvement.

Web Project: Informational Content
What kinds of information will be included?

Ideas. Are the ideas, materials, and products being posted generated by students or teachers? The more students are involved in the design of the task, the more they will take ownership of the project. Encourage students to become involved in decision making at all levels from the color of the background to the order of the index.
   Who will be involved with idea generation?
   Where will ideas be posted?
   How will you decide which ideas to use?

Information. What sources of information will be used? There's no reason to reinvent the wheel. If the information has been posted at another location, it's easy to link to it than to retype it. What unique perspective can you take on the information? Do you have primary source materials such as letters, diaries, stories, editorials, debates, or reports that your students have created that could be posted? Be careful when using publishing information from your textbook, trade books, or other sources. Review the copyright law before using materials from any source other than your own creations.
   Will students be creating original content for the project such as research reports, fictional stories, or drawings? As you collect information for your project, address the following questions.
   What kinds of information will be created?
   How will you decide what information gets posted?
   Who will read the information you present?
   Will users be able to comment on the information?
   Will users be able to add to the information?

Links. Will your pages link to other pages within your school or external resources around the world? Linking is a powerful tool and an important new skill. Students need to evaluate the quality of information at

Informational Content
   Ideas
   Information
   Links
   Activities
   Projects
   Lesson Plans
   Formats

Chapter 8: Planning Web-Based Learning Environments 161

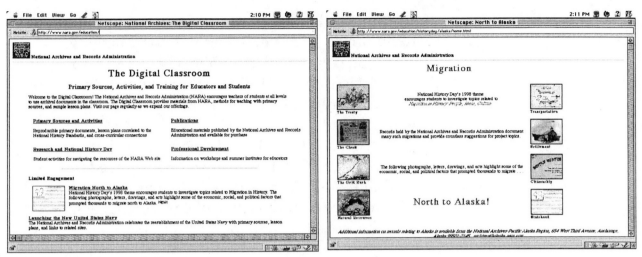

http://www.nara.gov/education/
Figure 8-7 National Archives.

other sites and decide whether the information is important enough to be linked to their site. Consider the use of primary source documents in your web pages. The **National Archives** (http://www.nara.gov/education/) has links to primary source documents as well as lesson plans and projects (see Figure 8-7). Figure 8-7b shows links to primary resources on Migration.

    What will the links look like?
    Will you use text links or an image map?
    Will the links be in a list or a paragraph?
    Who will check the links on a regular basis?

Activities. What will people do with your site? The web provides an opportunity for a very active learning environment where students can explore information, share ideas, and solve problems. You may wish to develop activities that make use of the information at other sites. On the other hand, your activity may not need external information to be successful. For example, if you're posting a short story you might not need external links.

    Who will be involved with the activity?
    Will you interact with other schools and students?
    What will you and your students be doing?

Projects. How is your web page connected to classroom projects? You may find that some activities require "on computer" use while others don't. You may be able to print out the web page and distribute a printed version as an alternative for people without web access.

    How much hardware and software is required?
    How many Internet connections are needed?
    Can the project be printed or downloaded?
    Are there materials that all participants will need?
    What's the timeline for the project?

Lesson Plans. Will teacher information be provided? There may be teachers who would like to learn more about your project. As a result, you may wish to develop lesson plans that will go with the web pages being developed by and for students. Again consider your audience. Do you envision students, teachers, or both using your pages? Develop lesson plans.

    Will all participants be the same age or grade level?
    What's the size of the class and the project?
    What student and teacher materials are needed?
    What's the expected learner outcome?
    Where does this project fit into the curriculum?
    What instructional strategies will be used?
    What's your plan for classroom management?

Formats. What's the best way to communicate information about your project? Text, tables, graphics, videos, audio, animation and many other media can be integrated into web projects. Consider the multiple intelligences of your children. How do they communicate best? Where do they need practice? The web is a great way to explore alternative communications.

    Will print materials be used?
    Who will develop the web pages?
    How will text and graphics be integrated?
    Will audio, video, or animation be used?

Informational Content

Describe a web-based project.

Answer the questions posed in the text for each of the following areas:

Ideas

Information

Links

Activities

Projects

Lesson Plans

Formats

Chart 8-3. Informational Content.

Web Project: Communication Types

Will your project be self contained or will it really use the power of the Internet as a communication tool? As you design pages, consider interaction. Can email, chat, discussion groups, or desktop video conferencing be used in your project?

Make connections to resource people in your local area as well as around the world. What kinds of information could you share? Why would students from other locations be interested in your project? Think beyond your classroom. What's the value of collaboration and sharing? What unique resources do you have in your local area that might be of interest to students in another part of the world?

Design active communication projects. Share information, then ask for input or feedback.

Go beyond simply posting projects. Ask for interaction. For example, the **Email Essay** project posted student projects and asked for email reviews. The reviews were then linked to the projects. Collect and share data from surveys or scientific experiments. Collaborate on writing or artistic projects.

Chart 8-4 contains a planning sheet for communication-type projects. Chart 8-5 contains an outline for a Call for Collaboration that you might post on the Internet. In Chart 8-6 you'll find a sample communication project.

Timeline: One Shot, Long Term, or Ongoing

What's the duration of the project? Do you envision a one shot project that is developed and posted or a year-long project with many phases?

One shot projects result in a one-time posting of information. You'll find lots of one shot activities as part of a culminating project at the end of a unit or as a reflection activity at the end of a field trip. For example, children in the United Kingdom went on a field trip to **Marsden Rock** (http://www.netlink.co.uk/users/itcentre/hilton/marsden/) and shared their

Chapter 8: Planning Web-Based Learning Environments

Communication Projects

As you plan for a communication-type project, answer the following questions.

Scope
    Who will participate in project development?
        local, regional (state, provincial), national, international
    Who is the audience for the final product?
        local, regional (state, provincial), national, international
    What is the impact of the project? Who cares? Why is this project important?

Technology Integration
    How will students use technology as an information tool?
    How will students use technology as a communication tool?
    How will students use technology as a creativity tool?

Student Involvement
    How will students be involved in project design and coordination?
    How will students be involved in collaboration with other groups?

Unique Experience
    How does this project provide a unique educational experience?

Chart 8-4. Communication Projects.

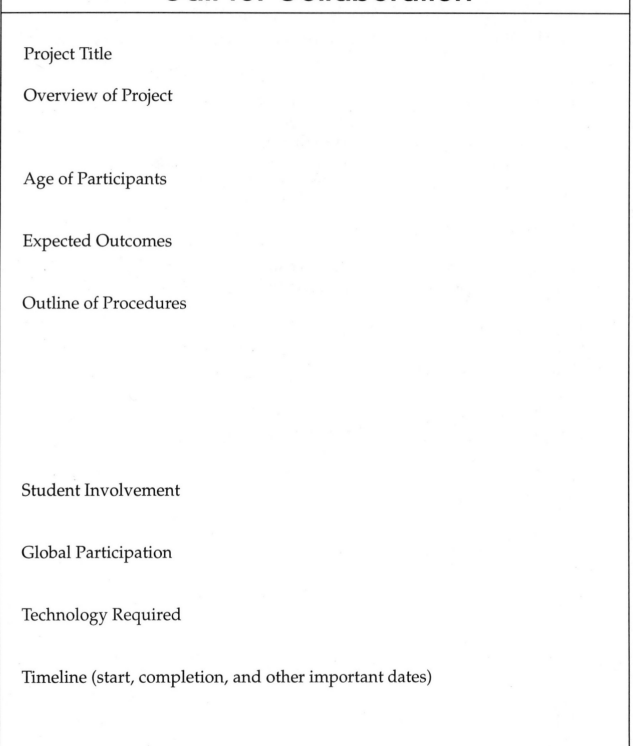

Chart 8-5. Call for Collaboration.

Sample Project

Topic:
Terrific Trees

Curriculum Areas:
Language Arts, Science

Age of Students:
8-12 year olds

Purpose/Overview:
Our fourth grade students are exploring the importance of trees in our world. We want to find out about the trees that grow in different parts of the world. We're interested in sharing information about the tree and pictures from different times of the year. We hope to post information from at least 10 different countries and 25 US states. The results will be shared on the web.

Time Line:
October 1:	Register classes
October 15-March 1:	Research by students
May 15:	Send information to me via email
April 1:	Distribute data to participants

Information Needed for Registration:
Teacher Name:
Name of School:
Age of Students:
Email Address:
Regular Mail Address:

Contact Information:
If you'd like to join us or need information, please contact me:
Ms. Susan Tree
Email: tree@usi.k12.in.us

Chart 8-6. Sample Project.

http://www.netlink.co.uk/users/itcentre/hilton/marsden
Figure 8-8. Virtual Field Trip.

Project Types
One shot
Long term
Ongoing

experience on a web page (see Figure 8-8). The page is not meant to be revised or updated. The **Food Chain** (http://avocado.dade.k12.fl.us/projects/foodchain/) is another one shot project where students posted the results of their inquiry project as a web page.

Long term projects can take a week, month, year, or longer to complete. They often post the skeleton for the project and add to it throughout the project as steps or activities are completed. These type of projects generally have a beginning, middle, and end, but take a long time to evolve. At Oakview Elementary the fifth grade class worked on the **Building Blocks of Civilization** (http://oakview.fcps.edu:80/~harris/96-97/agespages/) project throughout the year. As a new unit was completed the site was updated to include the new logo, pages, and links (see Figure 8-9). This ongoing approach to web development keeps the interest of outsiders and encourages revisits. It also keeps students interested in the projects by allowing small groups of students to work on the project throughout the year. This is particularly helpful if you have limited access to equipment.

Chapter 8: Planning Web-Based Learning Environments 169

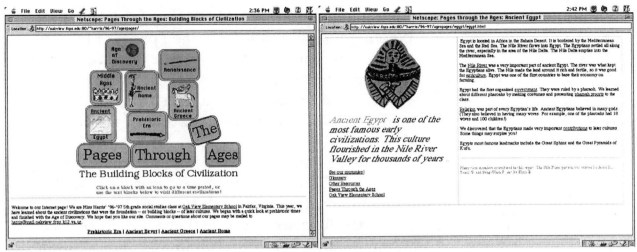

http://oakview.fcps.edu:80/~harris/96-97/agespages/
Figure 8-9. Building Blocks of Civilization project.

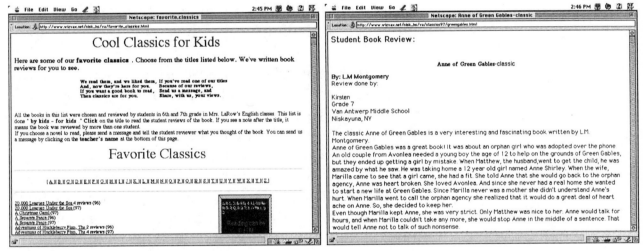

http://www.wizvax.net/nisk_hs/va/favorite_books.html
Figure 8-10. Cool Classics for Kids.

Ongoing projects continue to change and be revised. They're always a work in progress. For example, you could maintain a site that reports the weather and provides a new set of information every week. The **Book Review** (http://www.wizvax.net/nisk_hs/va/favorite_books.html) site was designed by seventh and eighth grade kids to share their book reviews (see Figure 8-10). A school newspaper would be another example of an ongoing project.

Planning Process
   Analyze Users
   Identify Purpose
   State Outcomes
   Organize Content
   Create a Plan
   Develop a Theme
   Design Layout
   Develop the Pages

Designing Web-based Learning Environments

Whether you plan your project on paper or in your head, it's important that you have a clear idea about what your web page will accomplish. Ask yourself: What function will this page serve? Who is likely to use it and why? What is the purpose of the page?

Analyze Potential Users. Start with an analysis of your users. To whom will you be speaking, sharing, and interacting? What are they like as explorers, web users, and learners? How do they typically behave when using the Internet? Will they be passive users or active participants within your web environment? What special considerations will need to be made based on the age, maturity, gender, cultural background, and reading level of the users?

Identify Your Purpose. Also ask yourself about the purpose of the page. What's your mission? What are you trying to accomplish and why? Try not to focus on the technology itself. If you find yourself saying that your mission is "to make a web page", you have a problem. It's not the web page that's important. The focus should be on the communication of information. Why are you creating the web page in the first place? Why should the audience be interested in your web page?

State Expected Outcomes. Consider the outcomes you expect. In other words, what do you want your users to accomplish from using the page? Do you want them to be informed on a topic or persuaded to take action on the issue?

Organize Your Content. Once you've identified your users, developed a mission, and created a clear set of outcomes, you're ready to select content for your page. What are the most important pieces of information? Can they be organized into categories? Can information be clustered together? Is there a hierarchy or sequence to certain pieces of information?

Think in nonlinear terms. Develop a concept map of your ideas. The center of your map or web will become the core page or index of your project. Each circle could represent a connected page or link to an outside resource. The more you plan now, the easier it will be to create the pages later. Many people like to create their concept map on poster paper. Others like to use the computer. A software package called **Inspiration** is a popular tool for organizing ideas. Your map will serve as the blue print for your project.

Inspiration can help you with idea generation, brainstorming, outlining, mapping, and other organizational needs.

Create a Preproduction Plan. Regardless of whether one or one hundred people will be involved with your project, it's helpful to begin with a preproduction plan. This plan will serve as a guide for your entire project. When developing a preproduction plan, be sure to include all your ideas, resources, and activities. By creating a master list of options, you have many possibilities to explore. At this point, you're not committed to any outcomes or activities.

Let's take the topic of Inventions. Chart 8-7 shows a diagram of concepts and objectives for the project. Chart 8-8 contains a list of resources including web sites, print materials, and CD-ROM. Chart 8-9 lists Internet-based activities that could be incorporated into the lesson. Although many activities are listed, only a few will be selected for implementation.

Develop a Theme. Your project will come to life quickly if you identify a theme, logo, metaphor, or analogy to go with your site. For example, you might design a cute creature such as your school mascot that will follow users through the pages. The kids at Oakview used a **Mad Scientist** (http://oakview.fcps.edu:80/~glazewsk/96-97/scientist/) theme for their science project (see Figure 8-11a)

Consider a logo or standard screen design such as a small icon to represent each major category or a different color to represent each page. For instance, if you have four steps in an experiment, use a giant 1, 2, 3,

Invention Project Planning

Inventions

Inventions have changed our world. Inventors often build on past ideas.

Disassemble and reassemble simple machines.
Create a chain showing the relationships among inventions and how past inventions lead to new ideas.
Compare and contrast past inventions.
Distinguish between copyright, patents, and trademarks.
Design a trademark.

Inventors

Inventors respond to the world around them.

Identify inventors who made significant contributions.
Match inventors with their inventions, time period, and location.
Describe the characteristics of an inventor.

Invention

Inventive Thinking

Inventive thinking combines curiosity, exploration or history, and creativity.

Identify characteristics of inventive thinking.
Apply inventive thinking to the development of a project.
Share inventive thinking approaches with others.

Inventing

Inventions are usually developed in response to a particular need.

Design an invention.
Plan for invention development.
Create an invention

Chart 8-7. Content.

Invention Project Resources

Web Resources

Albert Einstein Page	http://www-groups.dcs.st-and.ac.uk/~history/Mathematicians/Einstein.html
Canadian Young Inventor's Site	http://www.ideas.wis.net//cyif.html
Community of Inventors	http://medoc.gdb.org/work/invent.html
Creativity	http://www.quantumbooks.com/Creativity.html
Dead Inventor's Corner	http://www.discovery.com/DCO/doc/1012/world/inventors/week0896/inventors.html
Great Minority Inventors	http://www-groups.dcs.st-and.ac.uk/~history/Mathematicians/Einstein.html
History of Inventors	http://www.hfmgv.org/histories/projects.html
Invention and Design	http://jefferson.village.virginia.edu/~meg3c/id/id_home.html
Invention Dimension	http://web.mit.edu/afs/athena.mit.edu/org/i/invent/
Inventions	http://www.nationalgeographic.com/features/96/inventions/
Inventor Gallery	http://hawaii.cogsci.uiuc.edu/invent/Inventor_Gallery.html
Inventor Place: Hall of Fame	http://www.invent.org/inventure.html
Inventor's Site	http://mustang.coled.umn.edu/inventing/inventing.html
Inventor of the Week	http://web.mit.edu/afs/athena.mit.edu/org/i/invent/www/archive.html
Inventure Place	http://www.invent.org/
Leonardo da Vinci	http://cellini.leonardo.net/museum/main.html
Psychology of Invention	http://hawaii.cogsci.uiuc.edu/invent/invention.html
The Tech: Museum of Innovation	http://www.thetech.org/
Thomas Edison	http://userwww.sfsu.edu/~markd/TheFatherofLight.html
Wacky Patent of the Month	http://colitz.com/site/wacky.htm
Young Inventors	http://www.ideas.wis.net/cyif.html

Other Information Resources

- Aaseng, Nathan (1991) Twentieth Century Inventors. Facts On File.
- Binder, Lionel (1991). Invention. Knopf.
- Endacott, Geoff (1991). Discoveries and Inventions. Viking.
- Flatow, Ira (1992). They All Laughed. HarperCollins.
- Gardner, Robert (1990). Experimenting with Inventions. Franklin Watts.
- Haskins, James (1991) Outward Dreams: Black Inventors & Their Inventions. Walker.
- Invent It (Videocassette) (1988) Insights Visual Productions 401.
- Jones, Charlotte Foltz (1991) Mistakes That Worked. Doubleday.
- Lomask, Milton (1991) Great Lives: Invention & Technology. Scribners.
- Olsen, Frank H. (1991) Inventors Who Left Their Brands On America. Bantam.
- Richardson, Robert O. (1990) Weird & Wondrous World of Patents. Sterling.
- Turvey, Peter (1992). Inventions, Inventors, and Ingenious Ideas. Franklin Watts.
- Vare, Ethlie Anne & Ptacek, Greg (1993). Women Inventors and Their Discoveries. Oliver Press.

CD-ROM Resources

- Amazing Writing Machine
- Claris Home Page & ClarisWorks for Kids
- Microsoft Ancient Lands
- Eyewitness Encyclopedia of Science
- Leonardo the Inventor
- The Way Things Work
- What's My Secret #1 and #2

Chart 8-8. Resources.

Invention Project: Internet Ideas

Inventions
Explore student projects at Simple Machines (http://avacado.dade.k12.fl.us/simplemachines/)
Create ClarisWorks for Kids slide show invention chains to share on web page.
Post past and present inventions on a web page and ask users to compare and contrast.
In small groups investigate, copyright, patents, and trademarks. Create an "inventions helpline" web page for young inventors with Frequently Asked Questions about this topic.
Explore trademarks found on the Internet. Evaluate trademarks.
Coordinate a trademark contest. Ask kids around the world to contribute. Categorize the entries and post the trademarks.

Inventors
Explore inventors online.
Ask students to nominate an inventor for a special All Time Best award. Students must discuss the inventor, invention, and why they think it's important. Include links to online resources about the person and product. Vote online for the best!
Create a web timeline of inventors.
Invite an inventor to answer student questions through email.
Ask students around the world to vote on their favorite inventor. Track the location of the votes, the inventors location, and the invention. Is there a pattern?

Inventive Thinking
Explore web sites on invention and creativity.
Create a web page that contains the Keys to Inventive Thinking.
Share inventive thinking approaches online and ask others to join in.

Inventing
Explore sites for young inventors.
Post photographs of the invention process for others to see on the Internet.
Create a paper airplane site and ask other classes to join a paper airplane contest.
Post diagrams of student inventions.
Join an Invention project already in progress or start your own.

Chart 8-9. Activities.

Chapter 8: Planning Web-Based Learning Environments 175

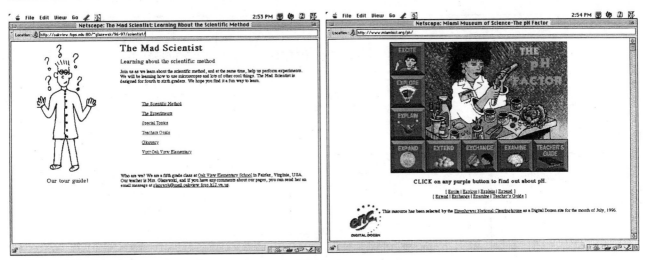

Figure 8-11. Mad Scientist science page and pH Factor project.

and 4 to draw attention to each area. Notice how the **Ph Factor** (http://www.miamisci.org/ph/) site uses the words Excite, Explore, Explain, Expand, Extend, Exchange to present the lessons (see Figure 8-11b).

Many people use metaphors and analogies as part of their sites. For instance, you might create a virtual field trip and use the information highway analogy. Many people design their site like a museum with different levels, rooms, and exhibits.

You could create a web site that uses a board game graphic as a main menu, a pie that shows the parts of the project, or a puzzle where users click on pieces. Use your imagination and make your site interesting and appealing to all ages.

Design Your Layout. Create a structure for your site. How will the pages be organized? Most sites are organized in a hierarchy. In other words, there's a core page that serves as the main menu, followed by a series of submenus and content pages. Consider drawing a diagram of the organizational structure to help with development of the pages.

Will the pages be self-explanatory or are they part of a larger project or unit of instruction? What will the pages look like? What fonts and sizes will be used? What will the headings look like? Will graphics and animation be used to support the text? Will the users

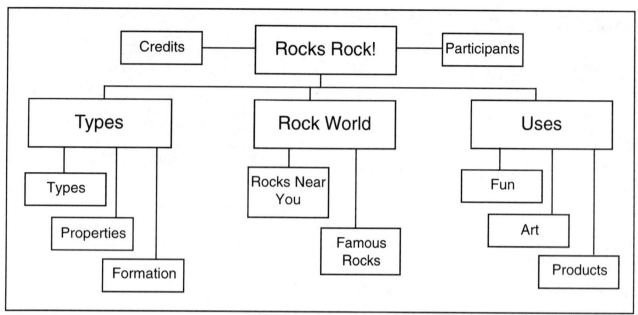

Figure 8-12. Diagram of web site.

be involved in some way? Will they answer questions, search for information, or be guided to additional information if needed? Where will users go for help?

Figure 8-12 shows a diagram of a project called **Rocks Rock!** In addition to three main areas, the site also links to a credit section and a participant list.

The **Types** section contains student reports and background information. It also links to lots of cool rock and mineral sites. This area is a great resource for all project participants as well as others who are interested in rocks.

The **Rock World** section contains data from two global projects. The first project is called **Rocks Near You**. In this project, students identify and chart rocks in their area and submit them to the master web page list. Students then compare the data to geological maps of the world. The second project called **Famous Rocks** asks people to write about a famous geological site in their area and share it on the website.

The **Uses** section highlights how rocks are used in our world including the areas of fun, art, and products. Part of this activity involved emailing people who work with rocks as part of their job and asking questions about their use of rocks. Students also took pictures of rocks in the community.

Develop the Pages. There are many categories of web pages that might be included in an informational or instructional web project.

About This Site
Core Page, Home Page, Index Page
Bibliography, Citations, Links
Subsection Pages
Supplemental Pages
Forms
Feedback
Help
Error
Navigation

Types of Pages
About This Site
Core Page
Bibliography
Citations
Links
Subsection Pages
Supplemental Pages
Forms
Feedback
Help
Error
Navigation

The first page that will appear in most projects is called the core page, home page, default page, or index page. It should welcome your users and introduce them to your site. This page must load quickly or users will become frustrated and leave. As a result, you need to combine an eye-catching, descriptive title and attractive contents with a fast loading system.

Limit your graphics to those that will have high impact. Carefully select a background, small graphics, and colored lettering to attract interest. You need to begin with an introduction and statement of purpose. These should provide a quick glance at the mission of your project. Next, provide an annotated index. You may wish to include a "what's new" and "awards we've won" section.

First Page
Core
Home
Index
Default

Most core pages end with a request for feedback, survey, guest book, or other tool to collect information from users. You may also wish to include links to software that is necessary to run movies or use your pages. Include contacts for the webmaster including name, surface mail, email, fax, and voice mail. Update and copyright notices should come last.

Notice the simplicity of the **Walt Whitman** (http://www.liglobal.com/walt/) page. The title and illustration is attractive without being distracting. The con-

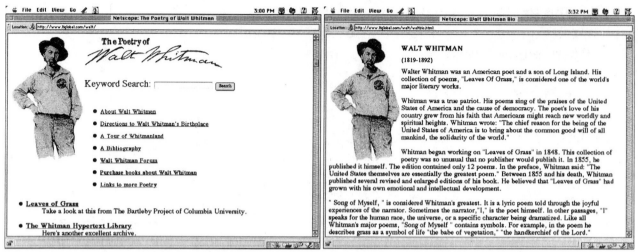

http://www.liglobal.com/walt
Figure 8-13. Walt Whitman page.

tents are simple, bold, easy to read, and presented in a logical order. On individual pages, the text is large and easy to read (see Figure 8-13).

The Blazers: Youth Services Community Club (http://home.earthlink.net/~penrose/Blazers/) mixes photographs and colorful graphics for an attractive introductory page. They provide an easy to use index across the bottom of the page as well as a mail center and guest book.

Overland High School (http://blazernet.ccsd.k12.co.us/) has a single core page that directs users to main areas. What are their major areas? Do you think this is adequate?

The **Stringtown Elementary School** (http://www.evsc.k12.in.us/schoolzone/schools/stringtown/string.html) page uses different colored pencils to highlight each grade level (see Figure 8-14). A pencil is also used as the school logo. As each classroom develops a page, the links will be activated. Notice that the community page uses the colored pencil logo as part of the heading on the page. The pencil is also used on other pages as well as in the "return" button.

Other informational and instructional pages should also contain an attractive title. This will be followed by text, graphics, sound, animation, and video information. Chunk information so that the text is not over-

Chapter 8: Planning Web-Based Learning Environments

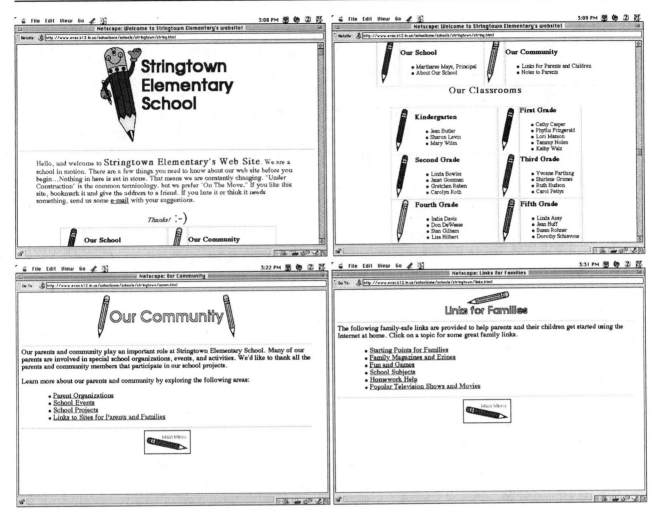

Figure 8-14. Stringtown Elementary School.

whelming. Be sure to include spaces between paragraphs and helpful headings and subheadings. Add interaction by including questions, activities, links, and opportunities to input information.

You'll also want to provide other kinds of pages. A review or conclusion page may be helpful. Also consider a credits page. Some projects require a help or map page that can assist users in navigating the project. **War Eyes** (http://tqd.advanced.org/2636/page.html) contains an About page, Mission page, and Conclusion page. These pages do an excellent job providing a context for the project.

Real World Considerations

Although planning is important, a spontaneous project can be exciting for learners. Students around the world shared the feelings of Israeli students after the assassination of Yitzahak Rabin. The world also shared their grief on the Internet after the death of Princess Diana. Canadian and US teens have shared their experiences following the devastation of floods and ice storms.

As you begin planning your project, consider how, why, and when you'll be using the Internet. You should be able to answer each of the following questions before you begin project development.

In your project, is there a need to:
- contact someone outside the classroom?
- seek outside advise or information?
- take action?
- learn more about others (i.e., cultures, people)?
- find an outside perspective?
- add or collect data from others?
- solve a problem using outside information?
- publish writings or artwork?
- identify a real-world example?
- locate authentic documents?
- gather and distribute information?
- share results?

Idea Exploration

Idea Exploration: Project Plan

Plan a project. Start with a preproduction plan including the content, resources, and possible activities. Create a layout for the structure of your web site. Also develop a logo or other visual elements that can be used throughout the project. While you're at it, develop a style sheet that includes the sizes and colors of your text including headings and subheadings. This kind of planning will help you develop a professional looking site.

Summary

Now that you've planned your project, you're ready to design your web-based materials.

Chapter 9: Designing Web Projects

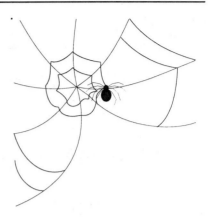

How should my pages be organized?
What background should I use?
Should I integrate audio, visual, and other cool multimedia elements?

In this chapter, you'll learn to design and develop web projects. Regardless of whether you're developing a school web site, classroom pages, or a project page, you want your pages to be informative, appealing, and effective.

Content

Carefully consider the presentation of information on your pages. Examine **World Safari** (http://www.supersurf.com/). The site was developed by a ten-year old and it's a great example of a colorful core page (see Figure 9-1). The page is constantly changing as new countries are added. The downside of this site is the contents. Although the site involves users in adding messages and discussing ideas, the countries information all comes from the CIA factbook and isn't very interesting. It could also use some graphics. As you select content, remember the importance of both visual and text elements.

http://www.supersurf.com/
Figure 9-1. World Surfari.

Choosing Information
　Compare
　Select
　Organize
　Express

Consider the following areas as you incorporate information into your pages.

Compare. How is the information from different resources alike and different? Why? Compare and contrast sources and types of information.

Select. What information is useful? Eliminate extra information and keep the most powerful ideas. Be sure to cite your sources.

Organize. What's the best way to arrange the information? Identify key ideas. Cluster information together into categories. Determine a logical order of presentation.

Express. What's the best way to communicate your ideas to others? Synthesize the information into new words, develop a picture, create a chart, design a timeline, or make a video.

In addition to the information you select for your page, also look at the quality of the sites you're linking to. Just because there's information, doesn't mean that you should link to the site. The information may not be useful to you or your users.

Chapter 9: Designing Web Projects

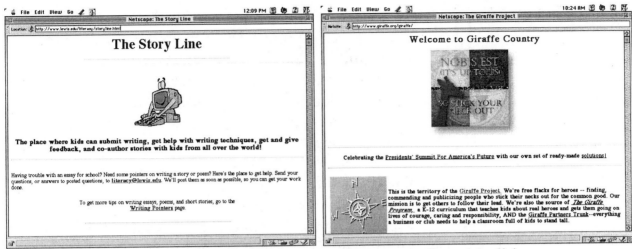

http://www.lewis.edu/literacy/storyline.htm   http://www.giraffe.org/giraffe/

Figure 9-2. Storyline and the Giraffe Project.

Accuracy. Is the information accurate? Is it frequently updated and continuously maintained? Are the sources credible and resources cited?

Usefulness. Is the information clear and meaningful? Is the information broad and deep?

Critical Thinking. Does the site challenge students to think critically, reflect on their learning, and address high level thinking skills?

Involvement. Are students actively involved using the site? Are they engaged in learning? The **Story Line** (http://www.lewis.edu/literacy/storyline.html) involves students in writing and even provides help (see Figure 9-2a).

Multiple Intelligences. Does the site integrate the intelligences of its users?

Rather than trying be everything to everyone, focus your attention on a single topic, theme, or unit for the content of your pages. Develop that area well before moving to the next topic. A series of "under construction" and poorly constructed pages is frustrating for a user.

Selecting Links
  Accuracy
  Usefulness
  Critical Thinking
  Involvement
  Multiple Intelligences

You may even wish to narrow the focus of your site to one specific project. Use a theme to draw interest. For example, **The Giraffe Project** (http://www.giraffe.org/giraffe/) focuses on people who are "sticking their neck out" for others. Their mission is to share the great things that people are doing for each other (see Figure 9-2b).

Organization

Consistency is the key to an effective web site. Users expect to find information in the same place throughout the site. For example, a heading may appear at the top of the page and a row of navigation tools may appear across the bottom. Creating a template will insure this consistency. In other words, design the outline of the page including the placement of separating lines, headings, technical information, and navigation tools. Then, make a copy of this page and fill in the information. Go back and use a copy of the template for each of your pages. Of course you may want to vary some elements to draw interest. For example, you might use a different color of text, background, or logo for each page with a particular topic or category.

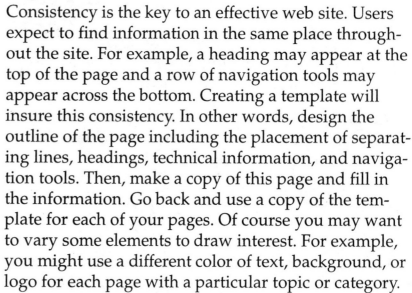

Organization is critical to the success of a web page. Create an overall plan for your project. You may organize it like a tree, web, table of contents, or organizational chart. Consider your content. What's the most logical way to present the information? Are there things that need to be presented in a particular sequence?

What Would You Do? is a webquest focusing on first aid issues (see Chart 9-1). A diagram shows a core page and six activity pages. A table at the top of the core page contains links to the six pages. A bar across the bottom of each information page also takes the user to the other pages in the project.

Chart 9-2 shows a project dealing with the **Middle Ages**. A diagram shows the relationship among pages in the project. A sketch of the core page and information pages is also provided.

Chapter 9: Designing Web Projects

What Would You Do?

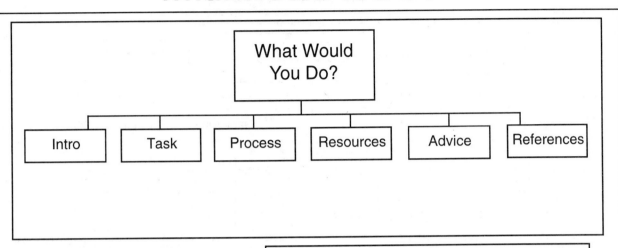

Core Page
The core page contains links to each stage of the webquest including introduction, task, process, resources, advice, conclusion, and references. The links are displayed on a table.

Information Page
Each information page contains a standard logo and title.

Across the bottom of each page is a long table that contains links to each of the other sections.

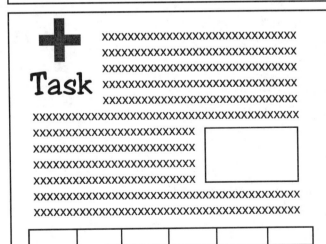

Chart 9-1. What Would You Do? Project.

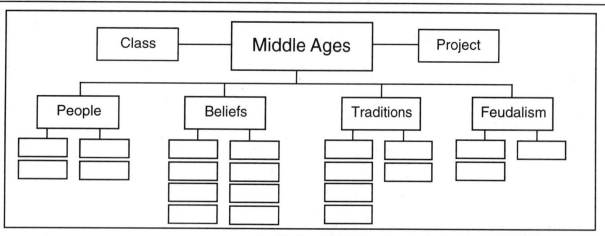

Core Page
The core page contains links to information about the class and project. It also links to the four major project areas and a credits page.

Middle Ages

About the Project
About Our Class
Middle Ages
   People
   Beliefs
   Traditions
   Feudalism
Credits

Information Page
Each information page has a standard graphic and text title. It also contains a short overview followed by the content of the page. The bottom on the page contains forward, backward, and main menu links.

Traditions

Overview

Content

Chart 9-2. Middle Ages Project.

Chapter 9: Designing Web Projects 187

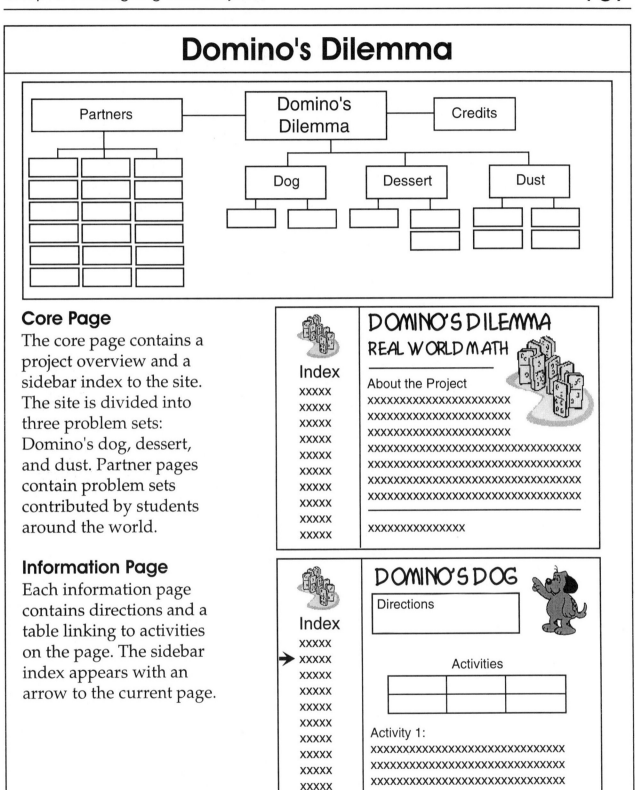

Core Page
The core page contains a project overview and a sidebar index to the site. The site is divided into three problem sets: Domino's dog, dessert, and dust. Partner pages contain problem sets contributed by students around the world.

Information Page
Each information page contains directions and a table linking to activities on the page. The sidebar index appears with an arrow to the current page.

Chart 9-3. Domino's Dilemma: Real World Math Project.

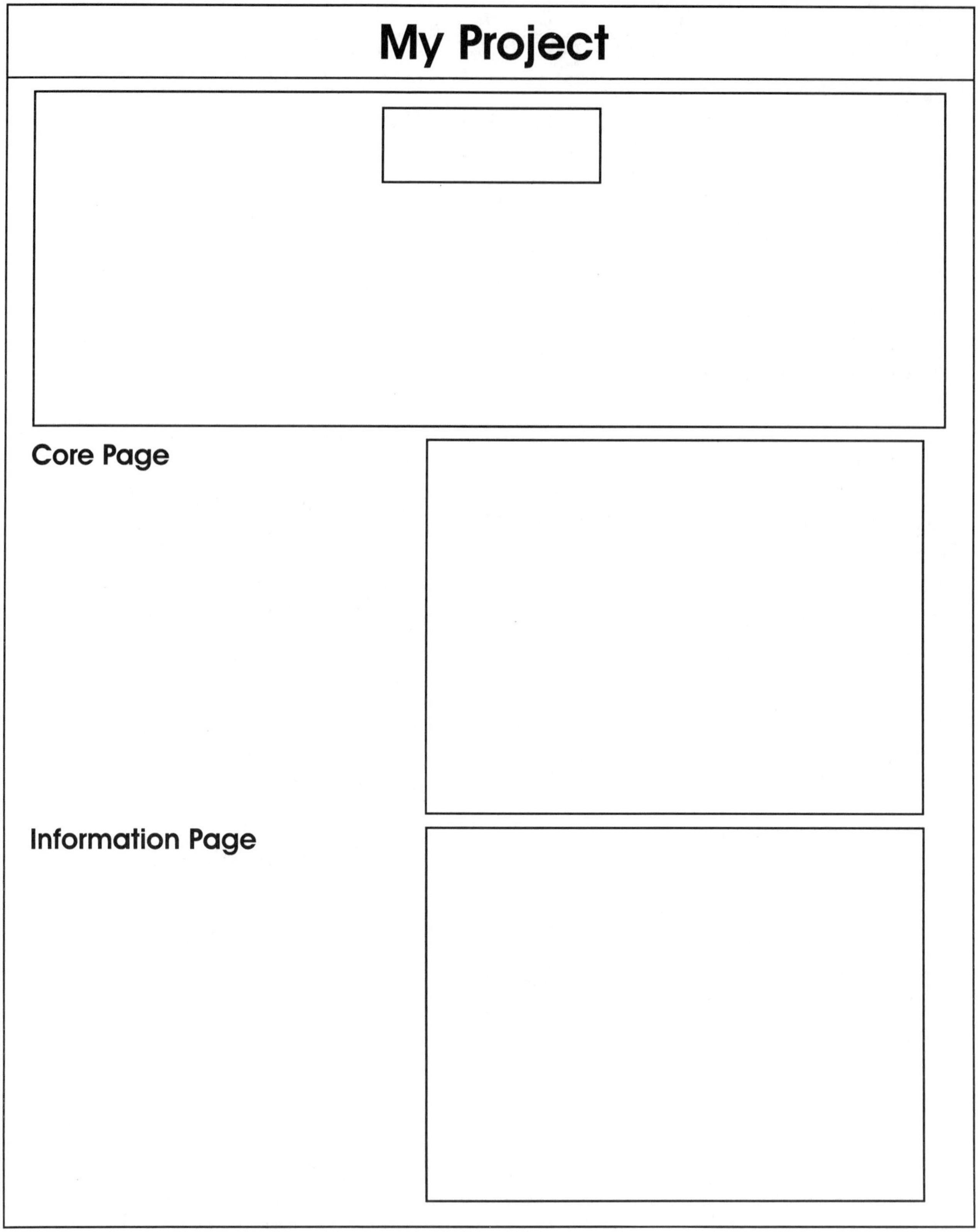

My Project

Core Page

Information Page

Chart 9-4. My Project Outline.

Domino's Dilemma is the title of the project in Chart 9-3. This real-world math project contains two elements. One section focuses on a standard set of math problems, while the other section posts the problems submitted by students participating in the project. Notice that the core page and information pages contain a side-bar index.

In each example, the diagram is helpful in creating a template for each information page. Use Chart 9-4 to do your own planning.

In addition to organizing information on pages, it's also important to carefully organize the folders and files that will store your information. Again, consistency is the key. The first page in an entire web site is generally given the name default.html or index.html. Beyond that you may wish to use the standard file names help.html, credits.html, and new.html.

Some developers like to use numbers in their system such as pic001.gif, pic002.gif, and pic003.gif. The problem with this system is that it's not very descriptive. You may wish to create a text document that annotates the list of picture files. If students will be involved, consider using their initials. Their folder might be name ks for Katie Smith. Her web pages would be called ksindex.html, ksfrog1.html, ksfrog2.html, and kspic1.gif. Some systems will only handle seven digit titles and three digit extensions.

Titles. Is a formal title included across the title area of the document? Is this title simple, yet descriptive? Are visually pleasing titles also included at the top of each page to identify the content? Highland Park in Austin Texas has lots of great examples (see Figure 9-3). Check out the title for the **Wildflowers of Texas** (http://www.hipark.austin.isd.tenet.edu/home/projects/first/wildflowers/wildflowers.html). It incorporates photographs. **A is for Austin** (http://www.hipark.austin.isd.tenet.edu/home/projects/first/aisfor/index.html) includes student drawings in the title area of the page. The **Patterns** (http://

http://www.hipark.austin.isd.tenet.edu/home/projects/first/wildflowers/wildflowers.html

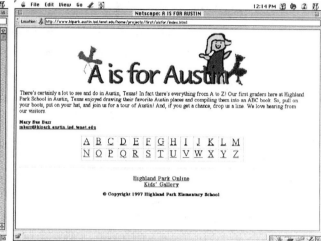

http://www.hipark.austin.isd.tenet.edu/home/projects/first/aisfor/index.html

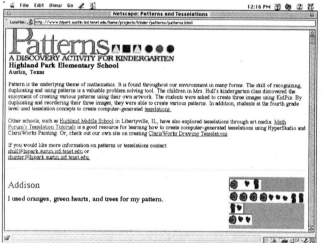

http://www.hipark.austin.isd.tenet.edu/home/projects/kinder/patterns/patterns.html

Figure 9-3. Austin projects.

http://www.hipark.austin.isd.tenet.edu/home/projects/third/castles/castles.html

www.hipark.austin.isd.tenet.edu/home/projects/kinder/patterns/patterns.html) page includes single geometric designs in the title. In **Castle Creations** (http://www.hipark.austin.isd.tenet.edu/home/projects/third/castles/castles.html), the title is aligned on the left and the overview is on the right.

Headings and Subheadings. Are headings and subheadings used to highlight sections? Do the headings relate directly to the content? Do the headings motivate and draw interest? Are sizes and colors used

Chapter 9: Designing Web Projects

to draw attention to particular sections? Are graphics or icons used consistently to help identify sections or areas of the project?

Chunk Information. Rather than using endless paragraphs of information, consider chunking information into small pieces. Separate paragraphs with spaces and use indentation to show levels of importance. Or, use tables and links to organize major areas. **The American School in Japan** site in Figure 9-4 (http://www.asij.ac.ap/) shows how both visuals and text can be used to organize a core page.

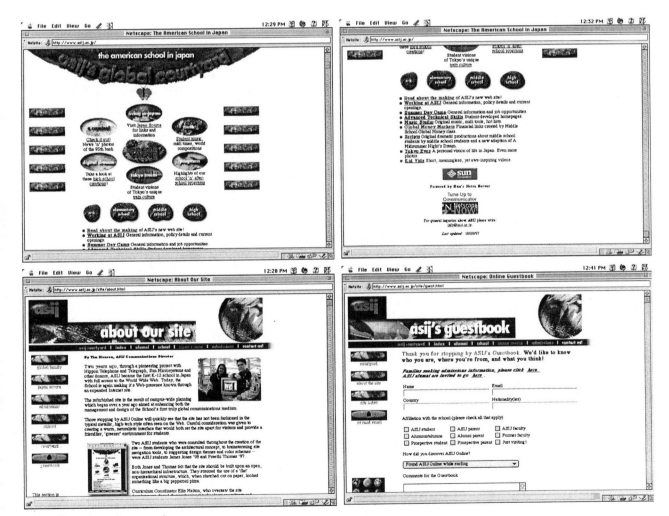

http://www.asij.ac.ap/
Figure 9-4. American School in Japan.

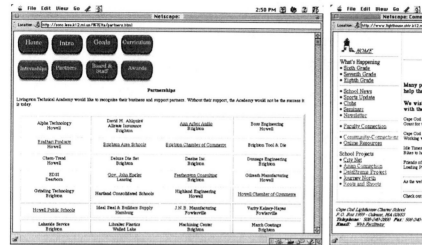

http://scnc.lesa.k12.mi.us/%7Elta/partners.html
Figure 9-5. Partners and sponsors.

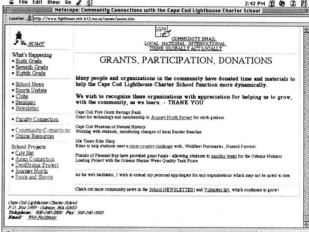

http://www.lighthouse.chtr.k12.ma.us/comm/comm.htm

Footers. Many webmasters place a line at the end of their document and then provide the types of information often found on a title page. Include the author and or webmaster on each page. Include names, addresses, email, and institution. The date of origin and updates should be included and annotated. In Figure 9-4b, thanks are given to hardware and software producers. In addition an email address is listed as well as the last revision date. Some schools even provide a page that discusses the development, mission, and use of the site. See Figure 9-4c.

Disclaimers. You may wish to include a disclaimer. In other words, you may wish to remind users that you aren't responsible for dated or inaccurate information. In addition, you could include a note about copyright and use of information.

Credits. It's a good idea to include a page or area for credits and acknowledgments. You'll want to include resources used in the project and give credit for audio, animations, or graphics used. You may also want to thank any sponsors. **Livingston Technical Academy** (http://scnc.lesa.k12.mi.us/%7Elta/partners.html) put their partners on a table as shown in Figure 9-5a. **Cape Cod Lighthouse School** (http://

Disclaimers

If the site is developed by students, indicate that the content was developed and presented in the original language of the students (i.e., misspellings, sentence fragments.)

Chapter 9: Designing Web Projects

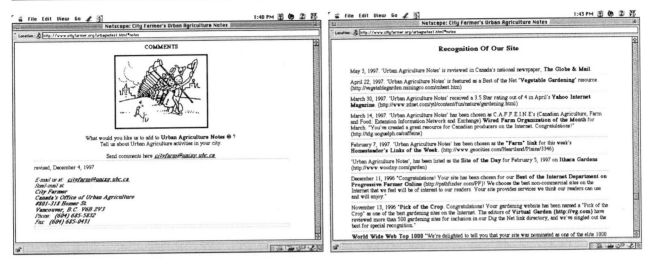

http://www.cityfarmer.org/urbagnotes1.html
Figure 9-6. Comments.

www.lighthouse.chtr.k12.ma.us/comm/comm.htm) in Figure 9-5b included a short paragraph about what each sponsor provided.

Contact Information. Be sure to include contact information somewhere in your web site. It could be a simple email address or you may wish to develop a comments form or a guest book (see Figure 9-4d). The **Urban Agriculture** (http://www.cityfarmer.org/urbagnotes1.html) page provides an email and snail address. It also posts comments from users (see Figure 9-6).

Contact Information
Sponsor name
Address
Webmaster name
Email
Fax
Phone

Links

Links are an important part of the web environment. They allow users to follow a train of thought, access additional information, or jump over irrelevant information. If you use lots of links, be sure to keep them up to date. Users hate "Link rot". Link rot happens when links aren't updated and lead to error messages rather than useful information.

There are four primary types of links. Examples are shown in the **American Dreams** webquest (http://town.pvt.k12.ca.us/Collaborations/amproject/student.html) shown in Figure 9-7.

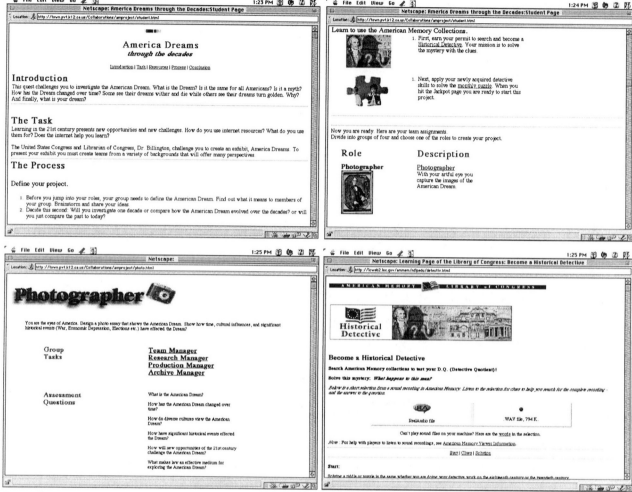

http://town.pvt.k12.ca.us/Collaborations/amproject/student.html
Figure 9-7. Links.

Link Types

Within a page
Different page,
    same site
Different page,
    different site
Other action,
    email, ftp,
    sound, movie

The first link involves movement within a single page. For example, a table of contents may be provided at the top of the page. Clicking on a topic or question will jump the user down the page to the particular topic.

Figure 9-7a shows the top of the webquest page. Users can click on the words Introduction, Task, Resources, Process, and Conclusion. When a hot word is clicked, the user jumps down the page to link.

The second type of link involves jumping to a different page within the same site. In Figure 9-7b the word "Photographer" is highlighted. When it is clicked, the user goes to the Photographer page within the

Chapter 9: Designing Web Projects 195

same site (see Figure 9-7c). Developers may use a table of contents, next and previous buttons, or a visual map to assist users in navigation.

A third type of link moves to another page on an entirely different web server. In this case the entire address will change. When using frames, the user may not realize they have moved to another site unless they study the status line while the page is being loaded. When the word "Historical Detective" is clicked in the example in Figure 9-7b, the user goes to the American Memories web site at the Library of Congress (see Figure 9--7d).

A final link involves other aspects of the Internet. Users might download a document such as a QuickTime movie or audio file, use ftp to download some software, or email someone using an email link.

The **MOTET: Music Online Telecommunications Environment for Teaching** project (http://nsn.bbn.com/motet/CurriculumIndex.html) incorporates audio files that are downloaded and played as shown in Figure 9-8a. It also links to sites where users can download software related to music (see Figure 9-8b).

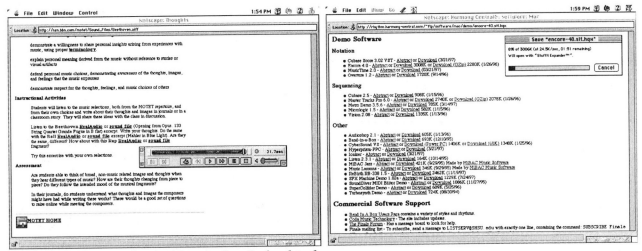

http://nsn.bbn.com/motet/CurriculumIndex.html
Figure 9-8. Music links.

Designing Links
Link Layout
Links Page
Navigation
Interaction
Feedback

Designing Links

There are many things to consider in designing your links. For example, keep the user informed. If they will be leaving the site, provide instructions for returning. Keep your links updated. "Mystery" links that go to the wrong page can be discouraging. If your program is under development, don't activate your links until the pages are done. It's frustrating and a waste of time for a user to link to an empty page with the words "under construction."

Link Layout. Some people like to place links in paragraphs, while others like to place them in lists. It depends on your goal. Sometimes the links are more meaningful within the context of an example or sentence. The user can choose to click for more information or continue reading. In other instances, you might wish to provide a link with a brief description or activity. Consider your users. Also, make it clear whether the link is "required" for understanding or simply an option.

Information should never be more than three clicks away. Don't build complex webs that require users to go through many menus before getting to information.

Links Page. Most schools provide some type of "favorite links" page. Consider a format that will be easy to use. For example, Caledonia High School (see Figure 9-9) has developed what they call their **WEBRARY** (http://www.caledonia.k12.mi.us/CHSlibpage/CHSlibpage.html) that is maintained by the School Library Media Center. This page contains lots of useful student links.

If you plan to include a "favorite links" page, be sure to keep it current. It is frustrating to go to a site and find that most of the links no longer function. This would be a good student project. Assign a student to check a particular page weekly or monthly to look for changes.

Chapter 9: Designing Web Projects

197

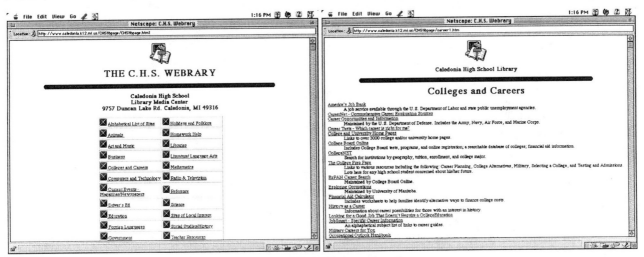

http://www.caledonia.k12.mi.us/CHSlibpage/CHSlibpage.html
Figure 9-9. Library links.

Navigation. Users must be able to easily find their way around your site. Every page should contain navigation tools. These are most frequently placed at the bottom of pages. Use icons to enhance your links visually, but also include a text option. Provide links forward and backward through linear sections of your project. In addition, provide links back to your main menu page, core page, or school site.

Check out the side bar navigation icons on the **Civil War** (http://www.rochester.k12.mn.us/john-marshall/overton/cwproj/main/civilframe.html) project page. The **Haiku** (http://mikan.cc.matsuyama-u.ac.jp:80/~shiki/) example uses a notebook analogy (see Figure 9-10a). An image map is used to present the notebook tabs on this core page. Explore the visual map used to provide organization for the **Revolutionary War** (http://www.rbs.edu/history/rbs/rbspage.html) project (see Figure 9-10b). In the **Ancient Greece** (http://oakview.fcps.edu/~smith/greece/) project, a student-produced drawing is used in the background of the table of contents buttons.

A table of contents is a logical way to set up a class project where student each posts their own web page. Examine the **Famous Americans Biography Book Reports** (http://www.inform.umd.edu/UMS+State/

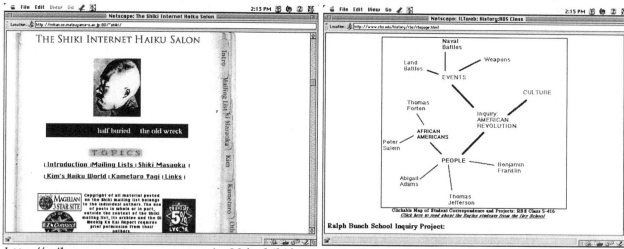

http://mikan.cc.matsuyama-u.ac.jp:80/~shiki/

http://www.rbs.edu/history/rbs/rbspage.html

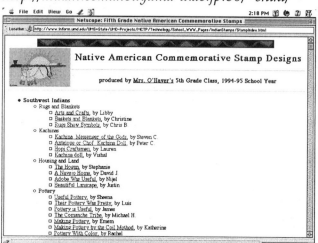

http://www.inform.umd.edu/UMS+State/
UMD-Projects/MCTP/Technology/
School_WWW_Pages/BookReportIndex.html

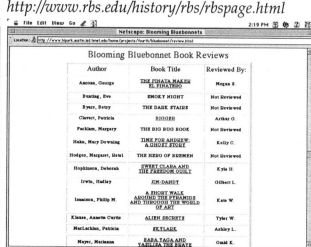

http://www.hipark.austin.isd.tenet.edu/home/
projects/fourth/bluebonnet/review.html

http://edweb.sdsu.edu/edfirst/sandiegozoo/
quest.html

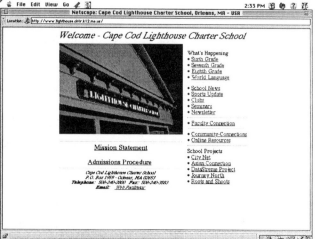

http://www.lighthouse.chtr.k12.ma.us

Figure 9-10. Navigation.

UMD-Projects/MCTP/Technology/School_WWW_Pages/BookReportIndex.html). They are accessed by clicking on a famous American. In the **Native American Commemorative Stamps** (http://www.inform.umd.edu/UMS+State/UMD-Projects/MCTP/Technology/School_WWW_Pages/IndianStamps/StampIndex.html) project an outline format is used to present pages (see Figure 9-10c).

Tables are also useful in presenting a table of contents (see Figure 9-10d). Examine the **Blooming Bluebonnets Book Reviews** (http://www.hipark.austin.isd.tenet.edu/home/projects/fourth/bluebonnet/review.html). As new books are reviewed, they're added to the table. **Loogootee Elementary West Homepage** (http://www.siec.k12.in.us/~west/west.htm) uses tables and popup lists. Do you like this way of organizing information?

You may wish to provide a number of different ways to access information. For example the **San Diego InternQuest** (http://edweb.sdsu.edu/edfirst/sandiegozoo/quest.html) shown in Figure 9-10e uses graphical buttons along the side of the page in addition to text links across the bottom of the page.

The key to navigation is access. Your navigation system should be simple and easy to use. Figure 9-10f shows a school in **Cape Cod** (http://www.lighthouse.chtr.k12.ma.us) with well-organized, efficient, "no-frills" school core page that's easy to use.

Interaction. Provide opportunities for users to interact on your page. Rather than a single link, provide a variety of choices. Incorporate polls, surveys, questions, and quizzes. **Ika's Online Fairy Tales** (http://www.ika.com/stories/menu.html) is set up for interactive reading (see Figure 9-11a). As children read the page, they can make choices regarding the story. For example, they can guess what happens next. Users can take a quiz at the **Chernobyl Nuclear Disaster** (http://tqd.advanced.org/3426/cgi-bin/Multiple_choice/multiple_choice_questions.cgi) site

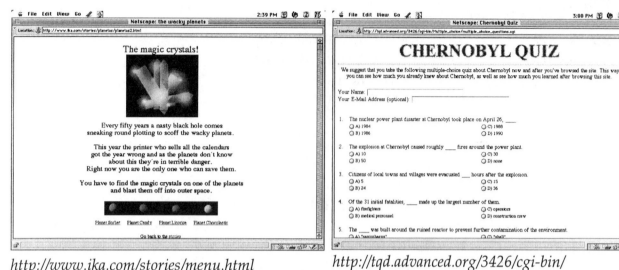

http://www.ika.com/stories/menu.html

http://tqd.advanced.org/3426/cgi-bin/
Multiple_choice/multiple_choice_questions.cgi

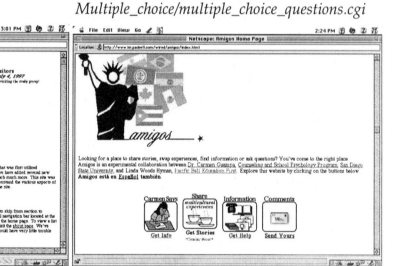

http://tqd.advanced.org/10335/

http://www.kn.pacbell.com/wired/amigos/

Figure 9-11. Interaction.

(see Figure 9-11b). **Interactive American History** (http://tqd.advanced.org/10335/) contains many interactive elements such as a concept map, outline generator, and discussion forum (see Figure 9-11c). The **Amigos** project (http://www.kn.pacbell.com/wired/amigos/) provides a chance for people to share ideas and concerns (see Figure 9-11d).

Feedback Pages. You may wish to provide an area for users to email you their ideas about your site. You could keep this information for personal use or post it.

Explore the page **"What Our Visitors Think"** (http://www.frii.com/~jreed/language/visitors.html) for a sample feedback page.

Text

Text is a logical element of a web page. You'll provide information, label diagrams, and provide help for users. You can enter text directly into your web page or store it in a word processing document.

Keep a style sheet showing the fonts, sizes, styles, colors, and indentation for each page to maintain consistency.

Text
Fonts
Scrolling Text
Justification

Fonts. The default font is dictated by the browser that the viewer is using. Although it's possible to change the font, the default works best in most cases. The sizes are relative. In other words, you can only make them larger or smaller but not dictate a specific size. You can use styles and colors to add interest. The font size of this paragraph is good for reading large chunks of information. Use the standard size +1. The next size larger or a bold style is good for headings and subheadings. Stick to two or three sizes and styles of text.

Think readability. If your font size is too large, the text will spread across the page onto multiple lines. If your font size is too small, your information will be difficult to read. The **Global Learn** site (http://www.globalearn.org/) does a great job providing pages that are easy to read by thinking about heading, subheading, and font sizes. They also try to make good use of white space by providing open areas on the page (see Figure 9-12).

Scrolling Text. If you have to scroll more than three or four screens, break up the page into multiple pages. Be sure to use headings if you have long scrolling pages. Headings can help a person find their place. It also helps if you provide a space between paragraphs.

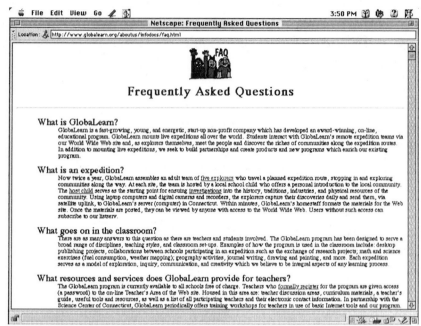

http://www.globalearn.org/
Figure 9-12. Text.

Justification. Left justified text is the easiest to read for multiple lines of information. **Bedford Lawrence High School** (http://www.kiva.net/~bnl/) contains some good information, but it's difficult to read because everything is right justified rather than left justified. Many web developers also center their text which also makes it difficult to read.

Graphics

If you're looking for ideas to add pizazz to your web pages, read the **Adding Graphics** (http://edweb.sdsu.edu/edfirst/web_learning/graphics.html) page. Photos, charts, graphics, and line drawings are all effective visual tools. Before you insert graphics, consider the need. Does the graphic add to, supplement, or distract from the purpose of the page? How long does it take to load the graphics? If the page loads too slowly users may get frustrated and give up.

The visuals you use should be relevant. They should also load in a minimum amount of time. If users don't begin seeing images in 10 seconds, they may give up and leave. Limit the number of graphics per page.

Background. Backgrounds can add to or distract from the atmosphere of a project. For example, the black background, red lettering, and photograph all contribute to the emotion of the **Chernobyl Nuclear Disaster** (http://tqd.advanced.org/3426/) page. In addition, the maps and diagrams throughout the site provide excellent illustrations of the ideas presented. The **Acid Rain** (http://earth.simmons.edu/acidrain/acidrain.html) page is very difficult to access because of the distracting background. The **Ellis Island Page** (http://www.i-channel.com/ellis/index.html) makes good use of a light background that relates directly to the purpose of the page (see Figure 9-13a). It lists the names of people who came through Ellis Island in white against a peach background.

You may also wish to try a border down one side of the page as shown in Figure 9-13b. The **Media Builder** (http://www.mediabuilder.com/) site provides lots of backgrounds and borders you can integrate into your pages.

Rather than a fancy colored background, consider using a white background with colored lettering and bright colored graphics. Or, use a very dark background with yellow or white lettering for emphasis. The key to backgrounds is contrast. Your background

Graphics
  Background
  Clip Art
  Maps
  Timelines
  Graphic titles
  Lines
  Bars, icons, logo
  Scanned images
  Captured images
  Digital stills
  Frames

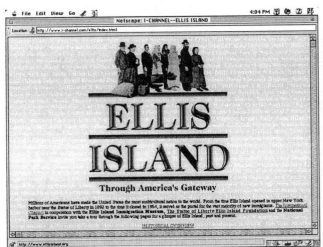
http://www.i-channel.com/ellis/index.html

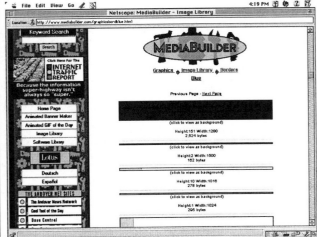
http://www.mediabuilder.com/

Figure 9-13. Backgrounds and borders.

Clip Art Sites

A+ Clip Art	http://aplusart.simplenet.com/aplusart/index.html
Animation	http://www.snowcrest.net/kitty/hpages/zebra.html?
Back to School Clip Links	http://www.cyberbee.com/bts.html
Barry's Clip Art	http://www4.clever.net/graphics/clip_art/clipart.html
Caboodles of Clip Art	http://www.caboodles.com
Clip Art Universe	http://www.nzwwa.com/mirror/clipart/
Clip Art.com	http://www.clipart.com
Jelane's Free Graphics	http://www.erinet.com/jelane/families/
Just Jane's Graphics	http://members.tripod.com/~jane2bob/
Library ClipArt	http://www.netins.net/showcase/meyers/library_clipart/clipart.html
Mining Co Clip Art	http://webclipart.miningco.com/
Rattle Snake Graffiti	http://www.fishnet.net/~gini/rattle/
School Pictures	http://www.bev.net/education/schools/admin/pics.html
Subject Area Resources	http://www.etc.bc.ca/tdebhome/subjects.html
Zia's Clip Art Sites	http://www.zia.com/kclip.htm

List 9-1. Clip Art Sites.

and lettering should be opposites such as black on white or navy on yellow.

Clip art. Clip art can add interest and appeal to your project (see List 9-1). Use clip art to illustrate book reports, stories, poetry, report covers, signs, multimedia projects, banners, papers, and homework assignments. **Just Jane's Graphics** (http://members.tripod.com/~jane2bob/justjane.html) contains lots of great graphics for kids (see Figure 9-14). You'll find icons, lines, bars, and all kinds of graphics. Be sure to check the copyright policy of each site. Some sites ask the user to include a citation when copying pictures. Some sites only let you copy a small number of graphics without an additional charge.

Chapter 9: Designing Web Projects

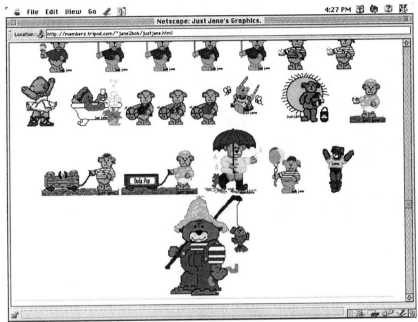

http://members.tripod.com/~jane2bob/justjane.html
Figure 9-14. Just Jane's Graphics.

Idea Exploration

Idea Exploration: Clip Art
Clip art is fun! The **Clip Art.Com** (http://www.clipart.com) site is a good starting place with dozens of popular links. You'll find lots of useful clip art at the sites provided.

In Netscape or Explorer you can copy or save most pictures easily. You click and hold your right mouse button on a picture and up pops a list of choices. You can also use software such as Capture to grab the picture. Once you've got the picture, you can put it in almost any document including a web page. Make sure you create a citation for where you found the picture even if it comes from a clip art source.

Create a web page with your favorite clip art or your favorite clip art sites. Use this page to quickly access the pictures or resources you need.

Maps. The **Global Temperature Project** (http://k12science.ati.stevens-tech.edu/curriculum/temp1/) contains a world map showing where in the world project participants live (see Figure 9-15). This can

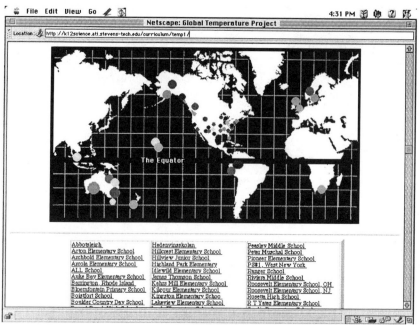

http://k12science.ati.stevens-tech.edu/curriculum/temp1/
Figure 9-15. Map of project participants.

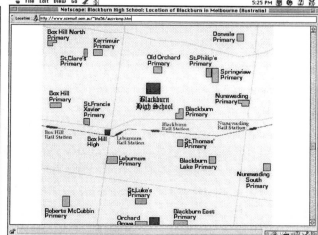

http://www.ozemail.com.au/~bhs56/ausvicmp.htm
Figure 9-16. Map that locates school.

draw interest to the page. You can also use maps to show the location of your school as shown in Figure 9-16. This page shows the location of **Blackburn High School** (http://www.ozemail.com.au/~bhs56/ausvicmp.htm) in Australia.

Timelines. A timeline is very helpful in understanding historical events and their place in history. The

Chapter 9: Designing Web Projects 207

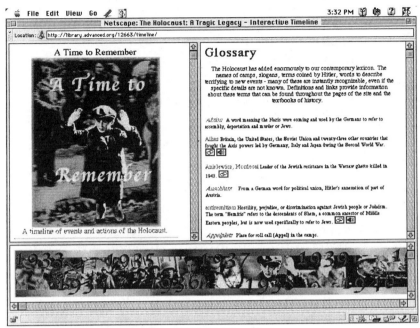

http://library.advanced.org/12663/timeline
Figure 9-17. Timeline.

http://www.frii.com/~jreed/
Figure 9-18. Graphics titles.

http://artsedge.kennedy-center.org/

Time to Remember (http://library.advanced.org/ 12663/timeline/) timeline scrolls across the bottom of the screen in Figure 9-17.

Graphic titles. Any paint or draw program can be used to make great graphic titles for your page. **Mr. Reed's Classroom** (http://www.frii.com/~jreed/) has a neat title with a graphic in the background. You can use the Cookie Cutter technique in HyperStudio or PhotoShop to get this effect (see Figure 9-18a).

Consider using a graphic in addition to a list of items in the site (see Figure 9-18b). Notice attractive introductory graphics at the **ArtsEdge** (http://artsedge.kennedy-center.org/). Use graphics to give your page a "look". Go to the **DK site** (http://www.dk.com/). You may recognize the style of the visuals from the books and CDs they produce.

Horizontal lines. Lines are an excellent way to separate areas of the screen. You can use the standard line that comes with most web development tools or surf the web for unique lines that incorporate color and graphics. In most cases the standard horizontal line can be made thicker or thinner to add interest.

Bars, icons, logos. Use icons with care. Make certain users know their purpose. The **Grandparent Stories** (http://www.best.com/~swanson/gm_stories/gm_storymenu.html) project makes good use of international flag icons. The flag represents the country of the story (see Figure 9-19).

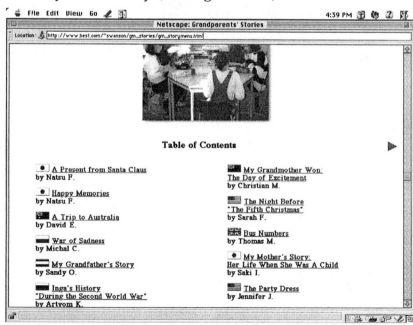

http://www.best.com/~swanson/gm_stories/gm_storymenu.html
Figure 9-19. Flag icons.

Chapter 9: Designing Web Projects

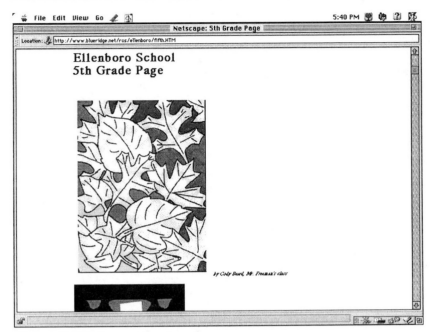

Figure 9-20. Scanned artwork.

Icons are also great for navigation. Try to repeat the same graphics rather than using lots of different graphics. Since a graphic only has to load once, it can appear multiple times without having to be reloaded.

Scanned images. Scanned artwork is an easy way to incorporate student-produced work into a web page. Figure 9-20 shows some fifth grade artwork that was scanned and posted on a web page (http://www.blueridge.net/rcs/ellenboro/fifth.HTM). Artwork created in chalk, crayon, marker, paints, pencil, and almost any other medium work well for web production. Rather than placing the full-size visual on the web page, include a thumbnail that can be clicked for a full-size view.

The **Timeline Project** (http://www.best.com/~swanson/fam_timeline/timelines.html) makes good use of photographs to record student projects. Try to keep photographs small for easy loading. Or, provide a thumbnail that can be clicked to view a larger picture. Be careful when using color. Use the least number of colors. In other words, rather than using millions of colors for a scanned picture, use thousands or 256. These pictures will load much quicker.

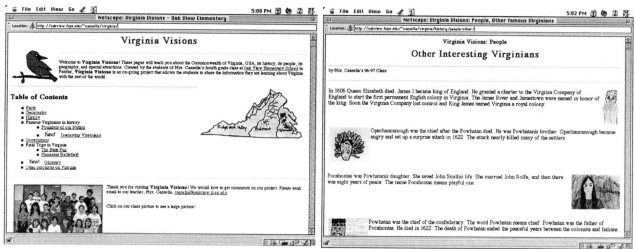

http://oakview.fcps.edu/~cassella/virginia/
Figure 9-21. Hand-drawn pictures.

Ask students to draw pictures using pencils, crayons, or markers, then use the scanned pictures in student projects (see Figure 9-21). The **Virginia Visions** (http://oakview.fcps.edu/~cassella/virginia/) project incorporates lots of student drawings. Notice how the student-produced images are laid out on varied sides of the screen on the **Other Virginians** (http://oakview.fcps.edu/~cassella/virginia/history/people-other/) page. Their **Manassas field trip** (http://oakview.fcps.edu/~cassella/virginia/special/manassas/) incorporates scanned photographs.

Captured images. In some cases you can save or copy images from graphics packages and place them directly into your web project. The **Johnny Appleseed** (http://www.hipark.austin.isd.tenet.edu/home/projects/second/ja/ja.html) project incorporated pictures produced by students using computer graphics software. The **Happy New Year** (http://wwfaxnet.com/nenga/index.html) project also used computer generated images.

Not all software allows you to easily copy or save pictures. However, you can usually use a screen grabber or capture program to copy a picture.

Chapter 9: Designing Web Projects

Charts, graphs, diagrams, tables. You may wish to build charts, graphs, diagrams, or tables into your project. For example, **Hilton Primary School's Bird Table** (http://www.netlink.co.uk/users/itcentre/hilton/birdtable/) page contains a table of information about birds. The **Poetry Garden** (http://sashimi.wwa.com/~uschwarz/poetry/grc000.html) uses a table for the main menu.

Digital stills from camera or video. Still pictures can be taken from a digital camera or video camera. The **Volcanoes** (http://met.open.ac.uk/heronsgate/projects/Volcanos/Volcanos.html) project shows the use of this type of picture in illustrating science projects.

Frames. Notice how frames were used for the menu and main graphics on **The Mysteries of Caminos Reales** (http://tqd.advanced.org/2832/) site.

Multimedia

Some schools use large graphics, animation, video, and sound to draw interest to their school. Unfortunately these elements can sometimes be overwhelming and distracting. They can also make the page load very slowly. Be considerate of your users. Use multimedia to add, not distract from the page.

Multimedia
  Sound
  GIF Animation
  Movies
  Applets
  Data Collection
  Software

Sound. Music, speeches, narration, and sound effective can bring a web page alive. One of the best examples of the impact of speech is the **Martin Luther King Jr.** (http://www.seattletimes.com/mlk/sound/) page. Listen to the excerpts from the speeches. There are many ways to incorporate sound into a page. Many pages now start with MIDI music such as **Grandpa Tucker's Rhymes & Tales** (http://www.night.net/tucker/). Does this draw interest or distract from the page? Also notice the use of the san serif font. Do you think this is easy or difficult to read?

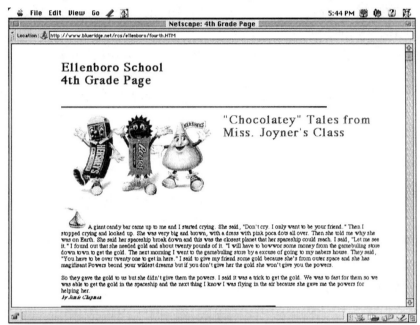

http://www.blueridge.net/rcs/ellenboro/fourth.HTM
Figure 9-22. Animation.

St. Christopher School (http://www3.sympatico.ca/saint.christopher/), **Mrs. Bogucki's 3rd Grade Class** (http://www.staffnet.com/hbogucki/aemes/default.htm), and the **Civil War Poetry and Music Page** (http://www.erols.com/kfraser/) begin their pages with music. Do you like this or do you think it's distracting? What about the musical selection? Remember your choice of music should reflect your project, school, or classroom.

GIF Animation. Animation is an easy way to draw interest to your site. Choose animations that contribute to your theme. For example, at **Ancient Sites** (http://www.ancientsites.com/) a fire is used on the introductory page. Figure 9-22 shows how an animated kiss logo is used at the beginning of each student story about chocolate (http://www.blueridge.net/rcs/ellenboro/fourth.HTM). On the other hand, they can also be distracting, so be careful.

Ask students to develop the GIFs for your page. The **First Internet GIF Animation contest** (http://

losangeles.digitalcity.com/animation/gallery.html) has lots of examples.

QuickTime movies. It's easy to include QuickTime movies in your projects, however this is not always a good idea. QuickTime movies can take a long time to load. It's recommended that you include a still picture. Then, users can click on the picture to play the movie as shown in the **Magnets** (http://met.open.ac.uk/heronsgate/projects/magnets/magnets.html) project. Also consider using very small screens such as the one in the **Smithsonian Magazine** (http://www.smithsonianmag.si.edu/smithsonian/issues96/oct96/undergroundrr.html) articles.

Applets. Applets are small JAVA programs. They can add cool features to your program, but they can also cause problems for users without the newest web browsers. Figure 9-23 shows a site called **Convomania** (http://www.mania.apple.com/) that is intended for teens with health problems and disabilities. In addition to cool graphics, scanned student projects, and interaction, the site uses a JAVA Applet to provide a refrigerator door with movable magnets for writing.

Data Collection. In some cases, you may wish to collect data from users. For example, Figure 9-24 shows a project called **LinkAge 2000** (http://library.advanced.org/10120/core.html) that focuses on aging. It contains a survey. You can also get users involved with chats, discussions, and other types of online information sharing.

Software downloads or plugins. Multimedia and hypermedia software can be used to design materials that can be run on the web or downloaded from the Internet. Explore **Henderson's Multimedia** (http://www.glenbrook.k12.il.us/gbssci/phys/THender/HCardInf.html) page for sample HyperCard and HyperStudio stacks used in his Physics classes. Try

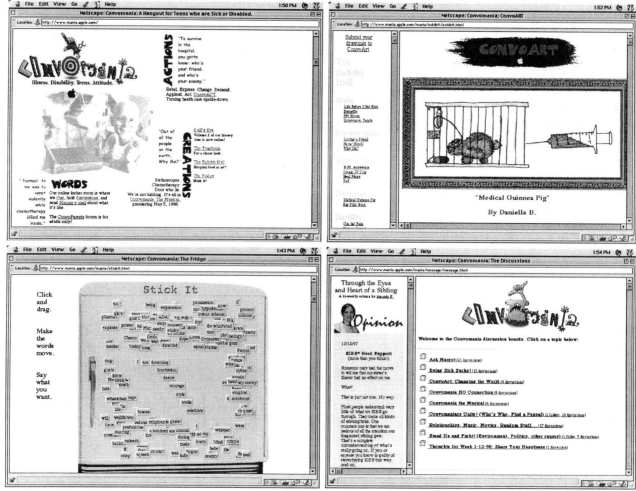

http://www.mania.apple.com/
Figure 9-23. Convomania.

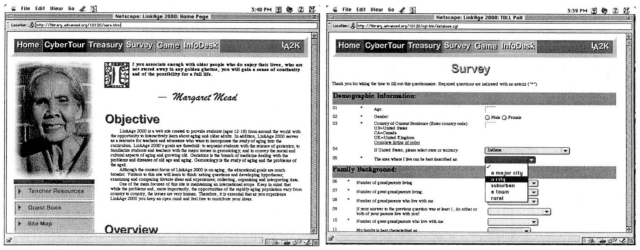

http://library.advanced.org/10120/core.html
Figure 9-24. LinkAge 2000 Survey.

some of **Percy Julian's** (http://kato.theramp.net/julian/hyperprogram.html) projects and **HyperCard** (http://www2.northstar.k12.ak.us/schools/upk/stacks/hypercard.html) science projects.

Idea Exploration: Design
Explore the award winning **Himalaya** site (http://library.advanced.org/10131/javamenu_final.htm) in Figure 9-25. Does it have the characteristics of good design? Why or why not? Try creating a diagram of the site.

Idea Exploration

Real World Considerations

Designing web pages can be lots of fun, but it can also be time consuming. Consistency is the key to an effective project. Design a core page and an information page. Use the information page as a template for all the content pages. Change the logo and information, but leave the basic design the same including the placement of the title and navigation tools. This consistency will make it easier for users to move around your pages.

Be careful when using Java and multimedia in your site. Many people have older browsers that can't handle these features. When possible, make these elements optional so a user can still enjoy your site even if they can't access these extras.

Summary

Designing your pages takes lots of planning and organization. Now that you've planned and designed your pages, you're ready to create them!

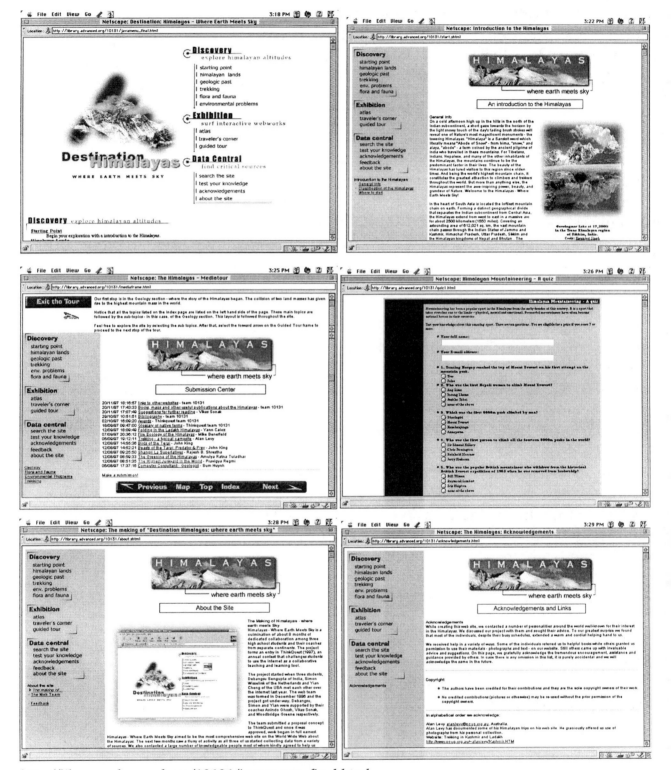

http://library.advanced.org/10131/javamenu_final.html
Figure 9-25. Himalayas Project.

Chapter 10: Creating Web Pages

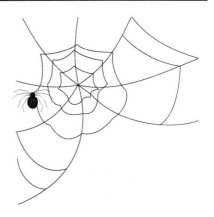

Can my young children create web pages?
What's the best web page development software?
Do I need to know HTML programming to make a web page?

In this chapter, you'll learn to create web pages. Developing web pages involves a combination of skills. Of course, you'll need some basic computer skills to get started. In addition, you'll need to learn a web development software package. Skills in instructional design, computer graphics, desktop presentations, desktop publishing and multimedia development are also helpful.

Read the pages in List 10-1 for background information about publishing on the web.

Web Development Resources

Publishing on the WWW	HTTP://www.ed.gov/Technology/Futures/mernit.html
Publishing on the WWW: Future	http://www.ed.gov/Technology/Futures/mernit.html
Internet Pages for K-12 Schools	http://www.newlink.net/education/class/doe/
Home Sweet Home	http://fromnowon.org/homesweet.html
The New (Electronic) Book	http://fromnowon.org/ch12.html

List 10-1. Web Development Resources.

Web Development Tools

Web page development is easy. Even primary age children can create their own web pages with very little instruction. HTML (HyperText Markup Language) programming is fairly simple to learn, but there are many web development tools available that don't require learning HTML programming language. **Adobe Pagemill**, **Microsoft Front Page**, and **Claris Home Page** are just a few of the many popular web page authoring tools.

Rather than doing the HTML programming ourselves, we use a web development tool. Most software is available for both the Macintosh and Windows platforms. This is one of the easiest ways to create a page because it is WYSIWYG (what-you-see-is-what-you-get) software. In other words, when you write, add links, create tables, or insert pictures they will appear on the screen just like in the final web page. The software will automatically insert the structural, graphical, and formatting tags into your web document. If you already know HTML editing, you can also add your own tags directly into the HTML code.

There are other ways to develop web pages. Many word processor and desktop presentation pages now provide web editors and web converters. A web editor allows you to insert HTML tags, while a web converter adds the necessary tag to change standard text and graphics into the web page format.

Some people are ready to go beyond simple HTML programming. The upper-level web programming language called JAVA allows programmers to go beyond placing text, graphics, sounds, and movies on a page. Programmers can write small programs called applets that will allow users to interact with the page, display games, animations, and other fun activities.

In addition to web development tools, you may also want to search the web for useful shareware utilities. For example, there are many GIF/JPEG converters that will translate any graphic into a visual that can be added to web pages. There are QuickTime converters

Web Development Tools

Adobe Pagemill
Claris Home Page
Microsoft Front Page

HTML

HyperText
Markup
Language

Chapter 10: Creating Web Pages 219

and sound resources that will help you configure movies and sounds for the web.

> Idea Exploration: HTML
>
> Explore some of the online web development resources (see List 10-2). Learn some basic HTML programming skills. There are a few things you can do using HTML programming that you can't do using the web development tools.
>
> Why might schools be interested in teaching HTML as an alternative to traditional programming courses such as C, Pascal, or BASIC? How do you feel about teaching high school student HTML programming? What are the advantages and disadvantages?

Idea Exploration

Choosing a Project

After exploring dozens of projects are you still having trouble thinking of a topic for your project? **The Web For Educators** (http://edweb.sdsu.edu/edfirst/courses/web_for_ed.html) will take you through the process of creating a cool educational web page (see

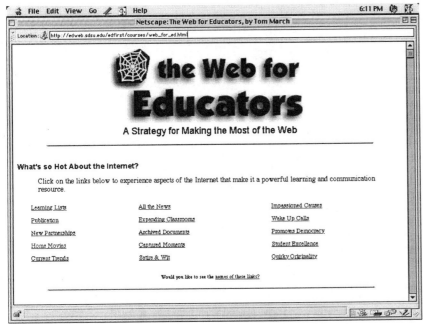

http://edweb.sdsu.edu/edfirst/courses/web_for_ed.html
Figure 10-1. Web Ideas.

Web Development Resources

Beginner's Guide to HTML	http://www.ncsa.uiuc.edu/General/Internet/WWW/HTMLPrimer.html
Composing Good HTML	http://www.cs.cmu.edu/afs/cs.cmu.edu/Web/People/tilt/cgh/
Copyright Tips for Web Page	http://www.siec.k12.in.us/~west/online/copy.htm
Create your own web page	http://www.smplanet.com/webpage/webpage.html
CyberTrail	http://www.wmht.org/trail/tender11.htm
HTML Converters	http://union.ncsa.uiuc.edu/HyperNews/get/www/html/converters.html
HTML Crash Course	http://k12.cnidr.org:90/htmlintro.html
HTML Editors	http://www.newlink.net/education/class/doe/editors.html
HTML Goodies	http://207.155.15.117/master.html
HTML Writer's Guild	http://www.hwg.org/
Internet Project Design	http://www.ilt.columbia.edu/k12/livetext/readings/telecom.html
Internet Development Tools	http://198.237.200.47/ESDPage/tools/tools.html
Making the Most of the Web	http://www.gsfc.nasa.gov/documents/making_most_www.html
Nick's Guide to Web Counters	http://www.futuris.net/nickp/counter.html
ProjectCool	http://www.projectcool.com/hiindex.html
School Web Maker	http://EDWEB.SDSU.EDU/EDFIRST/SchoolWeb/SchoolWeb.html
Top 10 Things NOT to do	http://cast.stanford.edu/cast/www/donts.html
Wizard's HTML Link Library	http://www.geocities.com/Heartland/Plains/3641/howtos0.html
Web Developer's Library	http://WWW.Stars.com/
Web Dev Home Page	http://indy.ael0.ocps.k12.fl.us/internet/webdev/index.htm
Web Developer's Library	http://WWW.Stars.com/Vlib/Providers/Style.html
Web Wonk: Tips	http://www.dsiegel.com/tips/tips_home.html

List 10-2. Web Development Resources.

Figure 10-1). Read **The Idea Machine** (http://edweb.sdsu.edu/edfirst/web_learning/machine.html) for help in developing and refining your web project.

Filamentality (http://www.kn.pacbell.com/wired/fil/) is a fill-in-the-blank interactive Web site that guides you through picking a topic, searching the Web, gathering good Internet sites, and turning Web resources into activities appropriate for learners. If you'd like to customize your web pages, go to **Beyond**

Chapter 10: Creating Web Pages

the Son of Filamentality (http://www.kn.pacbell.com/wired/beyond/).

As you formulate plans for your project, think about the ideas and information that will be integrated into the project. Ask yourself: Who should be involved with the development of the project? How long will it take to develop the project? Are hardware and software resources available for development?

Selecting Hardware and Software

It doesn't matter what platform of computer you use to develop your web pages. The following example will use Claris Home Page 3.0 on a Macintosh. If you'd like to give Home Page a try, you can download a trial version of the Macintosh or Windows software from the **Claris Home Page Site** at (http://www.clarishomepage.com/) (see Figure 10-2). The steps for creating your first web pages are the same regardless of the platform or software you choose.

http://www.clarishomepage.com/
Figure 10-2. Claris Home Page Site.

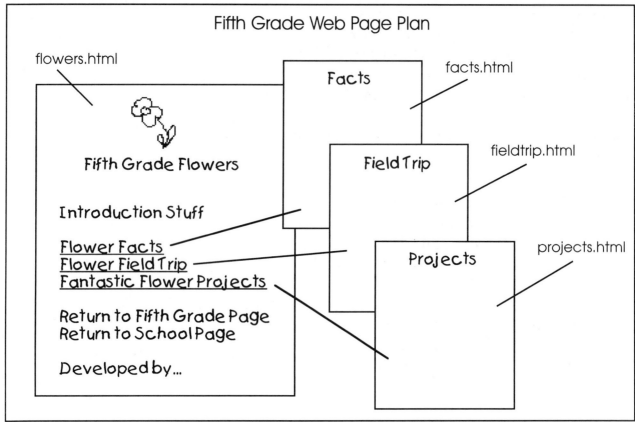
Figure 10-2. Fifth Grade Flowers plan.

Planning Your Pages

Planning is an essential first step in the development of web pages. Create a sketch of the pages and their links. If you find more than seven "chunks" of information on a single page, consider splitting the information into multiple pages with a "table of contents" page at the beginning as shown in Figure 10-2. The fifth grade class creating this project first planned a single page, then decided they had enough content for an introductory page plus three additional pages. The core page is called flowers.html and three additional pages are titled facts.html, fieldtrip.html, and projects.html. These pages along with all the images, sounds, and video will all be stored in a folder called flowers.

Before you begin developing web pages, it's important to get your computer desktop organized. Create a folder with a short, meaningful name such as flowers. All the pages, graphics, animations, sounds, and movies should go in this folder.

Chapter 10: Creating Web Pages

Setting Up Claris Home Page

A common problem with web page development is the storage of graphics. Even though your pictures, sounds, and movies will show up in your document on the screen, they must be stored as individual files along with your pages. For example, when you paste in a picture, Claris Home Page will automatically save the image in the Claris Home Page folder on your hard drive. It's best to save the pictures in the same folder with your web pages, so they will be easy to transport to your web server.

Claris Home Page provides excellent onscreen help.

Choose a topic from the 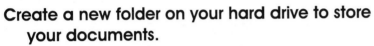 menu for help.

Create a new folder on your hard drive to store your documents.
We used the name flowers.

Follow the directions to install Claris Home Page on your hard drive. If you don't own the software, you can download a demonstration package from the Claris web page (http://www.clarishomepage.com/).

To open Claris Home Page:

Double-click on the Claris Home Page folder.
Double-click on the Claris Home Page icon.
A blank page should appear.

To set the preferences:

Pull down the Edit menu, select Preferences.
General preferences will appear.
See Figure 10-3.
Pull down the General option, select Images.
Click the Set... button next to Converted Images Folder:
Find the folder where your files will be stored.
When the folder is showing, click Select.
The new location should appear on the screen.
Click OK.

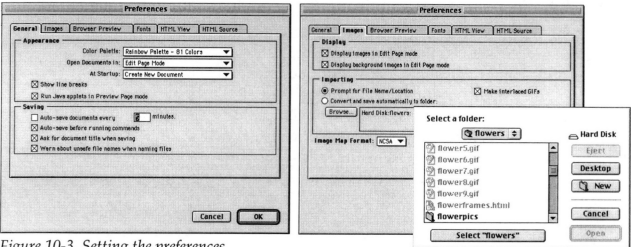

Figure 10-3. Setting the preferences.

Setting Document Options

Another preliminary activity is setting up the document options. You'll want to give your web page a title and also establish a background. The title you provide will be shown across the top of the web page when the page is running in a web browser such as Netscape. If you forget to provide a title, you'll be reminded when you save.

To enter a document title:

Pull down the Edit menu, select Document Options.. Click Parameters.

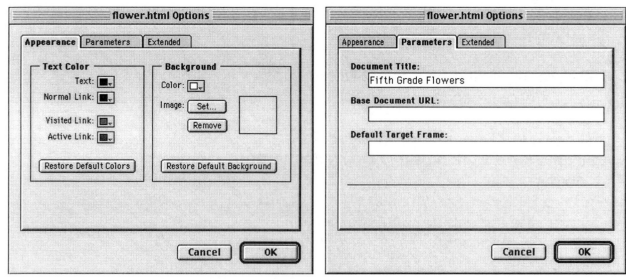

Figure 10-4. Document Options.

Chapter 10: Creating Web Pages

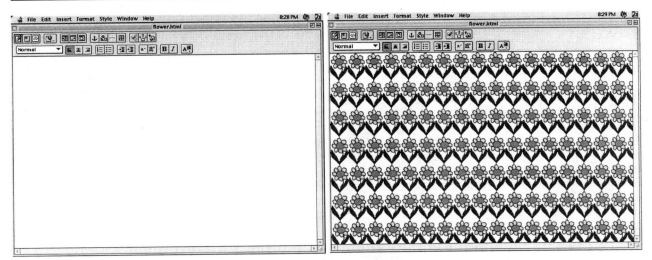

Figure 10-5. Setting the background color or graphic.

The Basic options will appear. See Figure 10-4.
Enter a title for your document and click OK.

The background is the area showing behind the text and graphics. You can select a color or use a graphic. Graphical backgrounds are seldom a good idea. They can easily overpower your graphics and make your text difficult to read. A light "ghost" image, watermark, or pattern is okay, but stay away from complex, bright graphics. Figure 10-5 shows a simple yellow background and an overpowering flowered background. An old-fashioned white background is my favorite because all text colors and graphics are easy to see.

To set a background color:

Pull down the Edit menu, select Document Options...
Click on the white box next to Color: to make a selection.
A color wheel will appear if you select Other... See Figure 10-6.
Select the color using the color wheel and the lightness setting using the scroll bar.
Click OK and click OK again.
Your background will appear.

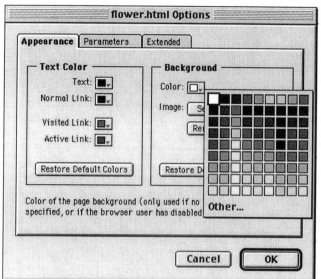

Figure 10-6. Color wheel.

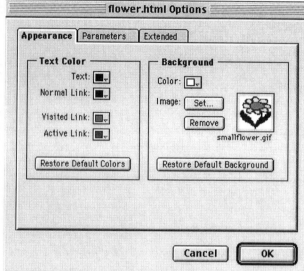

Figure 10-7. Setting Background Image.

To set a background graphic:

Pull down the Edit menu, select Document Options...

Click on the Set... button next to Background Image:

Find the image on your hard drive.
> If your graphic doesn't appear, you'll need to make it a GIF or Claris Home Page graphic first. We'll discuss this later in the chapter.

Click OK.
> The image will appear in the box.
> See Figure 10-7.

Click OK and the image will fill the background of your page.

To remove the background, click None next to the set option in the Document Options area.

Exploring Tools

Claris Home Page contains both a menu bar and toolbar to assist in web page development. The toolbar provides easy access to common tools and functions. The toolbar contains the basic toolbar, style toolbar, forms tool palette, and Image Map Editor toolbars. Figure 10-8 provides an overview of the basic and style

Chapter 10: Creating Web Pages

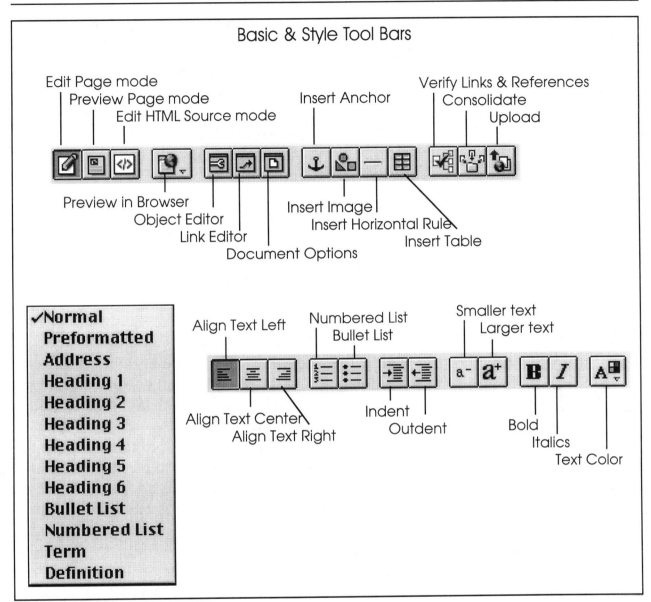

Figure 10-8. Toolbar overview.

toolbars. As you place the pointer over a button, the button's name appears to the right of the toolbar or under the tool.

Saving Your Document

Once you've completed your initial settings, you should save your document for the first time.

To save:

Pull down the File menu, select Save.

File Extensions

Some web servers use the .html while others use the .htm. In general, you'll use .html for Mac and UNIX systems and .htm for Windows.

Claris Home Page has a spell checker under the Edit menu.

Three Modes

Edit Page
Preview Page
Edit HTML

Adjusting Text Size

Highlight the text and use the a+ to make the text larger or a- to make it smaller.

The correct folder should appear, but double-check before saving.
Enter the name of the document including .html at the end and click Save.

Quitting Claris Home Page
When you're done working on your document, properly exit Claris Home Page.

To quit:

Pull down the File menu, select Quit.
If you haven't saved, it will remind you.

Editing Claris Home Page
There are three modes in Claris Home Page: Edit Page, Preview Page, and Edit HTML Source. When you open a document in Claris Home Page, it will appear in the Edit Page mode. This is the mode that you use to make changes to the page such as add text, graphics, and links. The Preview Page mode is used to view the page like it will appear in the web browser. The Edit HTML Source mode is used to edit, delete, add, or customize HTML code. Both the Window menu and the toolbar (see Figure 10-8) can be used to switch between modes.

Entering Text
Entering text is easy. It works just like a word processor. You begin typing at the blinking cursor as shown in Figure 10-9. We'll go back and add an attractive title later. The first section of your page should provide an overview to your web page or pages. In this case, it provides an overview to a fifth grade unit on flowers. Next, links are provided to other pages. Finally, page development information is found at the bottom of the page.

Once you've got some text, you'll want to do some formatting. You've got control over the relative sizes of text the end user will view. However, in most cases you don't have control over the font itself. You can

Chapter 10: Creating Web Pages

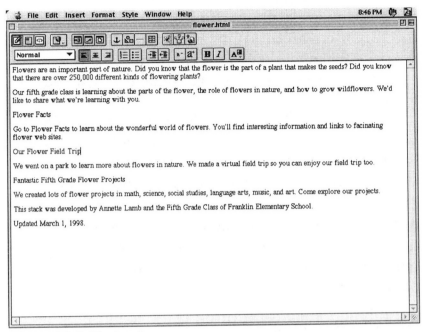

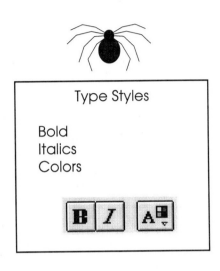

Figure 10-9. Text entry.

choose the size by selecting Heading 1 through 6 from the Format menu or using the smaller or larger font tools on the tool bar. The Normal size is 4. Sizes 5 and 6 are really too small to easily read off the screen. I prefer 3 for the body and 2 for the headings.

Explore the style options such as bold and italics. Although you can change the color of the font, be careful. For example, people are used to seeing new links in blue and used links in purple. If you select one of these colors, it may confuse users.

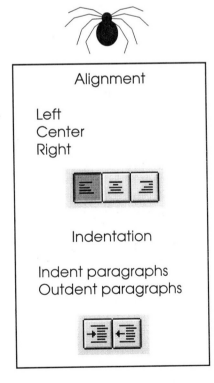

You can also change the alignment. For example, you can left, right, or center align text. You can also indent and outdent paragraphs. Review the tools available in Figure 10-8. The Format and Style menus provide other formatting options.

Inserting Images

Adding graphics can spice up your project, however don't overdo it. Graphics can take a long time to load on slow systems. Be considerate of your users. Use the smallest graphic possible to convey your idea. If you have more than seven photographs, consider creating two pages. Graphics can be a great addition, but they can also be a frustration.

Remember the graphics you insert will be linked to the page. Remember to move the graphics along with the page when you transport your project to your web server. It's easiest if everything is stored in a single folder.

When you add a graphic, the path to the graphic you are linking to is stored by Claris Home Page. You need to decide whether to store the relative path or the absolute path. The **relative path** is generally the best choice because you can easily move your files to a different computer without having to re-specify the links of the new location. The relative path defines the relationship between a page and an image appearing on the page. An **absolute path** always defines the location relative to the root level of your computer so the pathname doesn't change when a file is moved to a different location (MacintoshHD/flowers/flowers.html).

The Claris Home Page package provides lots of sample graphics in a folder titled Clip Art. Let's insert a picture. I'll insert an image next to one of my topics, flower facts.

Link Options

Relative path
Absolute path

To insert an image:

Click on the page where you'd like to insert the picture.
Pull down the Insert menu and select Image.
You can also click the Insert Image tool.
Select the image to insert.
Click Open.
The image will appear on the page.
To resize the image proportionally, click it, hold down the Shift key, and drag from the lower-right handle.

Once you've placed an image, you can use it throughout your document using copy and paste.

If you're worried about the amount of information on your page and how fast it will load, check the Document Statistics under the Edit menu.

Chapter 10: Creating Web Pages

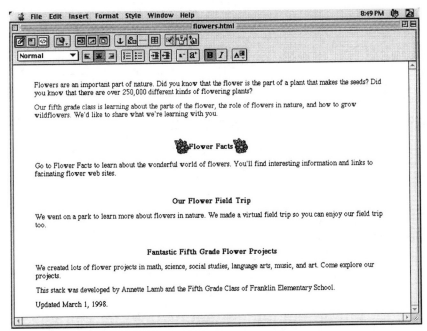

Figure 10-10. Inserting graphics.

If you're scanning pictures for use in Claris Home Page, save them in the pict format.

To copy and paste:

Select the picture.
Pull down the Edit menu, select Copy.
Click in the new location.
Pull down the Edit menu, select paste.
   See Figure 10-10.

Claris Home Page provides an image editor as shown in Figure 10-11. This allows users to place a border around the outside, align the image at the bottom, middle or top of the line, make the image transparent, resize the image, and other useful functions.

To use the image editor:

Double-click on an image.
   The image editor will appear.
   See Figure 10-11.
Try changing the alignment of the graphic from bottom to top.

Images must be in one of the two standard formats:
GIF (Graphics Interchange Format)
JPEG (Joint Photographic Experts Group).

Claris Home Page automatically converts PICT files on the Macintosh and BMP files on Windows into GIF format.

Transparent Images

If your image is white around the edges, set the Transparency.

Use the transparency tool  and the eye dropper to make the image transparent.

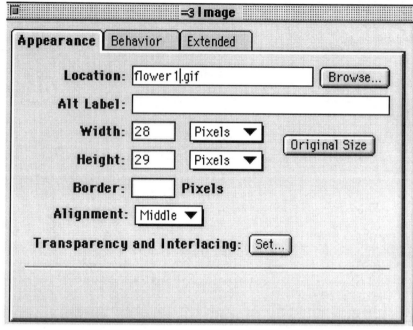

Figure 10-11. Image editor.

You can also copy and paste an image from another location. I created a graphic in **ClarisWorks** (see Figure 10-12), copied the picture, and pasted it into Claris Home Page (see Figure 10-13). I like using the paint option in ClarisWorks to create interesting titles with unusual fonts. The cool text is a paint graphic, so it can't be edited in Claris Home Page. You could also do your artwork in **KidPix**, **Photoshop** or any other graphics package. This is also a way to import scanned images.

Interlacing Images

Interlacing displays a rough outline of the entire image first, then gradually fills in the detail. Without interlacing the image comes up slowly, line by line.

To copy and paste an image:

Create the image in any software package, select it, and make a copy.
Open Claris Home Page.
Click where the image should be placed.
Pull down the Edit menu, select Paste.
   The image will be saved as a GIF graphic file in the folder indicated in Document Options. It will be given a number such image001.
To center the image, click the Center option on the toolbar.

Chapter 10: Creating Web Pages

233

Figure 10-12. ClarisWorks graphic.   *Figure 10-13. Inserting graphic in Home Page.*

Another way to add interest to your page is through the use of lines. The horizontal line tool lets you add lines of various thickness to your project. Use lines to separate major areas of your page such as your heading, key points, and web page information.

To insert a horizontal line:

Click where you'd like to add the line.
Click the Horizontal Rule option on the toolbar.
A line will be added.
Double-click on the line to see the options.
See Figure 10-14.
Increase the thickness of the line by changing the Height number.

No Images?

If you open your web page and no images appear, you may have a problem with the path. Check the Preferences and make certain images are being saved in the folder with your document.

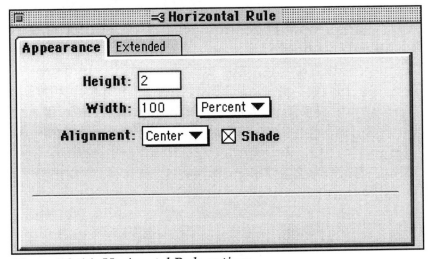

Figure 10-14. Horizontal Rule options.

Bars, Lines, & Icons

Besides graphics, you can also download bars, lines, and icons from clip art sites.

• • • • • • • • • • • • • • •

You can add pizazz to your project by importing graphics from lots of different sources. You can add scanned pictures, digital pictures, or clip art from CDs. Explore the Internet for artwork. You can find lines, bars, icons, and other images. Whether you find images in a book, CD, or on the web, make certain you check the copyright notice. Many sources allow educators to post their clip art on the Internet. Try one of the following sites to get started. You might also want to use a search engine and search for the words clip art.

Clipart.Com	http://www.clipart.com
Clipart Collection	http://www.ist.net/clipart
Icon Bazaar	http://www.iconbazaar.com

It's easy to collect pictures from the Internet. Just find the artwork and make a copy!

To copy a picture off the Internet:

Hold the mouse button on a picture.
    A menu will appear. See Figure 10-15.
Select copy.
Open your Claris Home Page document.
Click to place the document.
Pull down the File menu, select Paste.

Formatting Information

Sometimes it's nice to be able to place information into lists. Claris Home Page provides two types of lists: bullet and numbered. Unless your list has a particular sequence such as the steps in a process, top five reasons, or the best of something, stick to bullet rather than numbered lists. You'll notice that the lists will be indented as well as identified with bullets or numbers. Figure 10-16 shows a bullet and number list from the Flower Facts page. The numbered list is shown in Preview mode.

Lists

Numbered
Bullets

Chapter 10: Creating Web Pages

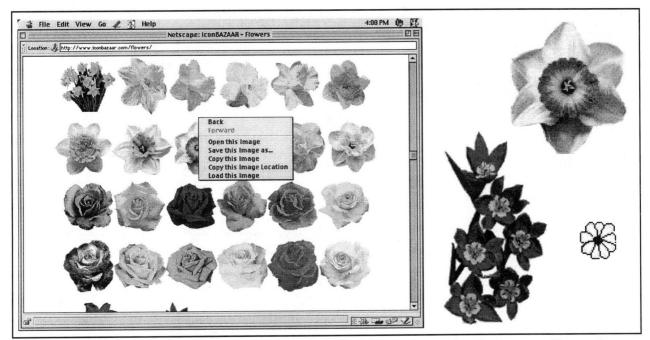

Figure 10-15. Clip art site and flower clip art from the Internet (www.iconbazaar.com/flowers).

To create a list:

Enter the items on separate lines.
Select the items by dragging over each line.
Click on the bullet or numbered button from the tool bar.

Notice that dots appear at the beginning of each line on a bullet list. A # appears at the beginning of each line on a numbered list. The # will be replaced by a number when the page is previewed.

Numbered lists can use Arabic numbers, Roman numerals, or letters. There are four additional ways to format information including term, definition, directory, and menu. Use the indent and outdent tools for further formatting. You can also nest the lists to provide subdirectory type listings.

Adding Links

The web is a hypertext environment. Users link information and ideas through the use of hot points. You can click on words and pictures to make connections

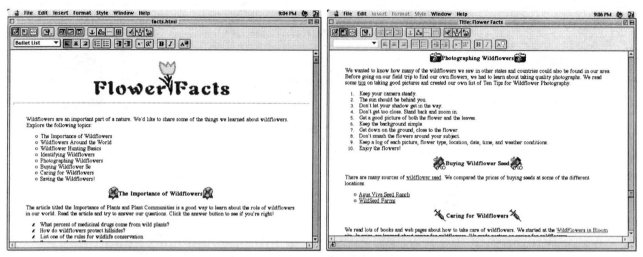

Figure 10-16. Bullet and number lists.

Links

Same Page
Same Site,
 Different Page
Different Site

between pages and information resources. The ability to add links is one of the greatest aspects of the Internet. There are three ways you may wish to use the linking capability of Claris Home Page.

First, you can move between pieces of information in the same document. For example, at the beginning of a long page you may develop a table of contents that allows a user to skip to a particular part of the page. The Flower Facts page will use this type of linking.

A second option is linking within your own site. For example, my project contains four pages that will be linked together. In this case, the system will be locating another file on the same web server.

The final option is linking to a remote site. You can link to web sites around the world. All you need is the web address or URL (Universal Resources Locator).

Linking within a Page

Let's create a link within a page. This is called linking to an anchor. For this activity, we'll use my Flower Facts page. You can create a link to an anchor so your users can jump to a specific spot on your page. Links can jump to anchors on the same page as the link itself or to anchors on other pages. You simply create an anchor at the location in your Web page where you want your users to jump to and then create a link to it.

Chapter 10: Creating Web Pages   **237**

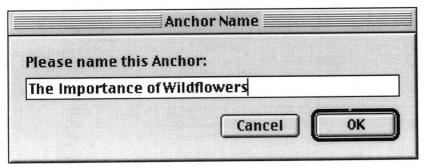

Figure 10-17. Anchor dialog box.

To create anchors:

Select the anchor text.
  Choose the location where the page will jump to. In my case, I will create an anchor for each major topic in my web page.

Pull down the Insert menu, select Anchor...
  The words you selected will appear in the box as shown in Figure 10-17.

Click OK.
  An anchor icon will appear on your Web page.

To link to the anchors:

Select the text or image you want to make the link to the anchor.

Pull down the Insert menu, select Link to URL...
  You can also click the Link Editor button on the toolbar.
  The Link Editor box will appear. See Figure 10-18.

Type the anchor's name in the URL text box or choose it from the pop-up menu.
  The text becomes underlined and the color of the text or the image border changes to blue to indicate the link. See Figure 10-18.

Try it!

Anchors

In addition to jumping down a page, you may want to create anchors to return back to the top of a page.

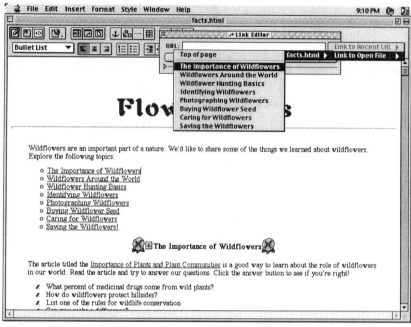

Figure 10-18. Link editor.

Linking to a Local Page

Beside linking to a particular part of a page, you can also link to another local page. Let's go back to our main web page, flowers. We need to link the flower.html file to the facts.html, fieldtrip.html, and projects.html document.

To link to other files:

Select the text or image that will be the link.
Pull down the Insert menu, select Link to file.
You can also select the Link to File button on the toolbar.
Select the name of the file, click Open.
The text becomes underlined and the color of the text or the image border changes to blue to indicate the link. See Figure 10-19.

Linking to a Remote Site

Probably the most exciting link is to a remote site. You can link to any web address on the Internet. It's easy to make mistakes when typing in web addresses. I recommend that you open Netscape and copy the URL di-

Chapter 10: Creating Web Pages

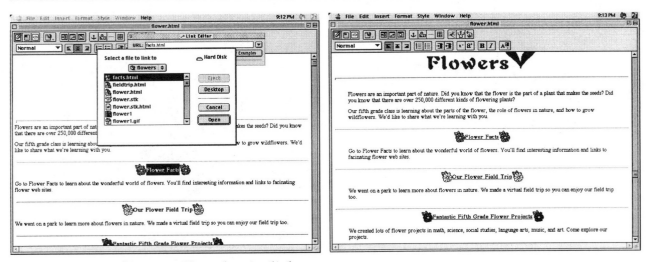

Figure 10-19. Linking to a file and active links.

rectly from the Location area. You can paste it right into Claris Home Page. Figure 10-20 shows some of the web sites that are links from the flower pages.

To link to other web sites:

Select the text or image that will be the link.
Pull down the Insert menu, select Link to URL.
You can also select the Link to URL button on the toolbar.
Enter the web address at URL:
The text becomes underlined and the color of the text or the image border changes to blue to indicate the link. See Figure 10-21.

Linking to Email Addresses

You've probably seen websites where the user can contact the webmaster through email. It's a good idea to provide this service at the bottom of your home page. In my case, this will be the bottom of the flower.html document. This is also the area where you may wish to place your snail mail address and page update information. This information is often placed in italic. The email link is easy to make.

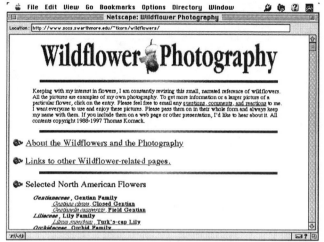

http://www.sccs.swarthmore.edu/~tkorn/wildflowers

http://www-wane.scri.fsu.edu/~mikems

http://www.duc.auburn.edu/~deancar/wfnotes.htm

http://www.duc.auburn.edu/~deancar/show1/index.htm

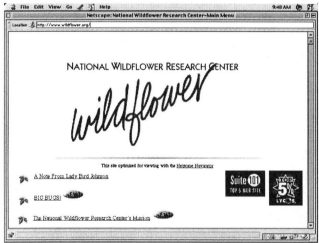

http://www.wildflower.org

Figure 10-20. Wildflower web sites.

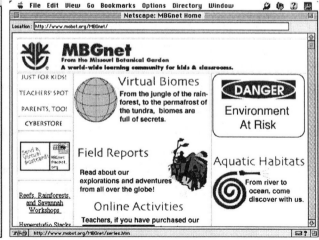

http://www.mobot.org/MBGnet

Chapter 10: Creating Web Pages

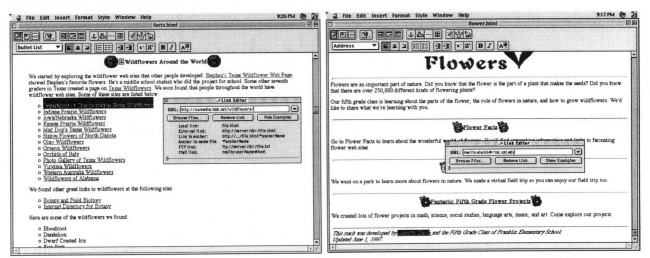

Figure 10-21. Linking to a URL.

Figure 10-22. Linking to an email address.

To link to email addresses:

**Select the text or image that will be the link.
Pull down the Insert menu, select Link to URL.
Enter the word mailto: and the email address.**
> The text becomes underlined and the color of the text or the image border changes to blue to indicate the link. See Figure 10-22.

Linking to FTP sites

If you become interested in adding sounds, animation, and video to your project, you may want to provide users with the plug ins they will need. You can do this by providing a link to an ftp site where users can download these resources. This link works the same way as the URL and email link except that the command begins with ftp:// instead of http:// or mailto:.

Creating Image Maps

You can link to and from images just like you do text. Simply drag over the image and make your selection. However there are times that you my just want to select part of a picture. In this case, you'll need to create an image map.

You can create client-side image maps and server-side image maps. Creating a server-side image map requires skills in HTML and web server programming.

Making a client-side image map is much easier. The HTML code resides within the Web page so you don't need to know anything about programming.

To create an image map, you need to assign hotspots to the picture. Hotspots are areas on an image map that viewers can click to link to different locations.

Before creating an image map, consider if it is really necessary. Client-side image maps only work in newer web browsers. If you create a client-side image map, I recommend that you also include a text option. In many cases, it's easier to simply create separate images. However in my case, I'd like students to be able to click on the parts of a flower. An image map would work good for this task. Let's start with something simple like clicking on three different flowers (see Figure 10-23).

Image Maps

client-side
server-side

To create a client-side image map:

Insert the image.
Select the image.
Pull down the Window menu, select Open Object Editor.
  The Object Editor will appear.
Click Behavior, Image Map and Edit.
  The image file opens in the Client-Side Image Map Editor.
Select the Rectangular Link or the Circular Link tool in the toolbar.
Draw a rectangle or circle over the area of the image that you want to be a hotspot.
  The Link Editor appears.
Type the filename or URL of the link in the URL text box.
  The name will appear over the image.
Add other links as needed.
  You can send the links forward or back as needed.

Chapter 10: Creating Web Pages

243

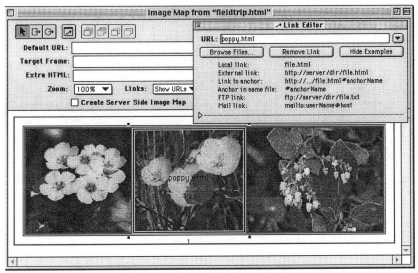

Figure 10-23. Creating a client-side image map.

Creating Tables

Sometimes you want an efficient way to organize information on a web page. Tables are an excellent way to present information. A table is made up of a series of rows and columns. A single block of information is called a cell and can contain text, images, lists, form elements, and other tables. You can even import tables from spreadsheet programs

To create a table:

Place the cursor where you want your table to appear on the page.

Pull down the Insert menu, select Table.
The Table Object Editor and table with two rows and columns appears.

Use the editor to add and delete rows and columns.

Drag the lines between the rows and columns to resize them.
See Figure 10-24.

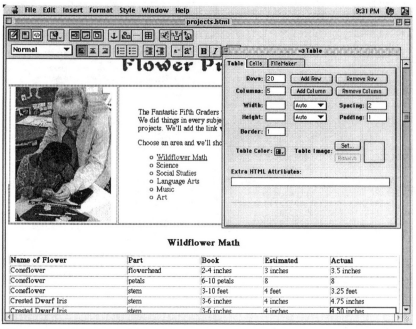

Figure 10-24. Creating tables.

You can change the background color of particular cells in a table.

To edit a table:

Double-click on the table border.
The Table Object Editor will appear.
Make changes.
If you set the border to 0, it will hide the lines of your table when you select preview. The picture and text at the top of Figure 10-24 are displayed in a table. The math information has a border of 1.

Use a table to create your core page overview. You can also use a table to create a column effect with text on one side and graphics on the other. Figure 10-25 shows a course page that uses tables for the course overview and calendar.

Adding QuickTime Movies

You can add QuickTime movies and other plug in files such as HyperStudio stacks. When you insert movies into your page, consider your audience. QuickTime movies require a special plug-in added to your

Chapter 10: Creating Web Pages   245

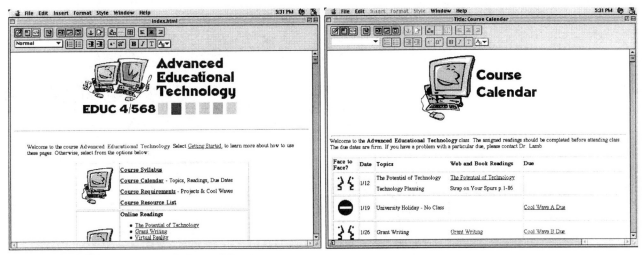

Figure 10-25. Pages containing tables.

browser to work. QuickTime, Video for Windows and MPEG are the three most common video formats on the Internet. QuickTime movies were originally developed for Macintosh, but because they are small in size, they are now common for all formats. QuickTime videos usually have a .mov or .qt extension. Microsoft's Video for Windows is less popular and contains the .avi extension. MPEG are small files using the .mpg or .mpeg extension. You can only add "flattened", cross-platform, QuickTime movies to your Web page. Programs like **Adobe Premiere** can save documents in this format. QuickTime movies can only be previewed in a browser.

Go to the CNN Video Vault (http://www.cnn.com/video_vault) and download a video. Place the video in your project folder.

To add a QuickTime movie:

Pull down the Edit menu, select QuickTime movie.
Select the QuickTime movie file.
Click Open.
> The QuickTime movie appears showing only the first frame. See Figure 10-26.

Double-click the QuickTime movie to open the QuickTime Movie Object Editor.

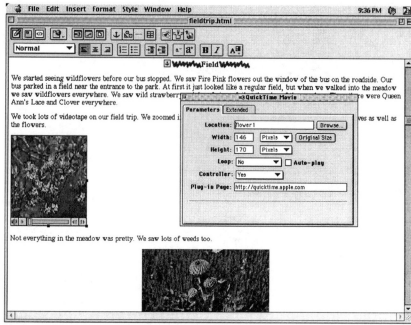

Figure 10-26. QuickTime movie.

Adding GIF Animation

The easiest way to add movement to your web page is the use of animated GIF files. You can download the tools to create your own files or download animated GIFs that have been created by others. GIF Builder (http://iawww.epfl.ch/Staff/Yves.Piguet/clip2gif-home/GifBuilder. htmliawww.epfl.ch/Staff/Yves.Piguet/clip2gif-home/GifBuilder.html) is a popular shareware package for creating GIF animation. GIF89a lets you compile multiple images within a single GIF file. This set of images can be used like frames in an animation sequence. Although you insert what appears to be a single GIF file into your web page, it will display multiple images in sequence like using a flip-book. The GIF file is downloaded once and played from the computer's cache. You can download several per page without one interfering with the others. Some sources of GIF Animation are found in List 10-3.

GIF Animation Station (http://www.dragonfire.net/~animated/moving/index.html) contains lots of small, fun animations. Some animation is just for fun. Tigger is a fun bouncy guy that might be

Chapter 10: Creating Web Pages

Video Sites

Yahoo Videos	http://www.yahoo.com/Computers_and_Internet/Multimedia/Video/Collections/
CNN Video Vaults	http://www.cnn.com/video_vault/
Video Links	http://members.aol.com/videolinks/index.html
Jesse's Movies	http://www.uslink.net/~edgerton/index.html
Video Oasis	http://www.geocities.com/SunsetStrip/1737/
AVI Movie Files	http://www.dragonfire.net/~animated/avis.htm

Gif Animation Sites

GIF Animation Station	http://www.dragonfire.net/~animated/moving/index.html
1st Internet Gallery	http://members.aol.com/royalef1/galframe.htm
Science examples	http://www2.ucsc.edu/people/straycat/cpa.html
Development Tools	http://www.killersites.com/5-tools
Creating Animation	http://members.aol.com/royalef/gifanim.htm

Applets

JAVA Applets	http://www.yahoo.com/Computers_and_Internet/Programming_Languages/Java/Applets/
Java Boutique	http://javaboutique.internet.com/
Mac Applets	http://www.mbmdesigns.com/macjava/
Gamelan	http://www.gamelan.com/
Cafe Del Sol	http://www.xm.com/cafe/applets.html
Chris Cob	http://www.ccobb.org/javalinks.html
Java Development	http://www.webdeveloper.com/categories/java/

Sounds

Yahoo Sounds	http://www.yahoo.com/Computers_and_Internet/Multimedia/Sound/
Sounds	http://sunsite.sut.ac.jp/multimed/sounds/
Historical sounds	http://www.webcorp.com/sounds/index.htm
Classic Waves	http://www.pnc.com.au/~bridgfam/wavepage.htm

List 10-3. *Videos, Gif Animation, Applets, and Sounds sites.*

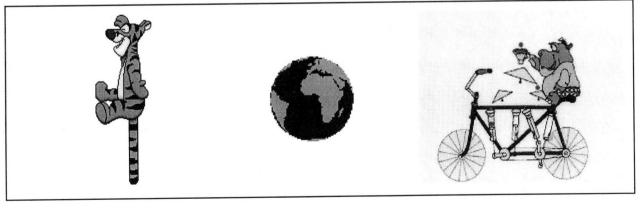

Figure 10-27. *Sample Animations.*

used for student motivation (see Figure 10-27). You could match the animation to a classroom topic or theme. For example, the earth could go with a geography project. **First Internet Gallery** (http://members.aol.com/royalef1/galframe.htm) contains animation by category. Some of the projects at this site ask that you contact the developer for permission to use their animation. Figure 10-27 shows how you could use animation in an instructional setting. It shows a hippo on a bicycle which moves by 4-cylinder engine.

To add a GIF animation:

Open your web browser.
Locate an animation you wish to use.
Click and hold image, select Save Image As.
Save the image, don't use copy or you'll only get a still image.
Save the image in your folder.
Open Claris Home Page.
Click where you want to place the animation.
Pull down Insert menu, select Image.
Select the image.
The still image will appear in the browser. You will need to view the page in the browser to see the animation.
View the page in the Browser.

Adding Applets

Another option for movement is JAVA programming, but this requires coding that can be difficult. If you want to give it a try, learn JavaScript. An alternative is to use the Applets that other people have prepared. An applet is a small computer program that can be inserted into Claris Home Page. Applets are used as counters, timers, and animations. Explore the Applets in List 10-3.

Don't try to modify the animation or make it transparent. This will freeze the image so it won't animate.

Chapter 10: Creating Web Pages

To add an applet:

Open your web browser.
Locate an applet you wish to use.
>You need to download all the .class files and any image or sound files.
>Follow the directions provided for downloading the applet.

Save the files in your folder.
Open Claris Home Page.
Pull down Insert menu, select Applet.
Enter the name of the applet next to the word Code:
>For example, you might enter the word AudioItem.class.
>Sometimes you need to specify parameters. This information goes next to Content: For example,
><param name=snd value="scooby.au">

View the page in the Browser.
>The applet should work in the browser.

Adding Other PlugIns

Plugs Ins have become popular extras in our browsers. Plugins are needed to run newer multimedia elements such as QuickTime VR movies, Real Audio and Video, or Macromedia Shockwaves. The end user must download these resource. They can sometimes be unstable, so think twice before requiring plugins for your project. If you do incorporate plugins, make certain you provide a link to a location where the plugin can be downloaded.

To add a plug-in file:

Pull down the Insert menu, select PlugIn.
>The warning message will direct you to select the data file, not the plugin itself.

Click OK.
Select the plugin data file.
Click Open.

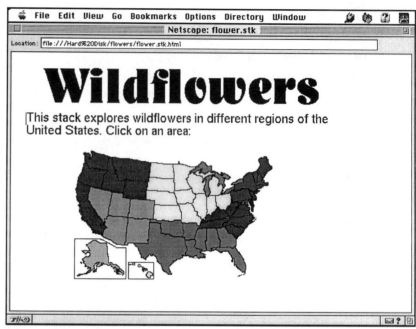

Figure 10-28. HyperStudio stack running in Netscape.

A rectangular box representing the plugin file appears on the page.

Double-click the box to open the Plugin Object Editor.

To play HyperStudio stacks, you can use the PlugIn option, or link to the HTML file that HyperStudio generates using Export Web Page. See Figure 10-28.

Adding Sound

There are a couple ways to add sounds to your document. You can use an applet or you can write your own HTML code. Create or locate a sound (see List 10-3).

Sometimes Claris Home Page has not provided the tools you need to add a particular feature to the page. For example, let's say you find a .au or .midi sound file you'd like to use. You can add it right into the code already created by Claris Home Page for your document. You can make either text or images "hot links" to the sounds.

Chapter 10: Creating Web Pages

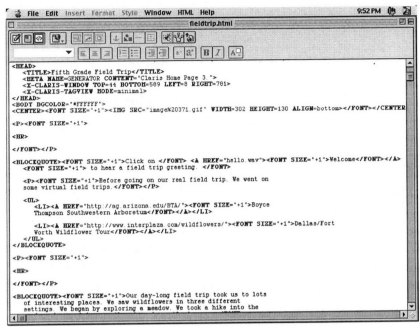

Figure 10-29. HTML code.

To add HTML code to play a sound:

Pull down the Window menu, select Edit HTML Source.
Or, click the Edit HTML Source button.
The HTML code will appear (see Figure 10-29).
Click where you wish to enter code.
Enter your code.
   <A HREF="hello.wav">welcome</A>

This code will tell the computer to play the file hello.wav file when the highlighted word "welcome" is clicked. Notice that this is the same code that is used to call a file or URL.

To add HTML code to play a sound at the beginning of your document:

Pull down the Window menu, select Edit HTML Source.
Click where you wish to enter code
Enter your code.

```
<BGSOUND SRC="x-files.mid" LOOP=1>
<EMBED SRC="x-files.mid" HIDDEN=TRUE
AUTOSTART=TRUE VOLUME=100 LOOP=1>
```

This code directs the computer to begin playing the file xfiles.mid when the page opens.

Creating Forms

You can use forms to conduct surveys, give quizzes, and play games. It's easy to make the forms. The problem comes in identifying the right CGI resources needed on your web server to collect and store the information. You can find links to CGI scripts and resources on the Claris Home Page technical support page (http://www.claris.com/support/ products/ clarispage). You can also write a JavaScript.

You can create only one form per Web page in Claris Home Page. Your form can contain text, images, tables, and other items, in addition to the form itself. Form elements include text areas, text fields, pop-up menus, buttons or checkboxes that the viewer can select, and a submit button that the viewer clicks to send their input to the server. You can also include a button for resetting the user's input. Passwords and other special features are also available.

JavaScripts are a great way to manipulate the contents of a form. For example, you can write a JavaScript that will send you the results of a student quiz.

Printing Web Pages

You can print the pages you create in Claris Home Page. You can print a page from the Edit Page mode, Preview Page mode, or Edit HTML Source mode. The page will print as it appears on the screen in that mode.

To print your Web page:

Pull down the File menu, select Print.
   The Print dialog box will appear.
Click Print.
   The entire contents of your Web page file will be printed.

Chapter 10: Creating Web Pages

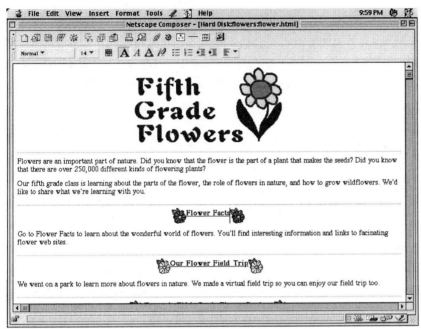

Figure 10-30. Netscape Composer.

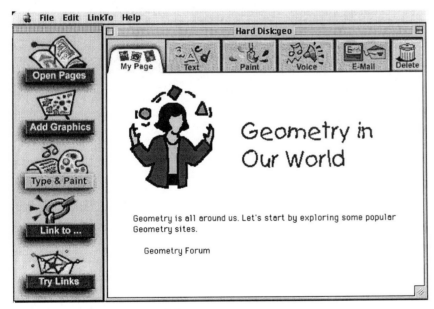

Figure 10-31. Web Workshop.

Summary

Although we used Claris Home Page in our discussion, there are dozens of web development tools available. Figure 10-30 shows the flower page in **Netscape Composer**. Notice that the tools area is very similar to Claris Home Page.

Some web development tools have been designed especially for children. Although you can use Claris Home Page with all ages, you may wish to try some of these specialized packages. Figure 10-31 shows a web development tool designed for kids called **Web Workshop**.

Don't get bogged down with the web development tools. Instead select an easy-to-use tool and learn the basics. For now, focus on the design and contents of your web pages. You can always learn the advanced features or a little HTML coding if you need to do something special at some point in the future.

Chapter 11: Designing & Developing School Web Sites

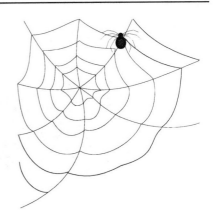

How often should our school site be updated?
Who should be in charge of our school site?
What should we put in our school site?

Each school has unique projects and activities to share. Make your school stand out. Your school site should reflect the pride of your school and community. Student involvement is the key to a learner-centered school. Be sure to get student input from the beginning. You may even be able to get students to run the entire site!

In this chapter, you'll learn to design a school web site. The design of an effective school web site depends on many factors. The **Bright Sites** (http://scrtec.org/bright_sites/characteristics/) page does an excellent job highlighting the features of effective school web projects. Carefully examine each of the links. Do you agree with their vision of effective design? Why or why not?

There are a number of individuals and organizations that evaluate school and teacher pages. Explore **Education World's Cool School** (http://www.education-world.com/cool_school/) and the **Classy Sites** (http://schmidel.com/7-12-Net/teachers.htm) pages. What criteria do they use to evaluate schools?

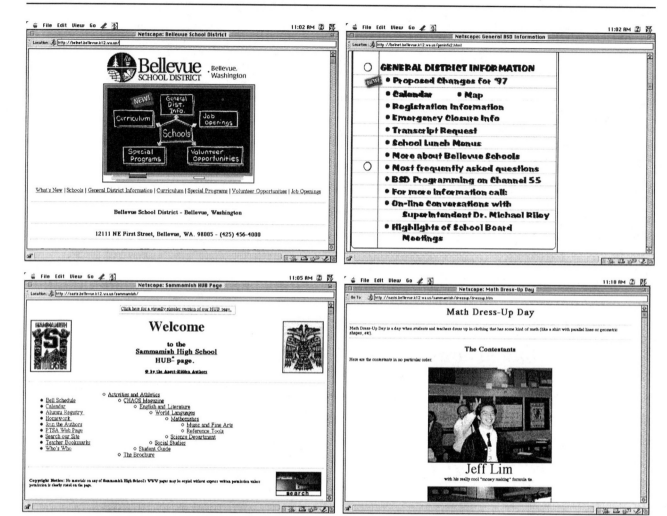

http://belnet.bellevue.k12.wa.us/
Figure 11-1. Bellevue Schools.

School Web Page Guidelines

There are many ways to design a school web page. As you go through the following guidelines examine a school such a **Bellevue Schools** (http://belnet.bellevue.k12.wa.us/) shown in Figure 11-1. Do they have an effective school web site? Why or why not?

Mission. Your site needs a purpose. Is the mission of the site clearly stated and apparent within the site? Does it relate to the mission of the school?

Chapter 11: Designing & Developing School Web Sites

Audience. Your site may reach many audiences including students, parents, teachers, administrators, community members and other interested Internet surfers. You'll need a core page that is general enough to be of interest to all audiences. Then, develop individual pages with a single audience in mind. If it's designed for kids, think about their interests and ability levels. If you have supplemental materials for parents or teachers, put those on separate pages.

Value. Your web site can play an indispensable role with your students, teachers, administration, and/or community. Is your site truly useful? Does it serve a function not available through other means? What makes your web page special? Why will people want to visit?

Appeal. The visual appeal of a page is a critical factor in web page design. Does the page look interesting? Is it a place you would like to return to another time? Does your site have a theme or attractive layout?

Ease of Use. People need to be able to get to your site for it to be practical. Is it easy to access your pages. Do they load quickly? Can users find their way around your page once they get there?

Creativity. Your school site should be unique and different than other pages on similar topics. Why reinvent the wheel? Why is your page different? What makes it original?

Organization. Your site must be well-organized to be used effectively. Can you move around easily? Is information chunked and presented in a logical order? The student project called **Geotopia** (http://www.best.com/~swanson/geo_nh/nhgeotopia.html) is well-organized (see Figure 11-2a). A table of contents provides an overview and links to the project page. In the **Interactive Mathematics** project (http://

School Guidelines
 Mission
 Audience
 Value
 Appeal
 Ease of Use
 Creativity
 Currency
 Response Time
 Technology
 Core Graphics

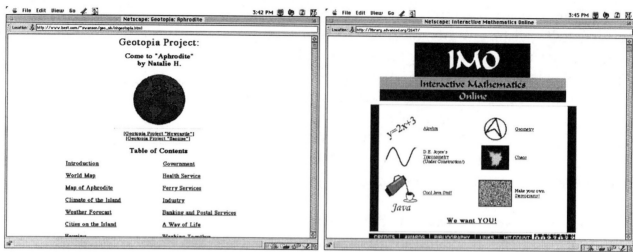

http://www.best.com/~swanson/geo_nh/nhgeotopia.html

http://library.advanced.org/2647

Figure 11-2. Organization.

library.advanced.org/2647/) notice how graphics and a table are used as part of the organizational structure (see Figure 11-2b). The **Dinosaur egg** (http://www.nationalgeographic.com/features/96/dinoeggs/intro.html) article provides some general categories and a suggested order rather than providing a linear article.

Currency. If you want repeat visitors, your site must be updated frequently. Be sure to include the date of revisions and icons to indicate new information. In addition, you may want to create an area for providing users with information about when the page was last updated and how it was changed. Some people provide a **"What's New"** area like Cameron School (http://cses.scbe.on.ca/index.htm) shown in Figure 11-3.

Response Time. Is the site responsive to the user's needs? You should be able to find useful information in 30 seconds.

Technology. Technology can play an important role in your site. A web page is more than text on a screen. Does your site make good use of the technology? Does it provide a graphic or picture when a visual is

School Web Site Design

Explore School Web Sites. Look for some of the following elements.

Mission

Audience

Value

Appeal

Ease of Use

Creativity

Currency

Response Time

Technology

Core Graphics

Chart 11-1. School Web Site Design.

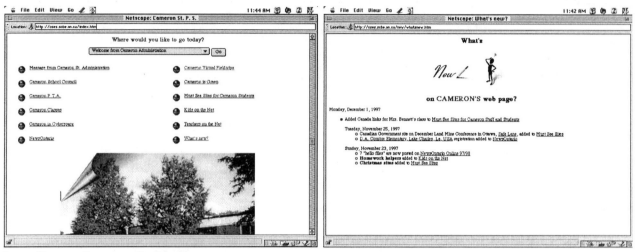

http://cses.scbe.on.ca/index.htm
Figure 11-3. What's new?

needed? Is audio used to stimulate interest? Is movement used to draw attention to a particular aspect of the screen. Do colors attract and bring emotion to the page? Is technology used effectively? Keep in mind that not everyone has the newest, fastest hardware and software. Avoid frames, JAVA scripts, special plug-ins and other techie toys that slow down or restrict use. **Loogootee West** (http://www.siec.k12.in.us/~west/west.htm) is a great example of a school that has suc-

Figure 11-4. Loogootee Elementary West.

Chapter 11: Designing & Developing School Web Sites 261

cessfully integrated some of these features (see Figure 11-4).

Core Page Graphics. The graphics on the core page particularly should reflect the focus of the site. Although a school building picture may be included, is that really the most important picture that should be presented at a learner centered school? Maybe you could include a school logo, hold a contest and include student art, or use a mosaic of students. **Hollywood Beach** (http://www.huensd.k12.ca.us/beach/) and **Challenger Elementary School** (http://scnc.hps.k12.mi.us/~chllngr/) use their school logo (see Figure 11-5).

School Site Elements
   Parents
   Community
   Instructional
   Achievements
   Classes
   Students

School Web Site Elements

Your school web site is more than endless pages of information. It should be organized into logical selections. For example, if your school has strong ties to parents and the community, develop a section for that particular audience.

Parent and Community Involvement. Your school should be connected with the community. Is there information that would be of interest to parents and members of the community? Even if a person didn't

http://www.huensd.k12.ca.us/beach/   http://scnc.hps.k12.mi.us/~chllngr

Figure 11-5. Hollywood Beach School and Challenger Elementary School.

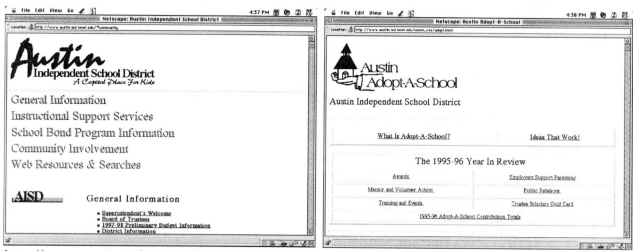

http://www.austin.isd.tenet.edu/
Figure 11-6. Austin Schools.

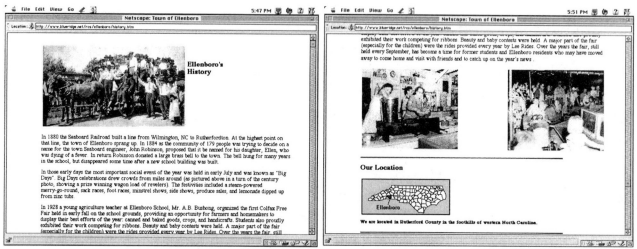

http://www.blueridge.net/rcs/ellenboro/history.htm
Figure 11-7. Ellenboro School Community.

have children in school, is there something that might draw their interest? Are there projects that involve the community such as a park cleanup, public library book drive, or local sporting event online? **Austin Independent School District** (http://www.austin.isd.tenet.edu/) has an entire section of their site dedicated to community involvement (see Figure 11-6). Some school pages include information about the community, its history, and location such as the **Ellenboro School** (http://www.blueridge.net/rcs/ellenboro/history.htm) in Figure 11-7.

Chapter 11: Designing & Developing School Web Sites

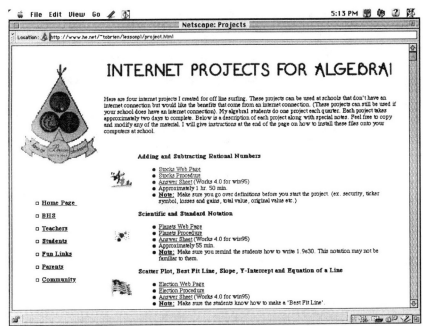

http://www.he.net/~tobrien/lessonpl/project.html
Figure 11-8. Project page.

Instructional Applications. Is there an instructional or educational use for your school web page? Does it go beyond lunch menus and sports scores to provide useful resources and activities for students? **Bremen High School** (http://www.he.net/~tobrien/lessonpl/project.html) contains an Internet Projects for Algebra page that provides on and off computer activities for students (see Figure 11-8).

School Achievements. Use your school web page to focus on the achievements of your students, accomplishments of your teachers, participation of your parents, special programs, and other things that are unique to your school. Explore schools that make use of the web for this type of self-promotion. **Bear Creek Elementary School** (http://bvsd.k12.co.us/schools/bcreek/) uses their web page to explain how their school is special. Learn about why they are a focus school.

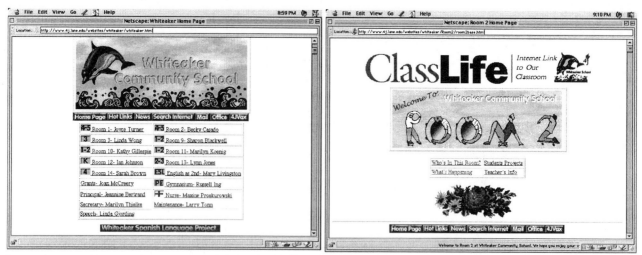

http://www.4j.lane.edu/websites/whiteaker/whiteaker.htm
Figure 11-9. Whiteaker School.

Class and Student Pages. Class pages are a significant part of many school sites. Figure 11-9 shows a menu and class page from Whiteaker elementary school. Although they're just getting started, they have a nice template for their pages established.

If class and student information is provided in the site, be sure you get permission from parents before including personal information and names of individual children. There are many reasons parents may be reluctant to have student names and pictures on the Internet. For example, some child custody documents prohibit posting student pictures. It's possible to use **PhotoShop** or other imaging software to "fuzzy" a child's picture when they are part of a group (see Figure 11-10d). If parents are concerned about use of names, children may choose to use a nickname on the web site.

When designing a class site, highlight those things that make your classroom unique (see Figure 11-10). For example, Mrs. Manion and Mrs. Walz team teach first grade and have include information about classroom management, activities, newsletter, and even child's writings and artwork about how they like their class organization.

Chapter 11: Designing & Developing School Web Sites 265

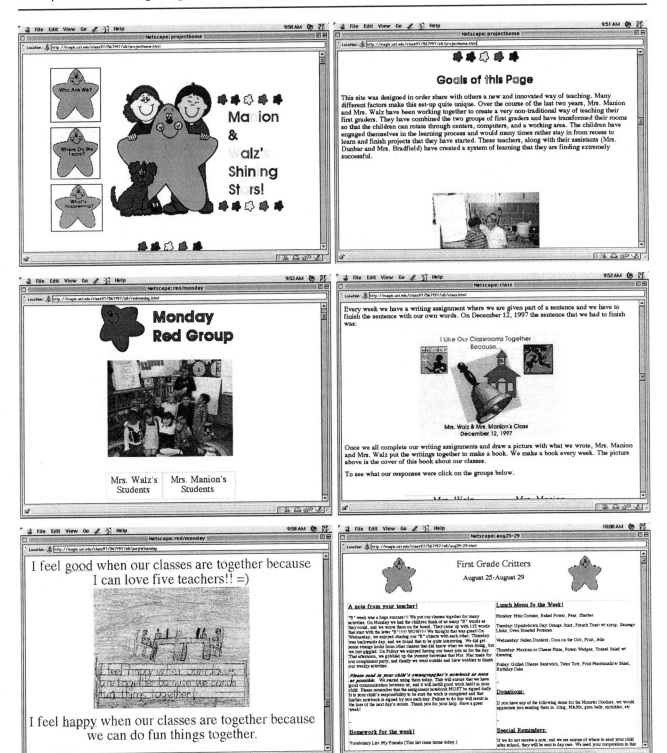

http://magic.usi.edu/class97/567f97/project.html
Figure 11-10. Walz and Manion Class.

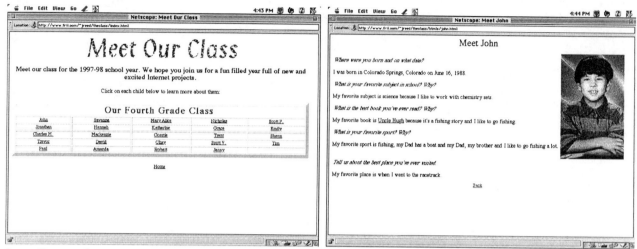

http://www.frii.com/~jreed/theclass/index.html
Figure 11-11. Meet Our Class.

Explore the **Class Page** (http://www.frii.com/~jreed/theclass/index.html) from Mr. Reed's class (see Figure 11-11). Do you like the pictures and short interview with each child? Why or why not? Could students have been more involved with the development of the page? Would this take more time?

Some schools are supporting student home pages. Many of these pages are developed in computer classes (http://home.att.net/~rushton/dria.htm) such as the one in Figure 11-12.

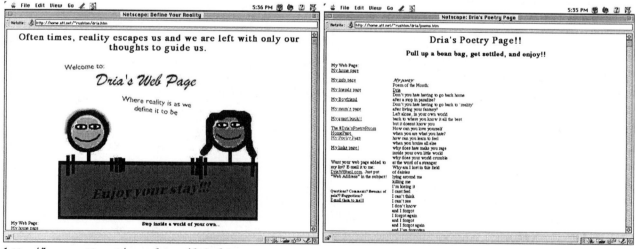

http://home.att.net/~rushton/dria.htm
Figure 11-12. Student page.

Chapter 11: Designing & Developing School Web Sites 267

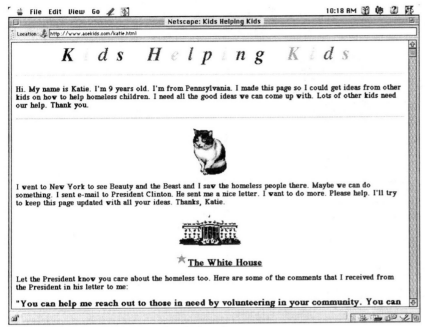

http://www.acekids.com/katie.html
Figure 11-13. Student home page.

Some of the most exciting student pages come from students who are taking action on issues. For example, Katie saw homeless people first-hand on a trip into the city to see Beauty and the Beast. She became concerned and developed a web page (http://www.acekids.com/katie.html). Katie has posted part of a letter from the President as well as letters from other people who are concerned about homelessness issues. Use pages like this to draw the interest of other students (see Figure 11-13).

Idea Exploration: School Analysis
Explore **Blackburn High School's** website (http://www.ozemail.com.au/~bhs56/main.htm) (see Figure 11-14). Is this an effective school site? Why or why not? Does this site have the elements discussed? Are there additional aspects and you like or dislike about the site?

Idea Exploration

Figure 11-14. Blackburn High School.

Chapter 12: Implementing and Evaluating Web Projects

How do I coordinate one computer and twenty-two students?
What's the best way to organize the project?
How should I group students and assign roles?

In this chapter, you'll explore classroom management considerations and evaluate web projects. You'll also evaluate your project and determine its effectiveness, efficiency, and appeal. Try out your project and see how it works. Revise your project as you go.

Getting Organized

Planning is a critical part of project implementation. Know your students and think ahead. If you're planning a large-scale Internet project, try elements with your class first to determine how much time the project will take. Also consider implementing a trial project with two or three schools rather than twenty or thirty schools your first time.

Use a wall or bulletin board in your classroom as "web headquarters." Include timelines, a layout of the site, a world map of participants, screen dumps from sites used, background information, and a responsibility chart. You may also want to post information in the lunchroom where all the students in the school can see

World Quilt: One Peace at a Time

Web Layout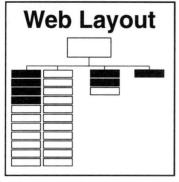

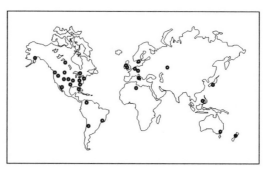

Job Board

Timeline

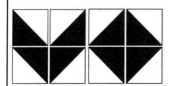 **Web Headquarters**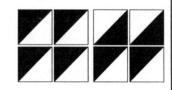

Topic:	World Peace
Overview:	Students at each site create digital peace quilt pieces representing what their country can contribute to the world.
Subjects:	Art, Social Studies, Math, Language Arts
Outcomes:	Apply design skills to the development of a digital quilt piece.
	Synthesis information about a country.
	Identify contributions of countries around the world.
	Create geometric patterns.
	Share concerns about world peace.
Ages:	10-14
Timeline:	10 weeks
Connections:	Countries around the world
Procedure:	Post a Call for Connections.
	Pinpoint participants on the map.
	Research additional countries not participating.
	Discuss unique aspects of each country.
	Develop digital quilt squares.
	Publish each digital quilt square as a thumbnail graphic.
	Develop a web page for each thumbnail, plus a core page.
	Optional: Contests for most unique, colorful, guess the country.

Chapter 12: Implementing and Evaluating Web Projects   271

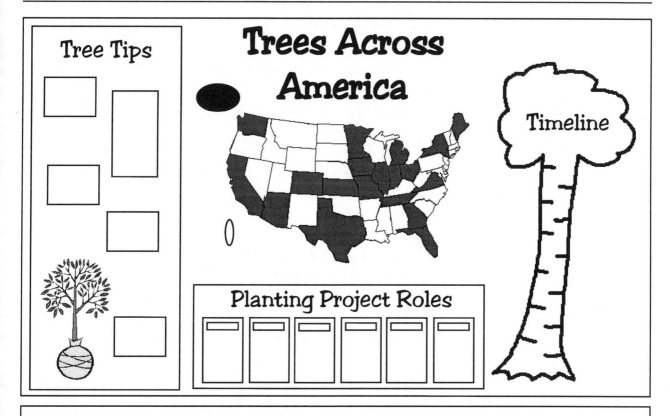

Topic:	Trees Across America
Overview:	Students at each site select a popular tree from their region, plant the tree, and report to the group.
Subjects:	Community Service, Science, Social Studies, Language Arts
Outcomes:	Identify trees of the region.
	Compare and contrast trees from different areas of the US.
	Plant a tree.
	Apply conservation practices.
	Discuss concerns regarding deforestation.
	Write persuasive communications.
Ages:	8-12
Timeline:	8 weeks (Spring time)
Connections:	States of the United States
Procedure:	Research and discuss history and issues in deforestation.
	Create web-based tree conservation public service pages.
	Post a Call for Connections. Pinpoint participants on the map.
	In small groups, identify trees of the region, report on each tree.
	Select and plant a tree from your state.
	Research and discuss conservation practices.
	Compare and contrast trees from different areas of the US.
	Optional: Photos of trees and chart containing tree info on web

your progress. This will get the entire school behind your project. Students love to see a map expand with participants from around the world or see a thermometer fill as project spaces are filled.

Chart 12-1 and Chart 12-2 show project bulletin boards and project plans.

Getting Organized

Timelines
Site Layout
Map
Screen Dumps
Background Information
Responsibility Chart

Timelines. Timelines, flowcharts, calendars, and due date postings are all ways to help you and your students keep track of the project. You'll be surprised how fast the time will go. Remember when a project falls behind it impacts all the schools involved. Keep on top of the project and develop contingency plans for slow downs and bottlenecks. For example, it may take twice as long as you anticipated for students to respond each day to email. You may need to use an additional email connection or ask a small group to volunteer after school to catch up. You'll have no trouble recruiting students. Try to incorporate your theme into your bulletin board. For example, a high school government class used pictures of race horses in their "race of the bills" project.

Your timeline should include milestones for the project, key due dates, and other important times that your class can anticipate. Involve students in the timeline by filling in dates or counting down days. Chart 12-1 contains a horizonal timeline while Chart 12-2 contains a vertical timeline in the form of a tree.

If you're the project leader, it's your responsibility to keep your participants on track. You may need a separate director's timeline. For instance, you need to send out confirmations before the project starts. You also need to send out reminders immediately before due dates.

In addition to the timelines, you might also want charts that show numbers of email messages, numbers of participating students or schools, and other interesting data. This is a great math activity for students.

Chapter 12: Implementing and Evaluating Web Projects

273

Site Layout. As students begin to develop web pages for the site. It's helpful for them to visualize the entire web project. There's probably a core page, credits page, participants page, FAQs page, and information pages.

Ask a small group to create a series of cards for each page that can be placed on the bulletin board. Or, direct the group to create a diagram of the site on paper and post it on the bulletin board. This visual representation will help students track their progress. For example, as each page is created or completed a sticker or checkmark could be added to the chart. Chart 12-1 contains an area called Web Layout for this purpose.

Map. Many web projects involve students from around the state or province, country, or world. It's fun to keep track of participants on a map. The World Quilt project uses a world map, while the Tree project uses a map of the United States. Some classes use pins or stickers to mark locations, while others color in the map or add an object such as a small leaf to the map.

Be sure all the students get an opportunity to interact with the map. Also consider placing a map in the hall or lunch room where everyone can see. Many projects also put a map on their website.

Highlight Your Map

Check off areas
Post pins or flags
Fill with color
Post stickers
Add objects
Add map pieces

Screen Dumps. Sometimes it's hard for students and parents to "see" the project as it progresses on the Internet. Consider posting screen dumps or create a print version of the web site in a notebook for people to see when they don't have access to the computer. You many even print out email communication and create a project diary or journal.

With a color printer, you can print beautiful representations of your project. For example, if you're working on an animals project, you might print out pictures of animals from a variety of sites and post them on your bulletin board. You could also post new web pages that have just been completed for your students to evaluate or just admire.

Background Information. Some projects require lots of in-class preparation and background information. For example, before your students jump into an online geometry problem solving project, they need a firm grasp of the math concepts. Use the bulletin board to post sample problems or review formulas or examples. In the Tree Project, students started by studying deforestation and conservation. An area of the bulletin board was dedicated to information related to these Tree Tips.

Responsibility Chart. Like any class project, you'll need to assign responsibilities. In a web project, there are many ongoing duties such as updating the map, checking email, posting information, researching topics, and writing articles. In some projects you may assign individual roles, while in others you may organize work groups with specific titles such as web weavers, email experts, tree tippers, and map makers. These roles could be for the duration of the project or they could rotate daily or weekly depending on the project. Charts 12-1 and 12-2 both contain responsibility charts.

Idea Exploration

Idea Exploration: Web Headquarters
Select a web project and brainstorm a list of things that might go on a bulletin board. Make a sketch of the bulletin board.

Classroom Management Considerations
Explore the following considerations in managing classrooms that are using Internet-based resources.

Ability Levels. For some students, the Internet is just too abstract. They may have difficulty understanding the organization of information and the concept of hypermedia. Consider a variety of projects to meet individual needs in the classroom. Some might access

Project Organization

Create a project overview.

Topic:
Overview:
Subjects:
Outcomes:

Ages:
Timeline:

Connections:
Procedure:

How will your project be organized? Brainstorm ideas in each of the following areas and sketch possibilities for a bulletin board for your project.

Timelines
Site Layout
Map
Screen Dumps
Background Information
Responsibility Chart

Chart 12-3. Project Organization

sites that require a lower or higher reading level. Some websites may have fewer or more illustrations to maintain motivation. Consider the needs of both your lowest and highest students. Planning can help students of all ability levels better understand the project.

Speed. Develop a realistic timeline for yourself and your students. Your project will become frustrating rather than fun if you and your students are constantly pressured by deadlines. Build in a cushion for problems or slow students.

You'll find that the time students take to develop and work with projects varies tremendously. Keep this in mind as you design your project. Build in remedial activities for slow learners and challenge activities for fast learners. Don't expect every student to read everything. Make it clear to students what's most important. Also provide a schedule so students know how to budget their time.

Know your schedule. Don't start something right before a break or at the very beginning of the year when it's hectic.

Classroom Management Considerations

Ability Levels
Speed
Grouping Students
Internet Access
Email
Computer Schedule
File Management

Grouping Students. In most schools there's simply not enough Internet access to provide one computer for each student. There's a good chance students will need to work in small groups. As you form groups, look for the natural leader. Work with these leaders to make certain they understand the importance of involving all group members. Also consider assigning roles that will rotate during the project so all students get a chance to use the technology and also to read, write, think, and share.

In the **Learning: Next Generation** project (http://home.on.rogers.wave.ca/eliza/learn/toc.htm) students designed schools of the future. They worked in small groups as shown in Figure 12-1 and collaborated with schools in different countries.

Chapter 12: Implementing and Evaluating Web Projects   277

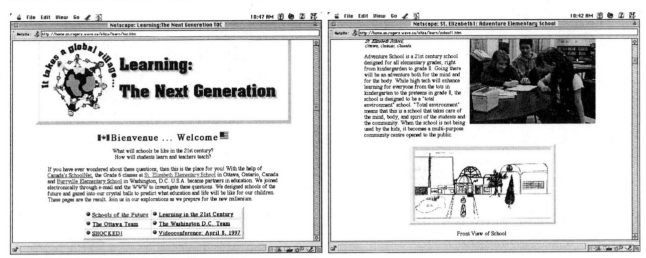

http://home.on.rogers.wave.ca/eliza/learn/toc.htm
Figure 12-1. Grouping students.

Internet Access. You'll find that the Internet can be really slow. This is particularly true during certain parts of the day. Sometimes you may lose your connection entirely or the site you need may be down. Look for the slow times and anticipate down times. Design off-computer activities that can be accomplished in conjunction with on-computer activities.

For example, let's say your students want to publish their projects at the **Great Kids** (http://www.greatkids.com/) network shown in Figure 12-2. Print out some good sample projects to show what other students have published. Also print out the publishing guidelines or criteria. You can publish on someone else's website even if you only have one web connection in your building!

Email. Email is often an important component of an Internet project. Before the project starts determine the email address you will be using. Don't use your personal email. Instead, get a class email address or an address for each small group. Decide what role students can take in project management. For example, students may be able to send out standard replies and post responses if they have a form letter or template to use.

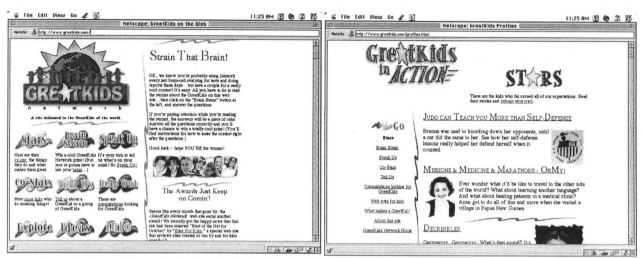

http://www.greatkids.com/
Figure 12-2. Great Kids in Action.

Use email to generate excitement in the project. Start with activities that will help students and classes get to know each other. You may even wish to exchange photos, audio greetings, and web sites.

At the end of the project, put a group of students in charge of thanking participants. You could also involve them in evaluating the project.

Computer Schedule. Be certain that students have adequate time to use the computer. Consider a rotation schedule that provides students at least 20 minutes at a time on the computer individually or in pairs. Be sure that you build in adequate time for groups to complete their daily work such as email or web page development. Some teachers use the morning for regularly scheduled activities and the afternoon for special projects. High school teachers often build a Monday/Wednesday or Tuesday/Thursday schedule for their students during project weeks and leave Friday for special topics.

File Management. Whether you have one computer in your classroom or a dozen, file management will be a major concern. Develop a project folder containing individual student folders and group work folders. If you have more than one computer you may be able to

Chapter 12: Implementing and Evaluating Web Projects 279

Classroom Management

Brainstorm classroom management concerns and strategies. What do you see as potential problems and solutions in each of the following areas?

Ability Levels

Speed

Grouping Students

Internet Access

Email

Computer Schedule

File Management

Chart 12-4. Classroom Management

share the folder over a network. Use a standard naming system to make management easier. Otherwise you'll end up with lots of files named "project" and "research."

Consider downloading web pages that you will be using regularly as information resources.

Idea Exploration

Idea Exploration: Voice of Experience
In **Tales from the Electronic Frontier** (http://www.wested.org/tales/) ten teachers share their experiences using Internet in the classroom. Start with **Why Tales?** (http://www.wested.org/tales/00whytell.html) to explore the purpose of the page. Read a tale and discuss the issues and questions submitted at the end of the tale. Discuss at least three things you discovered in the article. Describe examples of what you think might be helpful in implementing your own Internet-based project.

Formative Evaluation

Formative evaluation is the process of examining and revising a product before publishing. Always check your project on a variety of systems. Use different web browsers, a variety of computer systems, slow and

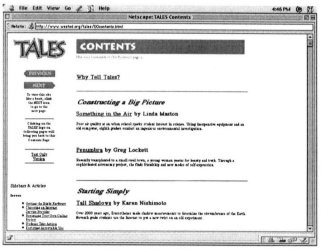
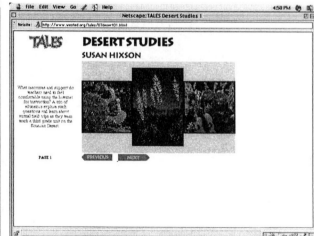

http://www.wested.org/tales/
Figure 12-3. Tales.

Chapter 12: Implementing and Evaluating Web Projects 281

fast Internet connections, small and large screens, and different computer platforms.

Before you post your project on the web, you'll want to do some extensive evaluation. Use the categories below in forming your own tool for conducting self-assessment.

- Layout
- Information Organization
- Technical Aspects: Speed, Complete Links
- Content Quality and Accuracy
- Typography
- Graphics
- Navigation
- Links within site
- Links outside site
- Contact information
- Interaction

It's a good idea to use multiple reviewers in this process. Consider a separate reviewer for each of the following areas.

Page layout. Ask someone to examine the overall look of your pages. They should look for consistency in the use of text, graphics, lines, and other elements. Is the page easy-to-read? What about the use of white space? Is the layout parallel between pages?

Rather than filling the screen with text, make use of white space. Indent text and include a space between paragraphs. Consider using horizontal lines between sections. If the page becomes more than three pages long, consider breaking it into pieces. Use the power of linking.

Organization & Sequence. Ask an average potential user to try the project. Is the content well-organized? Can the user sense a logic in the order and presentation of information? How long does the user take to make their way through the information? Is this important?

Web Page Evaluation Sites	
Blue Web'n	http://www.kn.pacbell.com/wired/bluewebn/rubric.html
CyberGuides	http://www.cyberbee.com/guides.html
Kathy Schrock	http://www.capecod.net/schrockguide/eval.htm
Primary Grades	http://www.siec.k12.in.us/~west/edu/rubric1.htm
Intermediate Grades	http://www.siec.k12.in.us/~west/edu/rubric2.htm
Secondary Grades	http://www.siec.k12.in.us/~west/edu/rubric3.htm

List 12-1. Web Page Evaluation Sites.

Evaluation Areas

Layout
Info Organization
Technical Aspects:
Speed, Complete Links
Content Quality and
Accuracy
Typography
Graphics
Navigation
Links within site
Links outside site
Contact information
Interaction

Content accuracy. An expert in the subject matter of the content should examine the page for accuracy. Is the information accurate? What about spelling, grammar, and writing style? Is the information appropriate for the audience?

Navigation links. Do the links work properly? Is the navigation easy to follow so users don't get lost in hyperspace?

High and low level. If students will be using the tool in a classroom setting, ask a low ability and high ability learner to try the program. Compare the length of time they spend with the program and the difficulties they encounter along the way.

Technical aspects. Ask a web developer to check the technical aspects of the program. Do graphics load in a reasonable time? Do sounds and movies work properly? Is the HTML code efficient?

Overall evaluation. Finally, ask someone to simply "look it over." What are their overall impressions? What do they view as the strengths and weaknesses of the pages? Did they find the site interesting or boring?

Use the information you collect to update your web pages. You may need to do a number of formative evaluations before you feel confident enough to place

Chapter 12: Implementing and Evaluating Web Projects 283

the project on the web for the world to see. You may wish to continue gathering feedback for revision even after posting the project. Consider adding a feedback link where users can email you with their suggestions.

Idea Exploration: Web Guidelines
Read **Cyberbee's** (http://www.cyberbee.com/master.html) guidelines for web masters (see Figure 12-4), **Maricopa Center for Learning and Instruction (MCLI)** (http://www.mcli.dist.maricopa.edu/) and the **Santa Cruz County Webmaster** (http://www.santacruz.k12.ca.us/~danielo/webmasters/wmResource.html) page. Also explore **TRC's Resources for Creating Your School Web Page** (http://www.trc.org/htmlpage.htm) materials. It examines policies and procedures for web page development. For other ideas about evaluating all types of information, skim the following sites: **Connections+** (http://www.mcrel.org/connect/plus/critical.html), **Critical Evaluation** (http://www.science.widener.edu/~withers/webeval.htm), and **Critical Thinking & Internet Resources** (http://www.mcrel.org/connect/plus/critical.html)
  Develop a policy for web page development.

Idea Exploration

Self, Student and Participant Reflection
Reflection is an important part of any project. Consider some of the following areas.

- How many students, teachers, and/or schools were involved with the project? How did you recruit these people? How could you expand the project next time? What would the implications of this expand?
- How were students involved in the project? Were students involved in all aspects of the project? How could you make the project more student-centered?

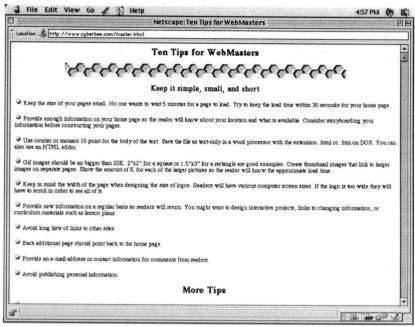

http://www.cyberbee.com/master.html
Figure 12-4. Cyberbee Evaluation Ideas.

What resources were most helpful in completion of your project? Were specific websites, listservs, or experts helpful? What will you look for next time to expand your project?
Was your project effective? What did students learn? How do you know? How did other classes benefit by participating? How would the project evolve to become even more effective in terms of student learning and collaboration?
What recommendations would you have for someone developing an Internet project?

In addition to evaluating the web pages, you'll also want to evaluate the project itself.

Get students involved with reflection. What were the strengths and weaknesses of the project? What would they do differently next time? What would they change? Try the following easy reflection tool:

The strengths of this project are...
The weaknesses of this project are...
Next time I'd...

Project Evaluation

Conduct formative evaluation on your project. Ask at least three people to examine each of the following areas and make recommendations.

Layout

Information Organization

Technical Aspects: Speed, Complete Links

Content Quality and Accuracy

Typography

Graphics

Navigation

Links within site

Links outside site

Contact information

Interaction

Chart 12-5. Project Evaluation.

Ask participants to become involved in the process of project reflection. What did they like and dislike about the project? Where did they need more or less time? Where were they frustrated? What did they think was fun? Was it useful? How? What about the timeline? Are there other suggestions they would make?

Site Sharing

Before, during, and after your project has been completed, share your web project with other students and teachers. Before your project begins, you'll concentrate on recruiting participants. During the project, you'll be looking for ideas and feedback. When the project is completed, you may wish others to come and see your work.

Many of the project sites listed in previous chapters provide a listing service to help you recruit participants. However if you're interested in advertising your site to the world, consider one of the national tools. For example, use **Submit-It** (http://www.submit-it.com/) to list your page with an endless array of search en-

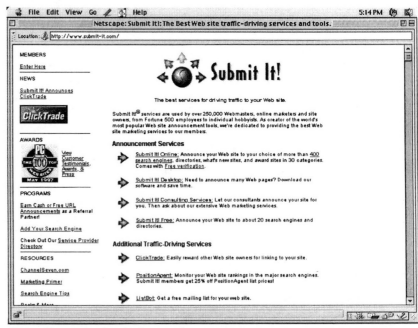

http://www.submit-it.com/
Figure 12-5. Submit-It.

gines (see Figure 12-5). **PostMaster** (http://www.netcreations.com/postmaster/registration/try.html) is a similiar site for web promotion.

You need to determine whether you really want to advertise your site. The more you share, the busier your web server will become. If you've got a powerful web server and want to maximize outside participation and exploration, you should regularly reregister your website with the popular search engines. This will ensure that your location appears near the beginning of search results.

Idea Exploration: Fun & Frustrations
Try out your project and see how it works. Revise your project as you go. Keep track of those things that work well and those things that need to be changed.

Write about the fun and frustrations of implementing this kind of project.

Idea Exploration

Summary

Schools are just beginning to see the potential of the Internet as a tool for accessing and sharing information. The only way to gain experience developing projects is to give it a try!

Join a project, develop a page, or create a school site. Ask others for help, learn from your experiences, and share your insights with others. Be a consumer, contributor, and a creator! Most of all, have fun! :-)

Personal Web Development Plan

Don't just read about projects, do it. Start small and begin today.

Develop a personal plan for web project development.

This semester I'll do ...

This semester I'll start planning ...

Within the next year, I'll ...

Chart 12-6. Personal Web Development Plan.

Index

ability levels 274-275
about me 74
absolute path 230
access 277
accuracy 183, 282
action 61, 138, 267
activities 161
activity projects 106-111
address 193
adjusting text size 228-229
administrative materials 17
administrators 17-19
Adobe Acrobat 52
Adobe Pagemill 13, 218
Adrian's Wall 50
adult education 20
advantages of newspapers 56
advertising 52
Advertising World 99-100
African American Treasure Hunt 107
After Andrew 137
Age of Imperialism 90
ages 154
aiff 60
Air Travelers 93
Alta Elementary 10
alternative products 142
American Dreams 193
American History 200
American Memory 99-100
American Revolution 34
American School Directory 21
American School in Japan 191
Americans 197
Amigos 200
Anatomy of Murder 120
anchors 237
Ancient Greece 197
Ancient History 140
Ancient Sites 212
animal habitats 28
animation 24, 65, 241, 246-248
appeal 257
Applet 213, 248-249
applet sites 247
Archaeotype 108
Art Gallery 76
Art Museum 119
art projects 57-59
Art Space 58
articles 49
ArtsEdge 208
artwork 74, 134-135
ask an artist 58
ask an expert 65, 130
assignments 26
athletics 19
Atlanta 3-4
au 60
audience 257
audience 47-48
audio 195
Austin 3, 15, 262
Australia 63
Australian sports 101
autobiographies 74, 87
aviation 34
Avocado Elementary 5
Aztecs 29

background 74, 177, 203-204, 225
background graphic 225-226
background information 274
balanced 24
Barney Bear's Travel 69
bars 208, 234
Barton Hills 16

Bear Creek Elementary 263
Bedford Lawrence High 202
Berit's Best Sites 74
bias 61
biodiversity 34
biographical sketches 142
biographies 30, 68, 103
Biology Page 119
Bird Table 139
birds 211
Blackburn High 206, 267
Blooming Bluebonnets 199
Blue and Gold Gazette 49
bmp 231
book buddy 68
Book Reviews 169, 199
bookmarks 102
boring 20
Boy Meets World 77
Break the Cycle 114
Bremen High 263
Brianna's Page 77
Bright Sites 255
Buchman's Class 35
Building Blocks of Civilization 168
buildings 1, 3-24
bullet lists 234
bulletin boards 269-272
butterflies 66

Caledonia High 196
calendars 272
Calkanimal 34
call for collaboration 166
call for participation 26
Camden Kids Literary Magazine 49
Caminoes Reales 121
Canada's class 36
Canoe Trip 136
Cape Cod Lighthouse School 192

captured images 210
case studies 112-114, 116
case study planning chart 116
Castle Attacking Weapons 141
Castle Creations 69
challenge activities 26
Challenger Elementary 261
challenges 131, 148
charts 211
chat 213
Chemistry 90
Chernobyl Nuclear Disaster 199
Cherry Creek 3
Cheshire High 17
Chico 3
Children's Book Forum 126
China WebQuest 108
chunk information 191
citations 204
Civil Rights 29
Civil War 26, 90, 197, 212
Claris Home Page 13, 218, 221
Claris Home Page
    anchors 237
Claris Home page
    animation 246-248
    applets 248-249
    background 225-226
    document options 224
    editing 228
    email 239, 241
    formatting 234
    forms 252
    ftp 241
    image maps 242
    images 229-230
    java 248-249
    lines 233
    links 235-241
    lists 234-235

modes 228
plug ins 249
preferences 223
printing 252
quitting 228
saving 227
setting up 223
sound 250-252
tables 243
text 228-229
tools 226-227
videos 244-245
ClarisWorks 232
class information 25-26
class magazines 50
class page functions 25-30
class pages 1, 19, 25-40, 88-90, 98, 264-267
class web pages list 35
classroom management 269, 274-280
classroom management chart 279
Classroom Web 21
Classy Sites 255
Claude Monet 58
client-side 242
clip art 204-205, 230, 234
clip art link list 204
cloning 108
clubs 5, 19, 50
Coal Creek Elementary 21
collaboration 125-131, 166,
collaboration planning chart 132
Collection of Poetry 68
College Campus Newspapers Online 53
color 209, 225-226
columns 46
committee 8-10
communication 125-131
communication planning chart 132
communication projects 165

community 5, 9-11, 87, 261-262
Community Leadership 139
community links 19
community newspaper 48
community projects 139
compare 182
Computer Art 90
computer class 87
computer schedule 278
concept map 171, 200
concerts 59
conclusion 106
Connections+ 283
consistency 184, 215
consumers 153-155
contact information 193
content 181-184
content accuracy 282
contests 131
contributors 155-156
control 14
converters 218
Convomania 213
copying and pasting 230
copying from Internet 234
copyright 59, 204
copyright issues 9
core page 177, 189
core page graphics 261
cotton 31
county 10
course pages 25-40
creating animation 246-248
creating forms 252
creating image maps 243
creating links 235-241
creating lists 235
creating tables 243-244
Creative Carnival 68
Creative Nexus 69

creativity 257
creators 157-158
credits 192
Crest Chronicle 44
Critical Issues Forum 126
critical thinking 183
critiques 28, 59
culture 34
culture studies 59, 61
Cupertino Junior High 22
currency 258
Cyberbee 283
CyberSpace Middle School 93

data analysis 65
data collection 130, 213
data comparison 65
data sharing 61
debate 30, 61, 65
deep 24
default 177, 189
democracy 109
demonstrations 65, 141
Dempsey Kids Art Galley 77
departments 19
Desert View High 5
designing class pages 35-36
designing school sites 255-268
designing student pages 78
desktop presentations 30
develop pages 177-179
developing large-scale projects 94
Diablo Valley Music 60, 136
diagram 175-176
diagram 184-185
diagram 211, 222
dioramas 57
digital camera 57, 141, 211
digital stills 211
digitize voice 86

Dinosaur Egg 258
Dinosaur Song 60
dioramas 31
disasters 84, 94, 121, 135
disclaimers 192
discussion 129, 200, 213
disk management 189
districts 1, 3-24
DK 208
Dogs of the North 156
Domino's Dilemma 187-188
download 213
download options 52
drawing 34
due dates 272
duplicate project 72

earthquake 121, 135
ease of use 257
Ecosystems 140
Eddie Blick 54
editing 80, 228
editorial guidelines 46
editorials 61, 68
Education World 255
EduStock 121
Egypt 138
Einstein, Albert 76, 104
Elanora Heights Primary 10
elections 94
electronic field trips 136
electronic magazine 41-56
electronic publishing 2
Elevator Tide to the Write 49
Ellensboro School 262
email 96, 193, 239, 241, 277-278
entering text 228-229
Environment 66
environmental concerns 138
Epatrol 138

Eric's page 75
essay 29
European Schools 151
evaluation 269-287
Evansville-Vanderburgh 3-4
Everglades 97
expand project 72
experiences 135
experimentation 65
experiments 130
experts 130
explorer 147
Exposer 52
express 182
extensions 148
ezine 2, 41-56

faculty 17-19
Falcon's Nest 5
Family History Project 126
FAQs 273
favorite links 196
favorite things 74
fax 193
features of newspapers 43-54
feedback 28, 177
feedback pages 200
fiction 30
field trip 164, 210
Fifty States 152
Filamentality 220
file extensions 227
file management 278
flags 208
flies 121
floods 135
flowcharts 272
folk tales 34
fonts 47, 201
Food Chain 168

Food Finder 101
footer 192
Foothill High 8, 9
foreign language 68
formative evaluation 280-286
formats 162
formatting information 234
forms 252
Fractal Projects 66
Fractals 90
frames 211
Freezone 41
ftp sites 241
functions 25-30

Gateway 45
Geography Scavenger Hunt 107
GeoNet Game 119
Geotopia 257
Geotouch 93
gif 231
gif animation 212-213, 246-248
gif animation sites 247
Giraffe Project 184
Global Learn 115, 201
global presence 10
Global Temperature Project 205
Global Zoo 93
grade level 154
Grand Forks 135
Grandma 34
Grandpa Tucker 211
Grandview Middle 8
grants 96
graphic titles 207
graphics 80, 202-211, 229-230
Great Kids 277
Greece School 58
grouping students 276
Guess Who? 127

guidelines 25, 46, 77

Haiku 197
handbooks 17
Happy New Year 210
Heart 114
Hello Dolly 108
Henderson's Multimedia 134, 213
Heronsgate 98
High School Central 21
higher order thinking 103
Highland Park Elementary 16
Hilton Primary Bird Table 211
Himalayas 215
history 16, 100, 262
History Net 100
hobbies 74, 86
Hollister's Third Grade Weather 140
Hollywood Beach 261
Holocaust 93
home page 177, 189
homework pages 19
Horace Mann Review 43-44
HORIZONline 47
horizontal lines 208, 233
hot lists planning chart 110
hot lists projects 102-105
hot points 102-105, 235
hotlists 30
Houston 32
HTML 13, 218-219
Hurricane Project 84
Hutt High 22
HyperCard 213, 215
HyperStudio 213, 215, 250
hypertext dictionary 106

I Have a Dream 127
icons 208-209, 234

Idea Exploration iv, 5, 24, 35, 38, 43, 53, 70, 73, 80, 84, 94, 102, 105, 109, 114, 131, 142
Idea Machine 220
ideas 160
If... 70
Ika's Online Fairy Tales 199
image editor 231-232
image maps 241-242
image problems 233
implementation 269-287
incidents 112
index 177, 189
Indian Hill Treasure Hunt 107
information 14, 160
information access 61, 65, 68
information resource 140
informational 99-111
informational content 160-163
Inklings 52
Inmates 127
inquiry 65, 136-137
Insect Project 65
insects 32
inserting images 229
instructional 112-124
instructional applications 263
instructional content 28-29
interaction 199
interaction pages 199
Interactive Mathematics 257
interactive projects 129
interdisciplinary projects 69-70
interest 74, 154
interlacing images 231
Internet access 277
Internet Integration Projects list 152
interviews 29, 34
Into Space 65
introduction 147

Index

inventions 171-174
investigations 61, 148
involvement 13, 183, 261-262
issues 61, 138, 155
issues newspaper 49
Ivan's Artwork 75

Japan 34, 135
JAVA 213, 218, -249
JavaScript 252
Jessica's Page 74
Johnny Appleseed 210
joint ventures 130
journal 89
journalism 68
Journey North 127
jpeg 231
Junior Seahawk 44
Just Jane's Graphics 204
justice system 120
justification 202

keyboarding skills 80
KidDay 68
KidLink 128
KidPix 232
Kids in the Hall 47
Kids Space 74
kindergarten class 36
King, Martin Luther 211

lab experiments 65, 139
Lakeway Library 19
large scale project planning page 94
large-scale projects 81, 83-96
layout 22, 24, 175-176
layout, newspaper 44-45
learner 147
learner-centered 4, 5, 80
learning advice 106

Learning Next Generation 276
lesson plans 20, 85, 162
letter 29, 68, 267
level 282
levels of control 14
levels of involvement 13, 153-159
library media center 19
library media specialist 8
Library of Congress 99-100
limiting pages 144
Lincoln 148
lines 208, 233-234
link layout 196
link rot 193
LinkAge 2000 213
linking to email address 239, 241
linking to ftp sites 241
linking to local page 238
linking to remote site 238-239
links 19-20, 30, 102-105, 160, 193-201,
    235-241, 282
links page 196
links within page 236
lists 102, 234
lists of links 102-105
literacy projects 68-69
literature study 68
Living School Book 93
Livingston Technical Academy 192
local pages 144
logo 14, 178, 208
long term projects 168
Loogootee Elementary 199, 260
Lorteria Cards 69
Louisville 19
lunch menu 17, 20

Mad Scientist 171
Magazine Collage 59
magazine list 54

magazines 2, 41-56, 91
Magnets 213
Manassas 210
Manion 264-265
Maple Sugaring 136
Mapquest 100
maps 16, 20, 61, 205, 273
Maricopa Center 283
Marketing 113
Mars Buggy 141
Marsden Rock 164
Maryland County Quilt 140
Masterpieces 69
materials 162
Math Links 105
math projects 65-67
MayaQuest 115
Melrose Elementary 15
Memories of 1940's 63
menus 24
Microsoft FrontPage 13, 218
Middle Ages 105, 184, 186
MiddleZine 91
midi 60
migration 66, 127
mini lesson 149
Minneapolis 11
Minnesota 3
Miraloma Elementary 22
mission 10-11, 256
mission statement 14-16
misspellings 80
Modigliani Project 134
Monarchs 66
Monster project 127
Months of the Year 128
MOTET 195
Mountain Men 153
movie review 29
movies 241

Mr. Reed's Classroom 207
Mrs. Bogucki's Class 212
Multicultural Calendar 128
multimedia creations 134-135
multiple intelligences 69, 183
museum 61, 119, 139, 175
music 19, 134-135
music files 60
music projects 59-60
music scores 59
Music Theory 124
Musical Composition 60
Mysteries of Camino Reales 211

Nagatsuka Elementary 8
NandoNext 44
NASA 99
National Archives 161
national debt 109
National Science & Technology Week 130
Native Americans 199
natural disasters 69
navigation 24, 197, 282
Netscape Composer 254
Neuroscience 90
Newcastle 76
news reporting 68
newsletters 61
newspaper 2, 19, 29, 41-56, 91, 169
newspaper list 54
newspaper web pages 55
NickNacks 125, 151
Noon Observation 66
numbered lists 234
Nutribase 100-101

Oakview Elementary 168, 171, 210
Ocean Expo 115
Oceans 155

Olympics 69, 94
one shot project 164
ongoing 169
ongoing projects 81, 83-96
Online Class 99
online magazines list 42
open Claris Home Page 223
opinion 68
oral histories 34, 61, 139
Orchard Park Odyssey 48
organization 24, 184-193, 257, 269-274, 281
organize 170
organize 182
outcomes 170
outdated 20
outline 200
OutPost 101 Space Station 94
Overland High 178

page layout 281
parent pages 20
parents 9, 11, 87, 261-262
Parker's class 37
participant 150
participant evaluation 283
Passports to the World 63
passwords 14
Patterns 66
Peace in Pictures 58
peer editing 68
peer review 38
peer writing 68
people information 17-19
people power 96
permission forms 18
personal web development plan 288
Peto's Class 25
Ph Factor 175
philosophy 5, 14

phone 193
photo essay 29
photographs 86
PhotoShop 232, 264
physics 32
Piano on the Net 124
pict 231
pictures 17
Pigeon Inquiry 136-137
Pitsco 151
planning 269-274
planning pages 222
planning, getting started 151-153
plug ins 249-250
Poems and Portraits 134
poetry 20, 68, 73,
Poetry Garden 211
Poetry Project 77
policies 17, 25
policy development 11-12
polls 61, 65, 130,
pollution 105
Poolgar 68
PopUp books 101
portfolios 35, 38, 85-87
Positively Poetry 77
Postmaster 287
Power River Coal Company 66
PowerPoint 30
practice 119
prairie chickens 31
preproduction plan 171
President's page 61
presidents 121
printing 252
problem solving 61, 65
problems 112
procedures 17
process 106
professional look 43-44

professional portfolios 85-86
programming 218-219
Project Central America 63
project evaluation chart 285
project idea chart 71
project idea pages 72
project organization chart 275
project pages 57-72
project selection 96
project sharing 28
projects 2, 31-34, 162
prose 68
public relations 10
publisher 148
publishing 131-142
publishing guidelines 46
publishing planning chart 133
puppets 57
Puppets from Around the World 134
purpose 35, 87, 10, 170, 256

Question of the Week 107
questions 199
QuickTime movies 213, 244-245
QuickTime VR 249
quitting 227
quiz 29, 89, 199

Raiders of the Lost Art 121
Ram's Horn Online Edition 52
ReadIn 68
reading guide 89
Real Audio 249
Real World Considerations iv, 20, 56, 72, 80, 96, 144, 180, 215
real-world experiences 135
realistic 72
reflection 283
relative path 230
reports 61, 65

research 58, 59, 61, 139-140
resources 19-20, 106
response time 258
responsibility chart 274
reviews 30, 68
Revolutionary War 63, 197
rocks 176
role playing 68
roles 147-150, 274
rotate 276
rubrics 26
rural 10

safe sites 19
San Diego InternQuest 199
saving documents 227
scan handwriting 86
scanned images 209-210
scans 58
scavenger hunts 106-111
schedule 276, 278
school achievements 263
school board 9
school corporations 3-5
school exploration 24
school information 14-15
school library links 21
school newspapers 43-54
school site contents 14-20
    people info 17-19
    resources 19-20
    school info 14-15
school site development 8-24
    control 14
    involvement 13-14
    policy 11
    purpose 10-11
    webmaster 12-13
school web pages, 23
school web site design chart 259

Index

school web site elements 261-267
school web structure 22, 24
schools 1, 3-24
SchoolZone 3-4
Science Fiction Writing 68
Science Inquiry Hotlist 102
science projects 65-67
science scavenger hunts 107
scrapbooks 102
screen dumps 273
scrolling text 201
sculpture 57
select 182
selecting hardware 221
selecting software 221
self evaluation 283
sequence 281
server-side 242
setting document options 223
setting preferences 223
setting up the page 223
shallow 24
sharing 58, 65, 68, 77, 134, 286-287
Shockwaves 249
short-term projects 81, 97-147
showcase art 58
Signs of Spring 128
Silverman's Class 35
Simple Machines 138
simulation planning chart 122
simulations 65, 120-122
single site projects 100-102
site activity pages 102
site evaluation 102
site layout 273
site sharing 286-287
situations 112
Slummit 50
small-scale projects 81, 97-147
small-scale, short term project charts 143

Smithsonian 213
Smoke Signal 48
snow 32
social action 61
social studies projects 61-64
software 52
software downloads 213
Solar System 90
Solar System Tour 115
sound 65, 211-212, 250-252

sound clips 59
sound files 195
sound sites 247
Southern PowWows 154-155
special features 50-51
speed 80, 276
spider logo iv
Spiders 156
sponsor name 193
sponsors 8, 9, 83
sports 5, 8, 101
St. Christopher School 212
staff 17-19
Stamp On Black History 154-155
starters 148
starting points 10
state agency 4
states 140
step-by-step instructions 89
storage space 18
Story Line 183
Story Problems 65
story starters 129
Storyteller Dolls 59
Stringtown Elementary 178, 264-265
structure 184-188
Student Ambassadors 94
student evaluation 283
student government 19

student involvement 60, 87, 153-159
student page development 80
student page list 74
student pages 18, 73-82, 264-267
student portfolios 86-87
student responsibility 37
student roles 147-150, 274
student web pages chart 79
students pages 2
style bar 227
subject samplers 106
Submit-It 286
Sunflowers 77
supplemental work 26
support 8, 9
Surf Rider 46
survey 28, 61, 65, 130, 199, 213

table 257
table of contents 197
tables 199, 211, 243-244
tacky 20
Tales from Electronic Frontier 280
task 106
Taton 52
teacher 8, 17-19, 148
teacher pages 20
teacher starters 129
teaming 144
technical aspects 282
technical writing 68
technology 258-259
technology access 80
technology coordinator 8
technology resources 96
telecollaboration 125
template 13, 106, 184
Tesselations 65, 66
testing 119
text 201-203, 228-229

text entry 228-229
text styles 229
text, newspapers 47
thematic units 94
theme 171
Tidal Passages 118
time 96
timeline 13, 29, 61, 142, 162, 164-170, 206-207, 272, 276
Timeline Project 209
titles 189
TJToday 47
tools 227
topic focus 49
topic pages 76
topical projects 93-94
transparent images 231
travel brochure 142
Travel Buddies 128
treasure hunts 106-111
trial project 269
trivia game 29
tutorial planning chart 123
tutorials 123-124
Twin cities 32
types of links 193-195
Tyrannosaurus Art 59

unit pages 25-40
unit projects 93-94
United Nations CyberSchoolBus 94
updates, newspaper 49
updating 13, 17, 20, 258
Urban Agriculture 193
URL 236
usefulness 183
users 170

value 257
video 141, 211, 213, 241

video sites 247
videos 244-245
videotape 86
Violinist page 75
Virginia 210
Virginia Indians 140
Virtual Earthquake 121
virtual elections 61
virtual field trip links 114
virtual field trip planning chart 117
virtual field trips 16, 61, 69, 99, 114-115, 117-119
Virtual Fly Lab 121
visuals 202-211
Vocal Point 49, 155
Volcano Simulation 120
Volcanoes 211

wall boards 269-272
Walz 264-265
War Eyes 139, 179
weather 140
Weather Wizards 94
Web 21, 66
web activities 147-148
web activities planning chart 111
web address 236
web contents 23
web development
    guidelines 11
    resources list 217, 220
    tools 218-219, 254
Web for Educators 219
web guidelines 283
web headquarters 269-274
web layout 22, 24
web page evaluation site list 282
web project, communication types 164
web project, informational content 160-163

web projects 219-220
web publishing 68
web quests 29
web site committee 8-10
web structure 22, 24, 184-188
Web Workshop 254
web-based learning environment 170-180
webmaster 12-13, 24, 43
webmaster name 193
webquest 106-111, 147, 184
webserver 88
Weird Guys Who Write Poems 73
Welcome to Wabash 63
West Terrace Elementary School 156-157
Wetlands 103
whales 157
What Would You Do? 184
What's New? 258
Where Are We? 128
Where on the Globe is Roger? 118
Whiteaker School 38, 263
Whitman, Walt 177
Who's Footing the Bill? 109
Winter Wonderland 135
Woodlands Secondary 22
World Safari 181
World War II 124
writing 134-135
WWII 69
WYSIWYG 13, 218

Xenophile Internet Science Magazine 49

Yahoo 53
Yamhill County 10
yearbook 19, 91
Yukon Quest 119

Zoo 157

Vision to Action Publications

Cruisin' the Information Highway:
Internet in the K-12 Classroom (2nd Edition)
   Annette Lamb & Larry Johnson

Get up to speed with basic technology, email, Web, Internet tools and resources, as well as, practical classroom activities and suggestions for leading the way onto the Info Highway.

ISBN 0-9641581-6-7   c1995, 1997 $23.95

Surfin' the Internet:
Practical Ideas from A to Z (2nd Edition)
   Annette Lamb, Nancy Smith & Larry Johnson

A practical guide for integrating Internet technology into the classroom. Contains unit and lesson ideas, resource lists, and reproducible activity sheets for a wide range of K-12 Internet projects.

ISBN 0-9641581-2-4   c1996, 1998 $26.95

Spinnin' the Web:
Designing and Developing Web Projects
   Annette Lamb

Explore and learn to create school sites, classroom pages, newspapers, projects, and individual pages. Design, development, implement, and evaluate web-based pages and projects.

ISBN 0-9641581-9-1   c1998 $26.95

Building Treehouses for Learning:
Technology in Today's Classrooms
   Annette Lamb

Focuses on the integration of traditional and emerging technologies into today's classrooms including CD-ROM, laserdiscs, video, desktop publishing and presentations, Internet, and multimedia.

ISBN 0-9641581-3-2   c1996 $34.95

MacPac for Teachers:
Hands-on Macintosh Applications
   Annette Lamb

A hands-on, step-by-step guidebook focusing o: Macintosh basics, ClarisWorks, HyperStudio, a: digitizing images, video, and sounds. A great companion to Treehouse for Learning.

ISBN 0-9641581-4-0   c1997 $19

The Magic Carpet Ride:
Integrating Technology into the K-12 Classro
   Annette Lamb

Focuses on integrating CD-ROM and student-produced multimedia technology into the class. Also includes hands-on instructions for HyperS and digitizing images, video, and sounds.

ISBN 0-9641581-5-9   c1997 $2:

Strap on Your Spurs:
Technology & Change Cowboy Style
   Annette Lamb & Larry Johnson

Contains strategies for designing, developing, implementing, and evaluating technology prog: in schools.

ISBN 0-9641581-0-8   c1994, 97 $2:

Videos
CD-ROM: An Introduction - $59.95
Introduction to HyperStudio - $59.95
Introduction to HyperCard 2.2 - $59.95
3 Part Series:
Internet in the Classroom - $59.95 each
   1 - Exploring Internet Resources
   2 - Integrating Internet Resources
   3 - Creating Internet Resources

Order Information

Vision to Action
Publishing & Consulting
Order & Distribution Center
PO Box 2003
Emporia, Kansas 66801
emailto: vision2a@cadvantage.com
website: http://cadvantage.com/~vision2a/
Voice Mail or Fax: 316 343 7989
Shipping & Handling Information in US
Send Check or PO to Vision to Action. Add 10% shipping/handling with $4.95 minimum.

Name: _____
Address: _____
_____
City, State, Zip: _____
Email Address: _____
Phone: _____
Order: _____
_____

Add shipping/handling:
Total: